Behind These Doors

Behind These Doors

Stories of Strength, Suffering and Survival in Prison

ALEX SOUTH

HODDER &
STOUGHTON

First published in Great Britain in 2023 by Hodder & Stoughton
An Hachette UK company

1

A CIP catalogue record for this title is available from the British Library

Hardback ISBN 9781399707558
Trade Paperback ISBN 9781399707565
eBook ISBN 9781399707572

Typeset in Monotype Bembo by Manipal Technologies Limited

Printed and bound in Great Britain by Clays Ltd, Elcograf S.p.A.

Hodder & Stoughton policy is to use papers that are natural, renewable and recyclable
products and made from wood grown in sustainable forests. The logging and
manufacturing processes are expected to conform to the environmental regulations of
the country of origin.

For my parents

Everything I do is because you have made me believe I can.

Introduction

'NO MOBILE PHONES, no chewing gum, no alcohol, no guns.' The list of prohibited items outside the prison: a big white-and-blue sign showing pictures of the things you can't bring in, positioned right outside the gate.

I remember thinking on my first day how the last one was a bit unnecessary. Because obviously, no one is going to try to bring a gun into a high-security jail.

Except, in 1994, someone did.

In fact, it was two guns, eight rounds of ammunition, three detonators and a quantity of Semtex explosives. These items were hidden inside the Special Secure Unit (SSU) of HMP Whitemoor, an area colloquially known as the 'prison within a prison', and from which it was considered impossible to escape. But on the night of Friday 9 September 1994, six of the ten prisoners in the SSU did escape. They used bolt croppers, rope ladders and torn bedsheets. They scaled wire fences, inner walls and outer walls, and made it to the fields surrounding Whitemoor. They weren't opportunistic; they weren't lucky. They were members of the IRA, and they were meticulous in their planning. Even now, nearly thirty years on, it's unclear exactly how they got the contraband in.

Fortunately, all of them were caught within a few hours – though not before a prison officer had been shot.

I knew all of this from my training course. I knew that I was standing only metres from where the bullet was fired, wearing a uniform only slightly modernised from the one that officer would have been wearing. I knew a prison dog had also been shot in the chase that ensued, and that a kilogram of explosives was later found in the grounds of the prison. But I pushed all of that to the back of my mind. The eight-metre-high perimeter wall is intimidating enough. So I told myself that it was a different era. An escape as audacious and violent as that surely couldn't happen now.

It's been more than ten years since my first day as a prison officer, but I can take myself back there in a second. I can hear the crunch of the grit as I walk from my car to the prison gatehouse, and I can smell the rock salt spread over the path outside. I can feel the heaviness of those clumpy black boots, fat laces and starched leather, the Prison Service crest woven into the tongue, the toe curved like a bulbous chin. The way the stiff material rubbed on my heel. I can remember the queue of prison staff waiting to be searched, the scuffed boots of the officer in front of me, the way my key chain gleamed with newness compared to his. And I can remember how dry my mouth was, how nervous I felt.

I knew what kind of prison officer I wanted to be. I wanted to be like Tom Hanks's character in *The Green Mile*, or Officer Patterson from *Prison Break*. Although I was new to this role, I wasn't entirely new to prison. I'd spent much of the last two years volunteering at a Young Offenders Institution, Littlehey in Huntington, mentoring teenage boys serving short sentences. I'd had a glimpse of how different officers worked and how they treated the prisoners in their care. So often, it seemed that the ones most respected around the prison were the ones who raised their voices the least. They were firm but fair, tough but kind. And they seemed to enjoy their jobs. That's how I imagined myself being if I were to become an officer. Looking back, I was shamefully naïve, but I was also curious and keen and determined.

So much time was being done behind this wall, so much life was being lived in one place. The tabloids say prison is hell on earth one day and a holiday camp the next, but I wasn't convinced by either claim. I'd lived half an hour from Whitemoor for my entire life, yet before I applied for the job, I'd never even known it was there. Since the escape almost twenty years before, Whitemoor had barely been in the news. The officers at the Young Offenders Institute had told me it was because lifers' prisons were different. They said that those prisons were quieter, more settled – until, of course, they were not. Those same officers told me that on the rare occasions when things did go wrong at Whitemoor, they went very wrong – yet I'd heard next to nothing about this maximum-security prison holding 400 of the country's supposedly most dangerous men. Whitemoor seemed like a strange paradox, as if it was simultaneously there but not there. Hidden in plain sight. The place both fascinated and unnerved me, and I wanted to see inside.

***

The queue inches forward, closer to the list of prohibited items and the staff enforcing it. Operational support grades, or OSGs, as they're known. As I enter the gatehouse, there is a room to my left that feels a bit like an office, with computers and filing cabinets and people clutching mugs of coffee. It looks like any other office – except they stand behind panes of bulletproof glass. To my right is the searching area. A pile of trays is stacked next to an X-ray machine, a smaller version of the conveyor belts you see in airports. I copy the officer in front of me and put my boots, bag, fleece and wristwatch in a tray. OSGs are the rank below officer, but they're integral to the fabric of prison life. Prisons couldn't run without them. If a weapon – or a phone or drugs – is going to get into a prison, it needs to get past the OSGs. They're the front line.

And the one searching me isn't taking any chances. She waits for me to walk through the X-ray portal, then snaps on some blue gloves. The underwire in my bra has set off the alarm. She searches my waistband, the cuffs of my shirt, my collar and my pockets, and uses a handheld metal detector to check there's nothing hidden in my socks. Another OSG searches my boots, fleece and backpack by hand, then passes them through the X-ray machine. It's the same process for everyone, from civilians to the governing governor. And at 6.45 on a Monday morning, there's a lot of people to get through.

There's been a lot of build-up to this moment for me. Six weeks of training and two years of volunteering. But now that I'm here, the adrenaline and nervous excitement is starting to drain away. In its place, I realise I'm beginning to feel distinctly uncomfortable. It's not the physicality of the place, it's not the bulletproof glass or rigorous searching procedures, it's the sudden realisation of what I'm about to do and where I'm doing it. Because Whitemoor isn't Littlehey. The men inside don't need someone to help them write their CV or plan how to budget. I'm not a volunteer anymore. I'm not a well-meaning civilian popping in for a few hours every week, with no disciplinary obligations. I'm conscious of just how new I look, my boots fresh out the box and my belt unmarked. Suddenly, I don't feel excited. I feel scared. The uniform feels big and ill-fitting on me. The responsibility does, too.

More gates, doors, cameras, ID checks. I lose count of the number of times I show my ID: to the OSG sitting behind a flimsy-looking desk who takes my tally, the little wooden disc with my staff number printed on it, and swaps it for a bunch of keys; to the senior officer curious as to why he's never seen me before; and to the staff in the control room, who stop me at each camera and check my face matches the picture on my ID. Many of the gates have small cameras installed; OSGs watch every person approaching and make sure they are who they say they are before releasing the electronic lock. It quickly becomes apparent that the wrong person getting in could be just as dangerous as the wrong person getting out.

'Clip your keys on to your chain now.' The guy next to me gives me a friendly nudge. 'Never leave the gatehouse until they're attached. Security.'

Security. That's what everything comes back to. It's the reason the outer buildings are all one storey, even though they're still an impossible leap from the perimeter wall. It's the reason all the corridors are identical, long stretches of brown linoleum and brick walls and rusting window frames and bars upon bars upon bars, stretching forward like rows of frozen soldiers. If a prisoner ever did manage to breach his residential wing, he'd be unsure which way to turn.

'First day already?' the officer asks me, as we step out of the gatehouse and into the open air. I recognise him from my induction week, before I went away for six weeks of training. His name is Brian, and he's been an officer here for nearly twenty years. Most of the staff have been in the job for a similar length of time. Everyone around me has that easy confidence of knowing this place inside out, as if it's an ordinary workplace, as if there aren't coils of barbed wire cutting into the sky. We pass through turnstiles activated by biometrics, my hand shaking a little as I press my fingerprint to the scanner, the cold stinging my cheek.

'So, how was training? You can forget everything you learned there; the reality's nothing like they tell you.' His smile is so broad that it fills his whole face. It puts me at ease. 'You've been assigned to A Wing, haven't you? Come on, I'll take you there.'

We walk side by side through a vehicle compound where the vans have ballistic armour, past where the batons and fish knives are held, through a maze of fenced walkways, past the little postbox on the wall, in which staff put security reports, and through more long corridors, which look out on to exercise yards. Cameras everywhere. Cameras and gates and bars, keys and chains and boots. People coming in, no one going out.

We come to a junction in the corridor: like the one outside the jail, the signs are blue and white, with crisp lettering. *Welcome to A Wing.*

'You ready?' Brian looks back at me. That smile again.

I don't know. I don't know if I'm ready.

I was twenty-two when I became a prison officer. It might seem like a strange career choice, especially for a young woman, but I was at a strange time in my life. Most people I knew were finding jobs after graduating, but I'd dropped out of my English degree after two months. University wasn't for me. I was desperately homesick, I didn't fit in with the nightlife culture, and I struggled with the constant influx of new people and new situations that everyone else seemed to find effortless. So I came home. I had a few different jobs around this time, trying to find something that resonated. I did stints in admin, recruitment and sales, but the only thing I stuck with was bar work, at the same place I'd been glass-collecting since I was seventeen.

It certainly wasn't a university education, but it was an education of sorts. The regulars who started with a Scotch at 8am taught me to listen and not judge. The ones who turned ugly after too much lager taught me to pick the battles worth having. The white powder left on the baby-changing table taught me that people will snort cocaine anywhere. My female manager taught me how to read a room, how to watch out for the men with wandering hands, and how to placate the ones who didn't like to be told no. I didn't know it at the time, but these were important skills. They served me well on Saturday nights in a packed bar, and they would serve me well on the landings in prison.

Working in the bar was fun and there were a lot of good times, but I don't remember being particularly happy. In fact, I felt a bit lost. I'd thought that life would be different after I left school, that the world would suddenly open up now that I had my independence, but it hadn't. Instead, I was a uni dropout, still living in the same town I'd lived in my whole life. I felt stuck.

I looked up local volunteering opportunities as a way of trying to alleviate these feelings. The mentoring role at HMYOI Littlehey was one of the first I saw, and I knew immediately that I wanted to apply. Here was something different, something unknown. And from the moment I started, I loved it. I felt committed to the young men I worked with, and I enjoyed the practical side of things: helping them to set up bank accounts or applying for a provisional driver's licence, for example. Becoming a prison officer felt like a natural next step. I knew that putting on a uniform would change things, but I still believed that the parts of mentoring I enjoyed so much, the relationship-building and the problem-solving, would be there in my new role.

I became a prison officer hoping to do good, to be compassionate and kind. And though there were undoubtedly moments where I fell short, I believe that, for the most part, I was all those things. But there was a lot I didn't know at the beginning. I thought I would see some version of evil, whatever that is, but it's one thing to wonder about it and another to see a home-made weapon plunged into someone's body. I also didn't expect to see so much good. I didn't know just how brave people can be. I didn't know that the people I'd meet inside would strengthen my faith in humanity as well as shake it, that their stories would shape how I see real life and what it means to be free. I didn't know how stress can infiltrate every part of you, or how prison can stay with you, even when you walk out of the gate. Sometimes the bars follow you home.

The IRA prisoners planned how to get out, but not how to stay out.

What follows is the story of the past decade of my life as a prison officer, and the mosaic of people, places and situations I encountered. It's the story of what happens when the alarm bell goes, but also of what happens after, when the sound still echoes in your head. It's the story of a young woman navigating what is an overwhelmingly male-dominated environment, and how loyalty can be found in the strangest of places. And it is an exploration of our modern-day prison system, and how jails are now, as ever, both a microcosm and reflection of society. Unsurprisingly, then, you will find that mental health, drugs and gang violence are all prominent themes in this book. But so are resilience, friendship and kindness.

The majority of prisoners in the UK will be released, and they will be released into our cities, towns and villages. Into your street and your community. It makes sense for us all to know what goes on behind those eight-metre-high walls, and to be invested in it, too. It could be your father, mother, child or friend who ends up there one day, or maybe even you. Walking the landings is not easy, for an officer or a prisoner.

If I could speak to that twenty-two-year-old woman now, I would tell her to hold her head a little higher and have confidence in herself. I would tell her that, for all her anxieties about violence and how to manage when the lights start flashing, she already has the skills to both defuse and confront those situations. I think most of us do. I have learned that empathy and respect go a long way, among both staff and prisoners, and we do ourselves a huge disservice when we abandon that way of thinking. I have learned that prison officers deserve far more credit than they are given, but also that a uniform itself does not guarantee emotional intelligence.

There is no question that I am a better person as a result of my time as an officer. I am braver, less judgemental and more understanding. But I am also more cynical, perhaps even a little paranoid, and painfully aware of the utter depravity of which some humans are capable. Despite this, I am so grateful for everything I have learned in this most incredible of jobs, and for the amazing people with whom I have had the privilege of working. Prisons are very tough places to work and live (I can confirm they are not, in fact, holiday camps), and I hope this book can be a testament to that and to the things that really go on inside, both wonderful and devastating.

It would not have been possible to write this book without changing names, places, genders, offences and other identifying features. Although everything I've written happened, some characters and incidents have been amalgamated, and I have changed details out of respect for those who would prefer that their stories remain hidden. For every incident that has an element of closure, there will be many more that remain ongoing. It may be uncomfortable to hear about the ways in which people suffer and try to survive, and the fact that some don't, but maybe that's the point. Prisons shouldn't be somebody else's problem. Perhaps the most uncomfortable truth of all is that you may recognise yourself in some of the people featured on these pages. There's something reassuring about the idea of people in prison being inherently bad, even evil, because then they become inhuman, the very antithesis of what we are. It makes it acceptable to not care about the people locked up and the ones holding the keys, because they'll never be us and their lives have no bearing on ours.

But that's not how it works. We've all driven too fast, drunk too much, checked our phones behind the wheel, maybe even thrown a punch on a night out. Life can change in a second; the consequences can last far longer. It might be nice to think that we're nothing like the ones doing time, but a dirty mirror is a mirror, all the same. Even if you don't like what you see.

PART 1

I

The Wing

*W*ELCOME TO *A Wing*.
The sign alone feels intimidating. It is a strange thing, to be welcomed to a place where no one wants to be.

The gate slams shut behind us. The 120 cell doors ahead of us remain closed. The wing is divided into three spurs – red, blue and green – each with forty cells, spread over three landings. The corresponding railings and cell doors are painted the colour of that spur, and one prisoner will later tell me how it's best for everyone if he isn't located on Red Spur. Something about staring at a red door all night makes him angry.

We've come through the main wing entrance on to the landing. There are framed photographs on the walls, snow-topped mountains with motivational quotes like 'The biggest mountain you will ever conquer is within yourself'. They hang next to anti-bullying posters and adverts for the Samaritans. And alarm bells. The alarm bells, big red buttons set in metal boxes, are fitted on every wall, in every room, everywhere.

We walk past an office marked 'CUSTODIAL MANAGER', and past another marked 'SENIOR OFFICERS'. These titles will soon be so familiar that I won't even bother to say them in full. Like everyone else, I'll abbreviate every possible term to its shortest version. Custodial manager will become CM, senior officer will become SO. In a place where every minute is accounted for, efficiency is everything. We keep walking, and my eyes are drawn to a large metal chair connected to a power socket in the wall. Brian notices me looking.

13

ALEX SOUTH

'That's the BOSS chair,' he says. 'If they've got anything metal plugged, that detects it.'

I look closer. 'Body Orifice Security Scanner' is printed on the side.

'Plugging' means what you think it does. Where you think it does. Many years from now, I'll listen as a prisoner tells me how he plugged five mobile phones in the visits hall at HMP Belmarsh, and I'll wince as he complains about the piles he now can't get rid of. But that's in the distant future, and right now I'm blissfully unaware of the reasons why someone might insert one phone into their rectum, never mind five.

BOSS chairs are used in prisons around the world as a type of non-invasive cavity search. They can detect metal even if it's concealed internally, so they're a useful tool in stemming the flow of mobile phones in prisons. Technically, there is no need for prisoners to have illicit mobile phones. There are three land-line phones on each spur that prisoners have access to, one on each floor. The prisoners have their own unique PIN to use, and they can top up their credit every week, but these phones are heavily monitored. The numbers prisoners can call are restricted, too, with good reason. While most prisoners who get hold of a mobile phone in jail will use it to speak to friends and family, there are many who use phones to organise further criminality, to harass their victims and to intimidate witnesses into refusing to testify against them.

Just as there's a demand for mobile phones, there's a market dedicated to circumnavigating the equipment that detects them. Later, I'll learn about the manufacturers that sell phones designed specifically to beat this equipment, or how some phones are disguised to look like car fobs, the kind that wouldn't arouse suspicion if a corrupt officer was to have one in his pocket. Some are no bigger than your thumb, and some are shaped like a bullet to help with – well, you know. But I'm new, and this is the first time I've ever seen a BOSS chair.

Right now, I'm just trying to find a space to sit in the staff breakroom. It smells like wet Monday mornings in here. Instant coffee and rain-soaked coats. The staff here are already a close-knit team, and I feel a bit out of place. But I won't feel like that for long; I'm about to spend a lot of time with these people, and much of it will be in this room. A lot happens here. This is where the security briefings are held twice a day. It's where countless cups of coffee are made, where *Bargain Hunt* is watched religiously, and where makeshift beds are constructed on night shifts. I'll laugh until my face hurts in this room, and, when things go badly wrong, I'll hold back tears in here, too. At first sight, it looks like the sort of breakroom you'd find in any workplace: a dozen tattered chairs, a couple of round tables in the middle and a dodgy-smelling fridge with a note about replacing the milk tacked to the door. Look a little closer, though, and there's a picture of the recent weapon find on the wall. A toothbrush with two razor blades melted into the head. And if you look just beyond that, at the windows lining one wall, you'll see the thick metal cages attached to them. They stop the windows from opening fully, so prisoners can't pass items from cell to cell. Items like a toothbrush with two razor blades melted into it.

I try not to stare at the picture of the toothbrush. It's there to keep staff vigilant, and ultimately to keep us safe, but it's not doing much for my nerves. Right now, I can't imagine a time when this environment won't feel daunting in every possible way. I'm in awe of the officers already in here, flinging off their coats and flicking on the kettle, clearly so comfortable with this room and the pictures of weapons and the BOSS chair and all the abbreviations I'm struggling to remember. But I will learn in time that being comfortable isn't always a good thing. There's a delicate balance between being comfortable and being complacent. Complacency is dangerous. So the pictures of weapons are important. They remind us of where we are. Not that I need reminding. I am very aware of where I am, who I'm with and what is expected of me.

I'm aware, in particular, of the potential for violence. I wonder how I'll handle it when it happens – what if I freeze? What if I forget all my restraint training? There were a handful of women on my training course, all preparing to become officers at jails around the country. We were still the minority, but it didn't feel like a big issue. Now I'm worried that it is. The officers in this room are all men. I'm fit, but I'm not particularly strong, whereas my colleagues definitely are. One is even a semi-professional bodybuilder. My instructor had told me not to worry about things like that; he'd said that restraints are all about control and not force. But that was in a dojo with padded walls and printed-out health-and-safety rules. Somewhere where I could practise and get things wrong and try again.

'Seats please, everyone.' A deep voice cuts through the chatter in the room, followed by the man to whom it belongs. 'You must be Alex.' He smiles at me. 'I'm Gavin, one of the senior officers here.' Gavin is big and bald, with faded green tattoos on his arms. He's holding an A4 notepad with 'OBSERVATION BOOK' printed on the cover. Or the 'obs book', as everyone calls it.

'Has everyone introduced themselves?' he asks me.

They have. They've asked me what I did for a living before, and said that prison probably isn't too dissimilar from a Saturday night in the bar. They've asked me how training went, and they've all said the same as Brian, that I might as well forget most of it. If any of them are thinking that I don't look the part, then they don't let it show. But it's all I can think about. I'm the only female officer on shift today, and I wish I wasn't. Everything from my ponytail to my voice to my diminutive stature makes me feel like I stand out.

'You'll be fine,' Gavin says, as if he can hear my thoughts. 'Just concentrate on learning the regime for the first week.'

He takes a seat at the front of the room and goes through the events of the last few days. 'The landings are looking a little dirty, can we make sure the cleaners are actually cleaning, please? We need to be checking in on Aaron as much as possible; this time of year is tough for him. It's the anniversary of his offence soon. And has everyone seen the pictures of the shanks on the wall? Found in the showers last Saturday.'

A shank is a makeshift prison weapon. Like the razor-blade-encrusted toothbrush, weapons can be manufactured out of almost anything in jail. Throughout my career, I'll see knuckledusters made from the rungs on an ironing board, a whip improvised from a TV cable, even a bar of soap fashioned into the shape of a gun and painted black. But it's the shanks, the ones with sharpened edges designed to stab or slash, that get to me the most.

Everyone listens carefully; you could hear a pin drop. Gavin won't go through it all again. There isn't time. Prisons run to a strict regime. Unlock, labour movement, lunch, bang-up, unlock, labour movement, exercise, dinner, bang-up, association, gym, bang-up. Routine is important. Not paying attention could be dangerous. People don't turn their toothbrushes into shanks for no reason.

'Now, let's get going.'

***

Red Spur. It's empty of furniture, except for a well-worn pool table at one end and a large commercial freezer at the other. Most prisons don't even have a microwave on the wing, never mind fridges and freezers. But Whitemoor is different from most prisons. Whitemoor doesn't serve the local courts and it doesn't take short-term prisoners. The men here are lifers, with very few exceptions. Because of this, they have access to the kind of facilities that a lot of jails don't offer, like kitchens on each spur for prisoners to cook their own food. The men store their meat, fish and ice lollies in these freezers, in clear plastic bags labelled with the name and number of the prisoner to whom they belong. The freezers are searched every day, and every day at least one bottle of frozen water is removed. The prisoners use them as weights to lift in their cells each night, but a solid block of ice could be a nasty weapon. If it's heavy enough to be used as a dumb-bell, it's heavy enough to knock someone out.

Above me is a platform of metal safety netting that stretches across the centre of the twos landing. It's there to catch prisoners who jump the railings as a form of protest. This might sound like a strange thing to do, but it happens a lot. The moment someone is on the netting, an 'incident at height' is declared, and specially trained staff are called to intervene if necessary.

Through the netting above me, I can see Brian on the twos landing, and another officer on the threes landing, both of them with keys in hand. The wing is quiet, just the occasional cough coming from behind a cell door. We're waiting for Gavin to make the call to unlock. When it comes, the wing will wake up. The prisoners will leave their cells and get ready for work.

'Unlock A Wing!'

And there it is. The first time I hear it.

Boots stride from door to door, keys click into waiting locks, heavy doors groan open, revealing the twelve-foot-by-eight-foot rooms behind them. The air is charged with the presence of all these men as they spill onto the landings. Musa with his slippers still on, Anderson in an all-red matching tracksuit, Eamonn with a chunky gold chain round his neck, Aaron with a purple scar round his, Peter in a stripy cardigan, Joseph in a foul mood. The smell of minty toothpaste and cheap deodorant, stale smoke and unwashed bedding. Patois, street slang, cockney rhyme, different languages entirely, some I recognise and some I don't. Red Spur is a different world, and I'm in the centre of it.

The same scene is playing out in jails round the country. Give or take half an hour, a broadly similar regime is taking place on G Wing at Pentonville, on the Category A Unit at Strangeways, the Dangerous Severe Personality Disorder Unit at Frankland, the Mother and Baby Unit at Bronzefield. The men's prisons, women's prisons, high-security and open prisons, young offenders' institutions and secure training centres for the kids under seventeen. All getting ready to be unlocked.

That first day, and several more after it, pass in a blur. A fog of procedures I don't yet understand, a layout I don't yet know, keys that all look the same and hundreds of names I'll never remember. I don't enjoy it. I feel completely and utterly out of my depth. All the normal stresses of starting a new job are compounded by the kind of job it is. It isn't just managers and colleagues watching me, it's 120 prisoners as well, and the ever-present threat of violence. The officers were right. Training hasn't prepared me in the slightest. I'm terrified.

Over time, it does get a bit easier. Gavin tells me to concentrate on learning all the prisoners' names and the regime, and not much else for now. A couple of weeks pass without incident, and some of my fear goes. I feel like I'm always just waiting for a fight to break out, but it doesn't. And yet, I'm still apprehensive. I still feel horribly out of place. I still feel nervous when we're about to unlock: a weird dichotomy between the cold metal of the keys in my hand and the hot anticipation of having to use them. It isn't like training college. The wing isn't a mock-up, the prisoners aren't dummies and safe words don't mean anything. Behind these doors is real life. Messy and chaotic and uncomfortable.

***

Relationships between staff and prisoners are a huge part of prison life. They're the reason things run smoothly – and when things don't run smoothly, they're often the reason for that, too. It can be hard to get the balance right, to be assertive but not abuse your authority, to be friendly but not a pushover. The power dynamics in prison are more complicated than you might think. It's more nuanced than just one group of people having the upper hand over another. Ultimately, prisons run on goodwill. There are many more prisoners than there are officers, and a uniform doesn't necessitate compliance. In fact, in some cases, it can mean the very opposite. So developing positive relationships is important. But that takes time. And inevitably, there's always going to be someone you don't see eye to eye with.

For me, at this moment in time, that person is Davis. He's twenty-two, and at the beginning of a life sentence. I won't pretend to know what that feels like. But if I thought being the same age might give us something to bond over, I was wrong.

I walk up the stairs at the end of the ones landing, passing Joseph on the way. He's tall and wide, his shoulders so big they seem to coax his head into a permanent stoop.

'Did you see it last night, Alex?' he asks.

He means the documentary about his case. It was one of the most high-profile trials in history, made notorious by the faces of the victims in photographs taken just hours before they were killed.

'Are you coming back on here after freeflow? Can we talk about it?' he asks.

These are the moments when I start to come into my own a bit. I can't pretend that I'm enjoying the job, because I'm most definitely not, but these are the times when I think that maybe, one day, I might. I'm not a fighter, but then no one's asked me to be. In fact, the things that my managers have asked of me are the parts of the job I think I could be good at. I'm a good listener. I like talking to people and getting to know them. It was only a few days ago that Roger described these skills to me as my 'greatest weapon'.

'It's a much greater achievement if you can talk yourself out of a difficult situation rather than having to draw your baton – and trust me, everyone else will thank you for it,' he told me.

So when Joseph asks if we can talk, I say yes. Part of me dares to hope that saying yes to these moments could be how I find my place here.

***

In the same way as the call to unlock signals the wing is waking up, the call to send on freeflow gets it moving.

Freeflow is the movement of prisoners from their wing to whatever activity they're scheduled to attend. And there's a lot on offer at Whitemoor: carpentry, painting, a recycling workshop, music engineering, IT repairs, education. But there's a strange irony to this. Whitemoor is a long-termers' jail. The majority of the men here are serving minimum tariffs of twenty years or more, and some of them are natural lifers. Even if they'll never use these skills in the outside world, though, there is great value in giving prisoners access to activities that are engaging and interesting. Boredom in prison is poisonous.

Brian stands at the entrance to Red Spur on the twos landing, leaning casually against the open gate, ticking off names of the prisoners as they line up. Officers are stationed at different points by the wing entrance, like checkpoints to be passed through. Roger is first, with the handheld metal detector, an ugly grey wand that skims the outline of the men's bodies and the soles of their shoes. Like most of the staff here, Roger's been a prison officer for a long time and he has the attitude to prove it: calm, careful and consistent. He tests the metal detector against his watch, listening for the shrill alert of machine against metal. His watch, all of our watches, cost no more than £28, because that's the amount the Prison Service will refund if your watch should break in an incident. Or at least, that's what I'm told, anyway. Mine is an old gold Casio with half the paint missing. The younger prisoners tell me it looks like the kind of thing a grandad would have.

I stand a few steps behind Roger, ready to do the rubdown searches after the prisoners have been wanded. Beside me is Jade, the only other female officer on duty today. She perches on a table by the railings, her radio turned up loud, waiting.

'ALL OUTSTATIONS, SEND ON FREEFLOW'.

With that, Red Spur gates open.

First up is Rafik. He's always first. For work, for lunch, for exercise, everything. While some prisoners are still in bed when the staff unlock in the morning, Rafik never is. He waits patiently by his cell door. His bed is always made and the chair is always upside down on the centre of his duvet. When I ask why, he tells me it's habit. He's been in and out of prison for a long time, and started off in the now-abolished Borstal system for young offenders. There, his cell had to be spotless and the floor always clear. Anything that wasn't bolted to the floor had to be on the bed. I don't ask what the consequences were if he didn't do it, but they were severe enough to keep him doing the same thing over thirty years later.

Rafik started off doing short stints in jail, mainly for selling drugs. But that's not where the real money is. So he worked his way up and swapped street corners and filthy crack houses for villas abroad, Cartier watches and, ultimately, a twenty-five-year sentence for drug importation. People aren't always what they seem. He trusted the wrong person and they set him up. They tapped his phones and had surveillance following his every move. So now he's here. In a cell not dissimilar to the ones he was in so many years earlier. A table, a wardrobe, bars on the window and a chair on the bed.

Rafik passes Roger's metal detector and stops in front of me, his arms raised like a human coat hanger.

'Good morning, Alex. How are you getting on?'

'Fine thank you, Rafik. Just getting used to everything still.'

He drops his arms and turns round. 'Has anyone been rude to you yet, Alex?' Arms up again.

'No. Everyone has been very polite.'

That's not strictly true. Davis has been rude to me. And so has Jason, from cell 12 on Green Spur. He may not say anything overtly disrespectful, but he had started staring at me a little too often, for a little too long – until the other officers noticed, and started staring back. I learned that his index offence was a string of prolonged, violent and premeditated attacks on women. But men like him, with that sort of attitude to female staff, are in the minority, and as many prisoners as officers have asked after my wellbeing.

Within seconds of the call to send on, swarms of prisoners have spilled from their respective wings into the main corridor. Freeflow is a chance for the men to catch up with their friends from different wings, to bump fists with the people they like, and bump fists a little harder with those they don't. There are easily upwards of a hundred men crossing the prison via the corridor, making this one of the busiest, and most volatile, times of the day. CCTV coverage supports the staff patrolling, but, in a prison in which almost everyone is serving a life sentence, it's tough to find a meaningful deterrent to violence. It's a bit late to worry about getting caught.

Jade and I make a good searching team; I do the rubdowns and she flicks through the folders and books that some of the men have with them. In fact, we make a good team in general. I look forward to the shifts we're on together. About forty per cent of the officers at Whitemoor are female, and Jade and I are two of the youngest, both in our early twenties. A lot of the things I'm experiencing at the moment, like finding my place in the team and dealing with misgivings about my physical abilities, are things Jade has already been through. She knows I'm worried about violence and how I'll handle it and, as a petite woman herself, she gets it. She tells me that after her first restraint, she was instructed to apply handcuffs, but couldn't get the key to work. It went on for so long that even the prisoner said he couldn't be bothered to fight anymore. When I tell her that I'm getting on fine and starting to feel more settled, she doesn't believe a word of it.

'Bullshit. You hate it. I did when I first started, too,' she says. 'But I love coming to work now. Just give it time. You'll find a way of working that suits you. Davis will stop being a prick eventually. He did exactly the same to me. You're a new face, and for some of these guys that's a challenge.'

Jade picks up a book by the spine and shakes the pages. Anything can be a hiding place, depending on what it is you want to conceal. Only last week, a particularly rotund prisoner from Green Spur lost his job in the main kitchens for stealing raw bacon and hiding it in between the rolls of his stomach.

When the last of the prisoners from Red Spur have been searched, Green Spur is unlocked. Then Blue Spur. Nearly ninety men come off the wing in total. One of the last to leave is Bolt. He's a well-known inmate throughout the entire high-security prison estate. It's not just the brutality of his index offence that's made him notorious, it's how brazen it was. Bodies in broad daylight.

The hierarchy among prisoners can be complicated. It can be related to the length of a prisoner's tariff, their reputation outside or their family connections. Sometimes offence matters and sometimes it doesn't, even when you wish it would. There are a handful of serious sex offenders on A Wing who are only safe here because of the protection their religion affords them. Religion is a big part of the hierarchy at Whitemoor.

Whatever the reason for it, Bolt is the one they all listen to here.

He's carrying a folder and some bulky textbooks with paper flags sticking out from the pages. Jade and I have swapped roles, so I check the books to make sure there's nothing concealed inside. They look similar to my own Open University books, with notes scribbled in the margins and whole paragraphs crudely highlighted. Conventional uni didn't suit me, but it turns out long-distance learning does. Bolt and I have spoken before about the degrees we're both studying for; his in sociology and mine in criminology. The conversation stalled somewhat when he told me why he wasn't allowed to study criminology himself. Apparently, it's a problem if you feature in one of the modules.

He's serving a life sentence for murder and attempted murder, but he very nearly wasn't convicted for either. The evidence was almost entirely circumstantial. No DNA was recovered, no blood-stained clothing, no weapons. Bolt's case took years to get to court, and, when it did, the trial cost over £4 million, and half the people giving evidence were in witness protection. So it's perhaps not surprising that the details have found their way into a textbook.

The value of higher education in prison can be contentious. The prisoners here don't pay for their Open University degrees, and that doesn't sit right with a lot of people. But from what I will come to see, their studies with the OU give these men a focus that was missing from their lives before.

'Big day today,' Bolt says, motioning to a bundle of A4 lined paper tucked into the next textbook. 'I'm handing in my essay.'

'You write your essays by hand?' I ask, unaware of how stupid this question is.

'Yeah, they're not that keen on giving us computers here.'

There are many reasons why I would not want to be a prisoner, but I'm adding this to the list.

The last few prisoners straggle out to the searching queues, having exhausted all possible excuses for why they shouldn't have to attend work. Those who stay are mostly wing cleaners. Armed with brooms, buckets and industrial-strength detergent, they sweep and mop the landings, change the bins and dust the railings. Somewhere this big, with this many people living in it, always seems to be dusty. It gathers in thick clumps in the corner of the netting and the tops of the window frames, despite the best efforts of the inmates assigned to get rid of it.

They roam the wings in their uniform of green trousers, pockets stuffed with J cloths. There's a cleaner for almost everything in jail: the ones landing, twos landing, threes; the showers, recesses and kitchens. Even the exercise yard. It's one of the best jobs a prisoner can have. As well as the green trousers, cleaners get more time out of cell, less supervision, and access to areas that are out of bounds to others. A trip to the bin compound can be more appealing than you'd think when you see the same four walls every day.

But, as I'll come to learn, there are other reasons why some people want a cleaning job so badly. It's the ideal cover for prisoners involved in the subculture. The stuff that goes on behind the scenes. Although I'm naïve enough at the moment to think there aren't phones or drugs on this wing, I'm wrong. Security is so tight at Whitemoor that a lot of the normal methods of conveying contraband into a prison are out of the question. There's no chance of launching a package over the perimeter wall here. But still, contraband gets in. Heroin, crack, weed, alcohol, phones, knives. And once inside the prison, it needs the right person to distribute the goods around the wing. Someone who can go between spurs, someone who's out of his cell when others aren't, who doesn't give the staff any grief and draws minimal attention to himself. A cleaner.

***

Everything that happens at Whitemoor is designed to be seen; the stairs have gaps between each step, and there are observation panels in every cell door. And yet, despite these measures, and the diligence of the staff, there are inevitably things that go unnoticed. Sometimes, the things that need seeing the most are the things that stay hidden.

No one's figured out why Joseph's moods are so erratic lately. There's speculation that he's on steroids, but he's passed every drug test. You can tell what kind of day he's having from the moment he's unlocked. You can tell from the way he walks and the look on his face and the snap in his voice.

'Was the documentary what you thought it would be?' I ask, as we stand side by side on the twos.

'Sort of, yeah. I knew they would try and make me out to be an animal. I expected that. It was hard seeing my mum on it, though.'

His mum had been interviewed on camera. Tears fell into her scarf as she talked about the son she knew and the man in the mugshot. She found it hard to reconcile the two. Joseph tells me he's innocent, that he had carried knives before – and used them, too – but not for this, not the thing they got him for. He says the CCTV footage is grainy, the key witness isn't credible, the whole trial was a mess. But he's here now.

'And I knew I probably would be at some point. There are two options if you're living that life. You're gonna get life or get killed. This is the better of the two.'

Get life or get killed. I'm struck by how the two halves of that phrase sound, as if they make perfect sense. 'Getting life' does anything but give someone life.

We talk about the crime itself and what it was like telling his mum that he thought he was going to be charged with multiple murder. We talk about the day he was arrested, and the way the feeling of the handcuffs snapping on to his wrists was different when the charge was murder. They felt more oppressive some-how, he tells me. Everything he says, he really thinks about. This kind of thing wasn't featured in the documentary. How he felt. What he was thinking when the lady juror in the yellow jumper mouthed 'Sorry' to him on the day they reached a verdict.

It's heavy stuff. Which is exactly why talking about it is so important. Officers are encouraged to have insightful conver-sations and tackle difficult subjects with prisoners – at least, as far as both parties are comfortable with doing so. There are versions of this conversation going on all around the wing, but up until now I've always been on the periphery. Stand-ing beside another officer as a prisoner opens up to them.

The documentary is a big deal; we'd all been briefed on it beforehand and advised to keep a close eye on Joseph. It isn't uncommon for prisoners to leave their cells in a foul mood the day after something about them has been aired on TV. They're seldom consulted in the making of these shows, and these are often men who like to be in control. Compared to the documentary, my conversation with Joseph isn't much, and it's quite possible that none of what he's saying is true, but that's not really the point. The point is he's talking. Emotions left bottled up can manifest in ugly ways. That's arguably the reason many of these men are in here in the first place.

With one word, Joseph went from a life outside to a life sentence inside. I wonder what that moment felt like for him, hearing the juror say 'guilty'. I ask him if he felt anything at all.

Sort of. He tells me that he felt numb when the verdict was read, but the numbness was still a feeling. Like feeling nothing and everything at the same time, as if all the rawest emotions inside him were filling him up, all that energy ready to spill from his mouth and his fists, but something buffered them just before they reached the surface.

Interestingly, he tells me, during that journey in the prison van from court back to jail after his life sentence had been handed down, he didn't think so much about the sentence itself or the years ahead of him, rising up like rungs on an endless ladder. He thought about school.

'All I could think on the way back to prison was what I was like in primary school. I was so happy, so into everything. Just a normal kid. I'd never have thought that I'd end up in prison for life. You look at a kid and you see the things they're into, you think about what they might be when they grow up. No one looks at a primary-school kid and thinks they'll be doing life for multiple murder.'

The killings weren't random. They were the latest in a long line of murders between two groups, going back and forth:

stabbings and shootings, homes set on fire with families inside. But when I ask how it all started, he can't tell me. He doesn't know who killed who first, or what it was over; he just knows that he couldn't be the one to stop. Nothing provokes vengeance as much as holding your friend in your arms while he chokes on his own blood.

A couple of cell doors down from Joseph is Ashley. They have the same accent because they're from the same area. Or nearly the same area. In a conversation that takes me a long time to get my head around, Joseph tells me that they're actually from rival areas. Ashley has, in fact, previously tried to kill Joseph by shooting at him in a crowded nightclub. Miraculously, no one was hurt. The police came but, of course, Ashley was long gone by then, and was never arrested for it. He's now serving a heavy sentence for attempted murder – gang-related again, but the target was someone else in Joseph's group rather than Joseph himself. And yet in here, they cook together, go to the gym together, attend religious service together.

In here, they're friends.

Joseph will be in his fifties when he's released, and Ashley not much younger. It's highly likely that neither of them will be allowed to go back to the same area over which they exerted so much influence. So it's impossible to predict if the rivalries that brought them here will naturally resume when they're out, but I'd make a good guess that they won't. There are new, younger men in their place now, ready to carry on their pointless war. Joseph and Ashley were big names once, but not anymore.

To an outsider like me, it doesn't make sense. And to an insider like Joseph, it doesn't make sense either. It might have done once, but not now. Because the people he lost his freedom for, the people he killed out of loyalty to, are the same people who don't write anymore, don't visit, don't send money.

Joseph and Ashley agreed to be civil in here because there are only five dispersal prisons in the country, and Whitemoor is the most settled. It's also the closest one to their home city, which makes it easier for their families to visit. Neither of them wants to transfer, but they both know the decision would be taken out of their hands if they were to cause trouble. Dispersal prisons are the most secure prisons in the country, and house the most serious offenders. Rather than having those men all located together, the dispersal system quite literally disperses them round the country. Wakefield takes predominantly sex offenders, so that leaves four others. Even if Joseph and Ashley were separated now, they would inevitably come across each other again at some point. Neither of them wants to spend the next twenty years inside always looking over their shoulder. So, for all these reasons, they agreed to be civil – but it turns out that they actually get on.

This truce extends to the visits hall. Although initially the security department would have had concerns about allowing two rival gangsters and their families to book visits on the same day, their respective families were prepared to put aside their differences, just as Joseph and Ashley were – for those two hours, at least. Joseph tells me that his toddler nephew refers to Whitemoor as 'Uncle Joseph's house', and asks why he never leaves. There are enough complicated emotions at play here. There's already too much to try to explain.

***

A week later, I'm sitting in the Blue Spur office flicking through a newspaper when I see someone I recognise. Bolt's face is staring coldly at me from the pages of a tabloid. A double-page spread. Fresh accusations from the Serious Crime Unit. It's pretty horrifying. I crunch on a breakfast bar and re-read the detective inspector's comments. They think Bolt committed more murders. I shake my head absent-mindedly, astonished.

'Good read?'

I look up to see Bolt's actual face.

'It's a bad photo, that. I wish they wouldn't use that one,' he says.

'It's not great,' I agree. 'Have you read this?'

'Yeah.' He passes me a frying pan to put back in the tool cabinet. Locked cabinets line the back wall of the office, with pots, pans, spatulas and ladles hanging on hooks inside them. Everything has to be signed out and signed back in before the end of association. The officers routinely patrol the kitchens, but the men here know how fortunate they are to have their own cooking facilities, and they don't abuse that privilege. In all my time at Whitemoor, none of these tools will ever be lost, hidden or used as weapons.

'You shouldn't believe everything you read, Alex. I didn't do the ones I've been convicted of, never mind those ones, too.'

I get up to put the pan away.

'It's in the paper because they haven't got enough evidence to actually charge me,' he continues. 'And they haven't got enough evidence because I didn't do it.'

I lock the cabinet. 'Everyone in here says they didn't do it,' I say.

Next to the picture of Bolt is a picture of a revolver with a silencer attached to it.

'I was involved in the lifestyle,' he says, 'but I didn't—'

Sammy, a Northerner with piercing green eyes, pops his head round the door and interrupts Bolt. 'Eh lad, what we having for tea? Alright, Alex?' He winks at me.

Bolt twists his head back to look at Sammy. 'Chicken curry. See if you can get some garam masala off someone, yeah?'

Sammy and Bolt are best friends. They're an unlikely-looking partnership, little and large, loud and quiet, Muslim and Christian, but rarely seen without each other. They're in a food boat together; Bolt cooks and Sammy's the pot-wash.

The prisoners who cook at Whitemoor are inventive with their food; they can make something out of nothing. There isn't a lot for them to work with, but somehow they make birthday cakes and banoffee pies, curries and marinades. That prisoner who once stole the bacon makes the best barbecue sauce I've ever tasted. Sammy might find some garam masala that's been left in the kitchen, but he's more likely to have to go to the cell of someone who's known to be a good cook – and if that's the case, he'll only take the spice if they're in there to ask. Aside from sex offenders, cell thieves are considered the lowest of the low. Still, Sammy is popular with everyone, Bolt even more so, so he won't have any trouble getting some garam masala. They'll just expect a bowl of curry themselves in return.

'Alright lad, in a bit.' We both watch as Sammy trots down the landing, yelling, 'Tikka masala!'

'*Garam*, you muppet,' Bolt mutters. He turns to me. 'Nothing is as simple as it seems, Alex. People get into that life for lots of reasons.'

'What's your reason?'

He sits down on the table, resting his elbows on his knees, hands dangling in front of him. 'My niece died. She went out one night and got shot.'

I don't know what to say. The man in the grainy mugshot sits in front of me, very real and very human. I ask him if he knows who it was that killed his niece. He says he does. I ask if they're in prison now, too, thinking the subsequent investigation and court case must be how he knows who's responsible. But there was no court case, he tells me. No one was ever even charged. And yet he knows exactly who did it.

'And no, they're not in prison.'

The air between us suddenly feels very thick. I'm not sure exactly what he's saying. But I'm very aware that Bolt does not appear to be the sort of person to know who killed his niece and let that lie.

bit of fear. It could be anything. A brawl or a stabbing or a hostage situation, or even a riot.

Anything.

They call it fight or flight, the way the human body reacts to these situations. Fight or flight, but never freeze. Freezing is not an option in prison.

On this occasion, I don't need to fight, but my adrenaline is still through the roof. I haven't seen a prisoner wielding a makeshift weapon before, covered in his own blood with his head split open. This is a first for me, and, despite the horror of some of the things I'll see over the next few years, it's a day I'll never forget.

Jade and I try to help the staff restraining Joseph, but the landing seems to have narrowed in the scrum of bodies that fill it. There's barely any room left. The alarm is still ringing, the red lights on the wall still flashing, even though the whole thing was over in seconds. Some prisoners lean over the railings to watch what's going on, but most have stepped wordlessly back into their cells. The majority had already left the wing for work, and I'll find out later that the timing was strategic. The men who attacked Joseph waited until his friends were gone.

I hear him tell the staff he's not going to fight, that it isn't about them. His words are merged and shaking.

Roger is talking to him calmly, his voice so steady, asking has he got anything else on him, just take it easy, is he hurt, where is the blood coming from, try to calm down. The shard of glass lies on the floor. I can see patches of a faded red logo. It's from a Pyrex dish. He's smashed a Pyrex dish. This isn't a carefully crafted shank; it's a frantic, last-minute knife, needed right then and there.

Boot prints have smeared blood down the landing. I notice with horror that they're mine.

'We need to lock up the spur now. Be careful, Alex – we don't know what's gone on,' Jade says.

35

We split up and take a landing each, locking cell doors, checking recesses and shower stalls. The gates to the wing keep swinging open as more staff arrive. Officers from all around the prison flood the spur to help us, many of whom I've never even seen before. The landings are a sea of white shirts.

Everyone checks on everyone else, making sure staff and prisoners are all accounted for. This is important. It's not unheard of for prisoners to cause an alarm-bell situation as a distraction from something else. With staff attention focused elsewhere, it can be an ideal opportunity to pass drugs or settle scores. So I count my landing diligently, tallying each individual man with a solid black line on my notepad, as if I don't trust my memory to make it to forty alone. With so many people watching and so much going on, I don't want to be the one who messes up my numbers.

'Happy with your numbers, Alex?'

I turn to see the custodial manager, tall and imposing in his immaculately smart uniform. I met him on my first day.

'Yes, I'm happy.' I show him my tallied notepad.

From the first time I spoke to CM Barnes, in one of the side offices by the wing entrance, I knew I never wanted to let this man down. Years of experience have earned him his rank and the respect that comes with it. On that first day, he'd told me in no uncertain terms that appearance matters, that my boots must be polished and my shirts ironed, that how professional I look on the outside will give me confidence on the inside. But now there's blood on my boots, and my hands are shaking.

Joseph sits on a chair at the back of Blue Spur ones landing. He alternates between sitting with his back straight against the back of the chair and leaning over, with his head lolling between his knees, frustration caught in his fists. The wound on his head is wide enough to reveal pink flesh: a long, deep cut running over the curve of his skull. The sort that couldn't be caused by fists alone. Some of the blood has dried already, leaving his hair matted in red clumps. I kneel next to him and ask him how he's doing.

He sighs and shrugs and laughs sadly. 'I'm fine. It's just jail, innit. Just jail. Is it bad? The thing on my head, is it bad?'

I peer at the top of his head. It's bad. 'No, it's not too bad. Let your hair grow a bit and you won't be able to notice. It looks like you took a bit of a beating, though.'

His swollen eyes meet mine. 'I did good, though, Alex. There was three of them and only one of me, and I didn't go down. I didn't hit the floor once. They call themselves fighters, but there was three of them and I didn't hit the floor.'

'Did they use weapons?' asks Bernard, standing next to us. Bernard is my buddy officer, given the task of showing me the ropes and getting me through my twelve-month probation period, although I'll still be going to him for advice years later. He's one of the best officers I'll ever work with. He started his career in the eighties at HMP Wandsworth, when the batons were wooden and the toilets were buckets. His voice still has the notes of a London accent never quite dropped, and he has a laugh that makes his beard dance. During our time working together, I'll never see a prisoner argue with him, or even try to. I'll never even hear him raise his voice.

'I don't actually know, Bernard. It just happened so fast,' Joseph says.

'What was it about?' I ask.

'No idea.' He's a terrible liar, but I get it. He can't tell me that.

The three of us sit quietly together, all of us thinking about the same thing, but so separately. We have all experienced the last thirty minutes in vastly different ways. I wonder how it feels for Joseph to look up and see a swipe of his own blood on the railings.

He shakes his head and exhales. 'I can't believe that happened, man.'

I suddenly remember the Pyrex dish. 'You smashed the dish, Joseph? The shard of glass was from that, right?'

'I just grabbed the nearest thing. I was just trying to protect myself.'

CM Barnes appears above us on the centre twos landing. He calls down that it's time for Joseph to go to Healthcare now; the corridor has been cleared of prisoners, and we can walk him there straight away.

'OK. Just let me put my shoes on properly,' says Joseph. The heels of his feet stick out of battered, bloodstained trainers. They must have come off in the beating. Or the chase. He fumbles with his shoes. It's only then that I notice how much his hands are shaking. Maybe that's why he'd balled them into fists before, so I couldn't see. A way to hold on to himself. He presses his heels down but the back of the trainer folds, his finger trapped between foot and fabric.

'Fuck's sake.' He shakes his head and tries again.

I look at his face and see that his eyes are wet.

'It's sweat. I'm so hot,' he mumbles, trying and failing again with his shoes. He's wearing navy blue socks. I don't know why that stays with me. I take his hand and put it on his lap. I put his shoes on for him.

'Thank you, Alex,' he says.

It isn't sweat.

***

That evening, we stand there in silence, looking down at the prisoners on the landings below. A game of table tennis takes place between two members of an organised crime gang; a group of friends chop and chat and chastise one another's culinary skills in the kitchen; Davis and Ahmet play a sloppy pool match with no recognisable rules; two middle-aged Jamaicans are engrossed in a tense game of dominoes in the corner.

Others lean on the railings like me and Bolt, watching nothing and everything.

Prison is a condensed version of all the best and worst bits of humanity. But no matter how bad my shift has been, I walk out of here at the end of it. They don't. Almost everyone here is a lifer. For them, there is no set finish time. Things can change in an instant. They could spend one night in their cell on the wing, and the next in Healthcare with staples in their head and two black eyes. The prisoners have to find a way to survive.

This world is new to me, but not to Bolt. He'd already left the wing for education when the assault happened. The general consensus among staff is that there's very little that happens without his say-so, but it's hard to see why he would want anything to happen to Joseph. The two of them are friends. Besides, Bolt always seems to be the peacekeeper around here. More than once I've seen him defuse potentially volatile situations. People listen to him.

It's evening association now; the two hours at the end of the day when the prisoners get to mix with each other on the wing. Joseph is staying in the Healthcare inpatients' unit, and his three assailants have been segregated. The blood has been cleaned from the floor. It's only the heavy iron padlock on Joseph's cell door that indicates something happened there. We now know that he was attacked from behind as he made a cup of tea in his cell. Due to the severity of the assault, his cell has been designated a crime scene and can't be opened until a specialist team of officers have attended to take photos and collect evidence.

I can see Bernard opposite, discussing recipes with a convicted terrorist. Roger is below me on the ones landing, deep in conversation with a man suspected of eating part of his victim's body. And Brian keeps checking the football score on BBC Sport online, and updating a prisoner nicknamed Henry VIII because he kept killing his wives. There are some extremely dangerous men in here. It might seem surprising that violent incidents aren't more common, but you have to consider how much time officers spend talking and getting to know these men. It's sometimes referred to as dynamic security, the idea that developing positive relationships with the prisoners helps maintain order and control.

But the staff I work with don't think about it; they just do it naturally. They know what to say and when to say it, and when to say nothing at all and just listen. I'm learning from the best. A few moments pass before Bolt and I both open our mouths to speak, but I get there first.

'Did you know that was going to happen earlier?' I say.

'No. I wouldn't have let it happen if I'd known,' he replies.

I believe him.

***

I leave the prison that day feeling much the same way I always do. Relieved that nothing went wrong, and glad to be making my way out into the fresh air. I walk through the long corridors, quiet and empty at this time, and through the vehicle compound, where a couple of OSGs are testing the engines. I pause at the baton lockers to find my own, hand in my keys at the gatehouse, go through the airlock, and then out into the car park. I allow myself to spend the drive home thinking about how the shift went, and if there's anything that I should perhaps have done differently. The further I go, the more able I feel to leave it behind, as if the prison's grip on me is loosening. The cages on the windows, the wire on the walls, the signs prohibiting bombs and weapons and drugs, all getting smaller and smaller until they're out of sight. Not completely out of mind, but I'm working on it.

The drive should take twenty-five minutes, but I get stuck behind a tractor that spits dried mud and onion skins on to my windshield. I could overtake, but the roads here are narrow, with sharp corners. It's not worth the risk, especially in my little black car that starts to rattle whenever I go above forty miles per hour. It took me three attempts to pass my driving test, and even now, almost five years later, the novelty hasn't worn off. I love the freedom of it. I love knowing that I can just get in the car and go, that I could wake up tomorrow and drive to Scotland if I wanted, for no reason at all.

Eventually, the tractor turns left and I turn right, into my hometown: a place that felt stagnant and boring not so long ago, but feels familiar and comforting now that I spend so much time in another world entirely. I drive past the bar where I used to work, past the Chinese restaurant where I go with my friends to celebrate every birthday, past the club where I spent far too much time in my teens, where the drinks were unnecessarily neon and the DJ randomly shouted, 'Are you ready?!' That club will be full later. Davis will still be in his cell, where I said goodbye to him half an hour ago. He'll still be there when people spill out of the club at closing time, when they jostle outside the fried chicken shop and queue at the taxi rank.

None of that for me, though. I'm always tired after work. Even when nothing has really happened, the intensity of being constantly alert, maintaining that state of hypervigilance, leaves me exhausted at the end of the day. So, I'll let myself into the flat above the barber's, which I share with two of my best friends, one a midwife and the other a social worker. We'll watch TV, and Hannah will flick through a dating app while Charlie cooks, or maybe we'll give up on that and get a takeaway. Or maybe we'll decide to go out after all. Maybe I'll have an hour to myself first, looking through my Open University stuff.

I can work and study. I can watch my lectures online or attend in person if I want. I can go out tonight or stay in. I can be with my friends or be by myself. I can go wherever I want, do whatever I want. But Davis can't. Nor can Bolt.

They'll still be there in the morning, when the officer on duty opens their door, and it starts all over again.

2

The Wing By Night

THE OTHER OFFICERS have already pointed out Aaron to me. Not that he needs pointing out. His neck is strangled by a thick purple welt that digs into the skin like a hideous necklace. He tried to hang himself a few weeks ago, and very nearly succeeded – the staff saved his life with seconds to spare. I've lost count of the number of people who tell me to check on Aaron more than is officially required, to look into his cell every time I walk past. I find myself pausing as I get to his door. I'm scared of seeing something I can't unsee.

He tells me, 'I'll be alright, Alex. Don't worry.'

But the rise and fall of his scar when he talks is all the reminding I need not to become complacent.

It's my first set of night shifts, and I've struggled more than I thought I would. It isn't the work that's taxing, or even knowing I'm the only member of staff on the wing. It's just staying awake. I've never worked nights before, and those last few hours before the day staff come in feel like torture.

As an A Wing officer, I spend my night shifts on the wing, just as I do my day shifts. It's a strange feeling being by yourself in a huge, open space leading on to lots of small, identically constructed rooms, all of them locked, each housing a single human. There are 120 men on A Wing with me, and yet I'm very much alone. I try not to let myself think how outnumbered I am. There's a TV in the staffroom that I could watch, but past 10pm there's not a lot on, and I prefer to be in the centre office anyway. The cell bell panel is in there; a grey box that lights up if any prisoners press their bell, showing the location of the cell. I don't want to miss a cell bell because I'm in another room. We're expected to answer cell bells within two minutes.

As you'd expect, staffing is significantly reduced at night. The expectation is that no doors will be unlocked. All I'm really here for is to check the prisoners are still in their cells throughout the night and answer any cell bells.

Some officers love nights. There isn't a whole lot to do. It's the reason some people specifically request night shifts for overtime; the overtime rate is higher than our normal pay, and you can easily spend most of the shift sitting down. It's easy money. But that's the same reason a lot of officers hate nights. If there's nothing to do, it can be very hard to stay awake. I started last night's shift feeling proactive and keen to keep myself busy. I checked all the showers and recesses for weapons, went through all the prisoners' outgoing mail and sorted it into piles, tidied the office and printed out the visits list for the next day. But very quickly, I ran out of things to do, and my enthusiasm waned. The clock eventually limped to 6.30am, moving as slowly as if someone had coated the hands in thick mud, and each flick of black plastic was a monumental effort that the clock must then pause to recover from.

By the time I'm back on duty tonight, word seems to have spread that I'm the night officer this week. The wing seems settled. Bolt is awake, sitting at his table with a textbook in front of him. Rafik is already fast asleep, one arm flung haphazardly out of bed, the TV remote balanced precariously in his palm. Almost all the prisoners have TVs in their cells. There's a handful who don't, due to poor behaviour. The threat of losing your TV is a powerful deterrent, and that alone keeps a lot of the prisoners from acting up. In Young Offender Institutions, there's often a set time for lights out when the prisoners have to switch off their TVs and go to sleep. But not here. Everyone at Whitemoor is over twenty-one, and all the cells are single occupancy. The prisoners are simply expected to use common courtesy when it comes to the volume of their TVs and stereos at night.

Most prisoners are showing compassion for Aaron. No one wants him to hurt himself, and everyone knows that the night hours are when it's hardest to reach him. Alone in his cell, it's harder to stop the darkness outside from darkening the thoughts inside his head. It might become easier for him to see a shoelace or the belt of a dressing gown and imagine it as a route to another world, or to nothing at all, just a finite end to everything that's come before.

In the Healthcare unit, these things would have been removed from his cell. The cell would have been clear of not just potential ligatures, but ligature points, too. Prisoners considered at high risk of taking their own lives are placed in cells with specially adapted furniture. The chair and table are made of curved plastic with no edges, impossible to tie a noose to. There's no glass, either; the window is Perspex and there's no observation panel, because there's no door. Just a clear Perspex gate, through which an officer observes the prisoner inside. All day, all night. These cells are called 'constant-watch' cells, because that's exactly what happens. Whether the prisoner is asleep, looking out the window, or sitting on the toilet, someone is watching them. There's no TV because the cable could be a ligature, and there's no kettle in case the prisoner intentionally scalds themself. They're not allowed a pencil in case they stab themselves, nor paper, in case they try to choke themselves by stuffing it down their throat.

Constant-watch cells are bleak and depressing to look at, never mind live in.

Unsurprisingly, most prisoners don't want to be in these cells. There's a powerful argument that placing someone in a constant-watch cell does more harm than good. I can't imagine that being put in a room that bare, with someone staring at you 24/7, does much to improve one's mental health. But the reality is that constant-watch cells keep people alive. If the person is determined to kill themself, then making that as physically difficult as possible is the priority.

Prisoners at high risk of suicide or self-harm have regular reviews with a multi-disciplinary team of officers and health-care professionals. Aaron engaged well in his reviews. He said he wanted to go back to the wing, that being with his friends, in his own cell, with his own possessions would help him. So first, he moved to a normal cell in Healthcare and then, after intensive consultation between his doctors, officers who knew him well and Aaron himself, he returned to the wing.

I don't know Aaron very well. He's shy, softly spoken, and seems trapped in his own mind most of the time. He's got a long sentence ahead of him and an extremely unpleasant offence behind him. Like the majority of these men, he's in for murder. A vicious and sadistic murder, quite different in its depravity from many of the others committed by men on this wing. He doesn't get visits, though he does have a good relationship with his parents. But they're approaching their eighties and frail, and the journey to Whitemoor is a long one for them. Aaron spends most of his time with the same two prisoners; Larry the wing painter, and Jamie, a ginger Traveller with a laugh that sounds like a horn. The three of them never cause the staff any problems. If anything, it's hard to stop Larry painting, and Jamie is consistently and unfailingly polite. Aaron doesn't ever really say much.

The details of his offence are enough to make me feel nauseated and angry and desperately sad. But I don't want him to die. Especially not here, in one of these tiny cells, at his own hands. I don't want to be the one who finds him swinging. I don't want to know that at some point during my shift, someone metres from me had made a noose with shaking hands, slipped it round their neck while balancing on a flimsy chest of drawers, tied and tightened a knot around cold bars, and stepped off.

I know a few officers who have found a prisoner hanging, some more than once, but most of the staff at Whitemoor haven't. Self-harm is rare here. Whitemoor is a good prison. Still, I've not been in the job for long yet; I have no idea of what's to come.

**

The sounds that normally characterise a prison wing are all gone at night. Chains and boots and keys in locks, shouts and laughter, the sounds of pots and pans in the kitchen and grunts from the gym – all gone. It's eerily quiet, aside from the occasional toilet flushing. When there's football on the TV, some prisoners will kick their cell doors after a goal, and everyone does it at midnight on New Year's Eve. But there's nothing worth getting out of bed for tonight. All the lights are off except the one in the office, leaving the landings dark. Too much light keeps the prisoners awake. I carry a small black pocket torch to do my checks with, angling it into the corner of the observation panel so it doesn't light up the whole cell. I just need to know they're in there. And breathing.

At 2am, a cell bell flashes. It's Peter. Peter is a sex offender. Normally, he wouldn't be housed on one of the general population wings, but a tenuous family link to a high-profile and well-liked prisoner on Green Spur has afforded him a degree of protection. Sometimes, that kind of association is all it takes to keep a prisoner like Peter safe. Most convicted sex offenders don't have that sort of buffer, though, and so they do their time on Vulnerable Prisoner Units. I know before I even get to his cell that Peter only wants me to come to his door because I'm young and female and basically something to look at.

'Are you alright?' I ask.

He stares at me, black stubble scuffing his chin and jaw. 'Yeah. Do you want to see some pictures of me?'

'No thank you, Peter. It's two in the morning. I think you should get some sleep.'

One side of his nose twitches. 'I shouldn't be here, you know. I shouldn't be in prison.'

'Well, maybe in the morning you can speak to the senior officers about that. Try and get some sleep, OK? I've got work to do.'

'So you're saying your work is more important than having a conversation with me?'

I think of Aaron, his dented neck, and the extra checks I won't compromise on. 'Yes, I'm afraid it is.'

'Peter, leave her alone now. Go to sleep.' Bolt's voice thunders across the landing.

'I actually need to sleep now. anyway,' Peter says, quickly, his demeanour changing considerably.

I close his observation panel and walk away. Bolt has done me a favour there. Maybe it's because he has a daughter about my age, or maybe it's just because we get on, but he knows Peter's behaviour is bordering on inappropriate, and he doesn't like it. Peter isn't a popular prisoner. He's tolerated because of who his cousin is. But even his cousin doesn't seem too keen on him; he seems embarrassed by him. Family connections might stop Peter getting assaulted, but they can't make him any friends. It's no secret that he's a convicted rapist.

Not all sentenced sex offenders go straight to a sex offenders' prison. There isn't the space. Not all of them go to Vulnerable Prisoner Units, either. A prisoner has to want to go to a VPU for their own protection. The staff can't force them, though unsurprisingly there aren't many sex offenders who fancy taking their chances on general population. If Peter's cousin wasn't here with him, I don't think he'd risk it, either.

When I get to Aaron's cell, I find him drinking a cup of tea and watching TV. One hand clasps the handle of a blue plastic mug, steam rising in delicate treble clefs. The other hand is thrust into his pocket. Grey socks cushion his heels as he rocks back and forth. I tap gently on the glass.

He nods and says quietly, 'I'm OK, Alex. I'm just gonna wait till this programme finishes and then I'll go to sleep. I'll be OK.'

I'll check on him every half an hour for the whole night. But it doesn't take half an hour to end your life, and I'm nervous every time I look in his cell.

The next night, though, I spend the majority of my shift at a different door.

The Exceptional High Risk prisoners need to be checked once an hour. They're considered exceptionally high risk for two reasons: their access to resources that could enable escape, and their risk to the public if they did escape. There are very few Exceptional High Risk prisoners in the jail, and Bolt is one of them. He's working on his next uni assignment, and my hourly visits give him a break. He's up until about 2am every night, hunched over a textbook and chewing on a highlighter.

I don't realise it at first, but our hourly check-ins are acting as a kind of inadvertent signal to Peter. As long as I'm talking to Bolt, Peter says nothing. But the first time he hears my boots walk past on my hourly checks, the first time he hears me open Bolt's observation panel but stay silent, that's when he knows that Bolt has fallen asleep. At 2am on the dot, seconds after I've checked on Bolt and seen the rise and fall of his chest beneath a yellow prison blanket, Peter's cell bell flashes. I don't have a choice, I have to answer it, but I hate doing it, knowing that in his head I'm not coming to his door in my capacity as a prison officer, but as a woman who has to stand and talk to him if he demands it.

'Peter,' I say firmly.

'I found this picture of me.' He holds up a photo of him in a boxing ring, staring fiercely at the camera. 'Did you know I used to be a professional boxer? That's why they all call me Bruiser.'

I haven't heard anyone call him Bruiser. I've heard some less complimentary nicknames go around for him, but not Bruiser.

'Peter, it's the middle of the night. Is there anything you actually need?'

'Yeah, I feel like talking.'

I know for a fact that he hasn't felt like talking to any of the male staff doing nights in the last few months.

'It's too late to have a proper conversation now.'

'Well I heard you just go speak to that fraggle. You don't mind speaking to him. Don't fucking bother. He won't do anything. He just pretends he's gonna string up for attention.'

He's talking about Aaron. He wants me to justify why I checked on the guy who tried to kill himself a few months ago.

'He hasn't pretended to string up for attention, Peter. I've barely spoken to him, anyway. Because it's the middle of the night.'

'I shouldn't even be in here, you know.' It's a refrain he repeats often. 'You know why I am? Because some stupid bitch lied.'

The knot in my chest tightens. Because that's not what I read last night. I read that a young woman barely out of her teens bit her lip until it bled to stop herself from crying out, trying not to wake her baby while Peter did what he did to her. I think about the multiple calls to police in the days before, domestic violence alerts, panic buttons installed, footprints in the garden. I don't want to hear his version of events. He thinks he is entitled to women, their attention and their bodies. I read enough last night.

'I'm going now, Peter. Go to sleep, please.' I shut the flap and walk away.

He kicks the door. 'That's not a good idea, you know. Walking away from me is not a good idea.'

I'm not really sure what he means, but half an hour later I find out.

He's cut himself. Snapped a CD into pieces and used one of them to slice a thin slit into his upper forearm.

Prisons are full of people prepared to tear open their own flesh to quieten the noise in their heads. Female prisons have it far worse than male establishments; men will generally resort to interpersonal violence, whereas women are more likely to turn their pain inwards.

'Why have you done that?'

'Because you walked away from me.' He's standing over the sink. There's blood spattered round the bowl and three dark droplets on the floor beneath. 'I said I wanted to talk; I said you shouldn't walk away.'

I need to somehow convince him to pass the shards of CD to me under the cell door. I can't leave him in there with a potential weapon that he's already used on himself, but equally I can't open the door when he's got a weapon. If it was daytime, a team of officers kitted out in personal protective equipment, with helmets and shields, would be deployed to remove both prisoner and weapon. But there aren't enough staff for that at night, and the CM won't want to call staff in unless he absolutely has to. His last ten years in prison mean that Peter knows this too. He's got what he wanted; I'm back at his door. Eventually, he agrees and passes the fragments under the door. Dried blood skims the edge of one of them, a smudged thumbprint dulling the shine of its surface.

'Thank you. Do I need to be worried? Are you going to cut yourself again with something else?'

He presses his face into the glass. 'So, what do you want to talk about now? We've got all night,' he says.

The knot in my chest rearranges itself. I don't really know how to handle this. It's becoming clear that Peter will do whatever it takes to make me talk to him. I can't see how I can walk away without risking him cutting himself, but I can't stand here all night – and there are other people I need to check on. I also need to report the self-harm to the night CM. I kick the shards of the CD further away, so he won't see me the curve of my body as I bend down to collect them.

'I need to go to the office now. A nurse needs to check your arm to make sure you're OK, so I'll give them a call.'

'No, they fucking don't. I don't want anyone coming to check me. Don't call a nurse.'

I call a nurse. And the night CM. Then I go back to his cell. I'm the only member of staff on A Wing, so there's no one else who could go in my place, but I wish there was. I haven't been in this sort of situation before. I could always ask for Peter to be moved to a different wing during the day tomorrow, but I know I need to challenge this sort of behaviour effectively rather than hide from it. Because it certainly won't be the last time.

He claws dirty fingernails into the wound, pinching and scratching to draw more blood, then pinches the cut together and holds it over the sink. Dark red blood drips into the porcelain. He mutters something inaudible to himself, pinching harder and squeezing blood from the strip of exposed flesh. The actual wound itself isn't bad – it's like a wider, dirtier papercut – but watching him try to make it worse is grim. I'm not really bothered by blood, that isn't what horrifies me. It's his commitment to forcing my attention, even if this is what it requires.

I watch as he puts the plug in the sink and turns the tap on to a steady dribble. He flicks the water over the blood, drip on to drip, then uses his index finger like a stumpy whisk, mixing water and blood. He's diluting it to make it seem like there's more blood than there is. Realising this makes me feel a bit sick, I turn away and rest my back against the wall. I don't want him to see me; I'm only standing here to make sure he doesn't harm himself again while I wait for the CM. But every time I glance into his cell, I see things that could be turned into weapons: table legs, a tin of tuna that could be put in a sock, the kettle, even shards of plastic from the light fitting if he decides to smash it.

Slamming gates and jangling keys snap me out of this train of thought. The CM throws open the office door and pauses as it smacks into the wall, trembling on its hinges. Every time I've spoken to Peter, it's been in a whisper, as I've been trying not to wake up anyone else. That seems a bit pointless now. I'm not sure Mr Button could make more noise if he tried.

He switches on the wing lights – not just for Peter's landing, but for every landing, flooding the wing with artificial brightness. Strips of light appear under cell doors, eyes peer through the gaps between door and frame. This is exactly what I was hoping to avoid. It seems Mr Button has a different plan in mind. He strides towards me with a huge smile on his face.

'This him?' he asks, gesturing to Peter's door.

'Yes.'

'Right, young man. What's the problem?'

'There's no fucking problem. I told her not to call anyone. Go away.'

Peter is not happy. He told me not to get anyone, and I've gone and done the opposite. Not only is there no longer a young woman talking to him, now there's an enormous man instead.

'You're bleeding,' says Mr Button. In a very loud voice.

'It's nothing, I'm fine.'

'Why have you self-harmed? The nurse is on her way.'

'I don't want to see the nurse. I'm fine. Go away.'

'Do you remember me, Peter? We've met before.'

'No, I don't. Why are you shouting? Go away.'

Mr Button isn't quite shouting, but he's not far off. He's certainly not making any effort to keep the noise down.

'We met when you were on B Wing. About six months ago. I was on nights then, too, and Miss Morris was the night officer for that week. You kept calling her to your door, and when she didn't come as quickly as you liked you cut yourself with some plastic. Remember?'

Peter says nothing.

'Maybe you can't remember who Miss Morris is? She's a young officer on B Wing, long blond hair. You wanted to talk to her. A *lot*. Am I jogging your memory? You'd been fine the week before, when Mr Brown was on nights, and, as far as I recall, you had no issues the week after when another male officer was on. But you stayed up the whole night when it was Miss Morris.'

I didn't know this. Officer Morris works on B Wing. She's older than I am, and far more experienced. I realise then that this isn't about me; it never was. Things like this will happen throughout my career, shows of control or intimidation or manipulation that feel very gender specific. The way I deal with these situations will change. I'll become more confident, more assertive and far less tolerant. But for now, just realising this is enough.

It isn't about me. It's about Peter and the way he views women. It's his problem, not mine.

I'm not the only one interested in what Mr Button has to say. His words seem to have breathed life into the spur. Anyone who is awake is listening, ears pressed to cell doors. And it suddenly becomes clear: Mr Button wants them to hear. His loudness isn't accidental.

The other prisoners shout and bang their doors, pissed off at being woken by this, of all things. It's now after 3am, and they aren't blaming me or Mr Button; they're blaming the man who seems to have a predilection for young women he knows are on their own.

Peter isn't stupid; he knows exactly what the CM is doing. But this time, he doesn't say anything back. No matter how angry he is, getting into an argument means keeping everyone else awake, and that's not a risk worth taking.

So he stares at Mr Button. Who stares back. And insists that the nurse take a look at Peter's cut through the observation panel, despite his protests that he's fine.

I'm relieved that Mr Button's here, but I feel a little embarrassed at having had to call him in the first place. I know from the radio that none of the other wing officers have required assistance. And I'm conscious of all the other things Mr Button needs to be doing in his capacity as CM of the entire prison during the night. He needs to visit all four wings, Healthcare and the segregation unit, and conduct management checks on the prisoners under constant watch. The officers seated outside their cells have to write observations every fifteen minutes – 'breathing noted', 'currently lying on right-hand side', etc. – and Mr Button has to check and check again that they aren't even a minute out. And after that, he'll put on his thick black Prison Service coat and woollen hat embossed with the Queen's crest, and the matching gloves with the leather cuff that they'll stop issuing to new staff a year from now, and he'll trudge across the prison, out into the cold, and across to F Wing.

F Wing is the prison within a prison. It's a small, self-contained prison completely separate from the main jail, with its own exercise yard, its own segregation unit and its own wing. Just ten cells. For the most dangerous men in the entire prison system. The prisoners housed on F Wing are typically men who have killed in custody, but there are also terrorists whose suicide bombs failed to detonate, and organised criminals so wealthy that they've featured on the *Sunday Times* Rich List.

Mr Button might pause at the Close Supervision Centre to have a quick coffee and a chat with the officers; then he'll make his way across to the gatehouse, using his radio to let the OSGs in the control room know every time he goes from one place to the next. The control room is staffed 24/7, and the OSGs inside monitor the prison CCTV continuously. They'll watch Mr Button as he crosses the jail. They'll watch him and they'll watch the skies, staying in constant communication with the police in case the police helicopter is deployed, the only form of aircraft permitted to fly above the prison. They'll adjust the external cameras to investigate every time the Geofencing alarm is activated, a form of digital technology that triggers an alert any time movement close to the perimeter wall is detected.

Mr Button needs to oversee all of this. And he's not the sort of man to cut corners. So he could probably do without Peter making superficial marks on his arm because I don't want to have a cosy chat with him at two in the morning.

But maybe that's the end of it. Peter hasn't pressed his cell bell again. It would appear that Mr Button's loudness has silenced him.

For now, at least.

***

The walk from the wing to the car park seems to take forever. I step on to the main corridor, the same one the prisoners take to go to work and education round the corner, past the segregation unit, past Healthcare, past a side office where Mr Button would have sat doing his paperwork throughout the night. Until I called for him, that is. Past a heavy wooden door that opens on to another corridor, the floor of which is covered with plush carpet instead of linoleum. This is where the governors' offices are, with proper coffee machines and filtered water dispensers. I keep going. I'm so tired.

As I stand in the airlock, whose electronic doors whine as they slowly inch closed, I'm praying I don't get a search on the way out; numbers are generated randomly and, if my tally matches, I'll have to stay an extra five minutes for a rubdown.

My arms feel like lead – I'm not sure I could actually raise them high enough for the search – and my eyes are stinging, outraged at still being open. Thankfully I'm waved straight through, out into the car park that's been carpeted by a thick layer of grit. Streetlamps dim as the sky wakes up, slowly thawing the darkness into a medley of purples and oranges. It's stunning, the kind of sunrise you only really see in the countryside, and only if you're up early enough. If the prisoners were to look out of their windows now, they'd see it too.

This is the closest I'll get to daytime. The day is my night, and it goes by too fast. A standard set of night shifts consists of seven nights followed by seven days off. Just one more shift to go. Although, as I'll find out, readjusting my body clock will take up at least half of my week off.

***

Two hours until my last night shift, and I'm not up for it. It was dark when I got into bed, it was dark when I woke up, and it's freezing. Just getting out of bed felt like stepping into a fridge. I don as many layers as Prison Service uniform will allow and step out of my flat into the brisk evening air. Frost has settled on the asphalt like glitter, as if nature is getting ready for Christmas too. Walking to my car takes me past the clock tower, the chemist and the local off-licence, their brick frames adorned with Christmas lights, shop windows dangling streamers, mince-pie deals and flu-advice posters. It's so normal and quiet and peaceful round here. It feels a world away from life sentences and prisons within prisons and rooms with Perspex doors. But all that and plenty more is only twenty-five minutes up the road.

Whitemoor is a miniature city, built of names, colours, languages, cultures, religions, troubles, biases and pointless feuds. It seems somewhat ironic that such a microcosm of diversity should exist so close to what is perhaps one of the most old-fashioned towns I've ever been to. It's not just the diversity of Whitemoor, but the volatility of it, too – the heavy potential for violence. It feels out of place here, nestled amidst the fields: a violently stark reminder of reality, of the knife crime, gun crime, gang wars, terrorism and torrential anger that bruises modern society – if you choose to see it.

The steering wheel feels like a belt of ice between my hands. I know these roads so well. The rural debris that lingers on them – a fallen turnip or dead deer – is often the only sign anyone else has been there. The roads are empty tonight, the residue of the day's tractors stretching before me, despondent crop fields either side, a lonely petrol garage nestled beside a potato factory. I'm more cautious than usual. It's icy tonight, and I've slid on one of these corners before.

Driving through Warboys takes me through Chatteris and on to the A141 into March. March is a fenland town, a shamble of aged buildings, thatched roofs, green riverbanks and winding rivers that make me feel like I'm stepping back in time. The prison is just visible from here, but only if you know where to look, beyond the ditches glazed over with sparkling mud and past the fields. I turn right on to Twenty Foot Road, which runs alongside the Old River Nene, the water's surface like a still blue ribbon, peaceful and unmoving, saying nothing of the cars that have tumbled into it in the past. These roads can be deceptive, a staccato of potholes and bumps and sudden corners. I've got into a weird habit of rolling down the windows whenever I drive on this river road, so I have an escape route if the car does go in. A slab of cold air smacks my cheek as I do the same thing tonight. Two more right turns, and the prison looms into view.

From a distance, it doesn't really look like a prison. Whitemoor is surrounded by fields, with a river on one side and a disused railway line on the other. It looks like a cluster of high-mast lights and nondescript buildings. But up close, and especially in the dark, it has a more sinister feel. The perimeter wall is over eight metres high and solid concrete. Once you're through the gate and into the prison grounds, every building is topped with coils of razor-tipped barbed wire. There are signs warning you to stay away from the patrol dogs, and more signs prompting you to check that you've locked the gates behind you. Every physical element of this place is designed to remind you of exactly where you are.

Barely fifteen minutes later, and I'm saying goodbye to Jade as she heads home for an evening infinitely more pleasant than mine. She stays on the wing while I do my preliminary checks, trying each cell door to make absolutely certain they're definitely locked. Peter doesn't even look at me when I get to his. Given his strategy last night, this doesn't feel particularly encouraging. Once Jade is gone, I feel a bit isolated. I know I'm safe, I know Peter can't physically get to me from behind his door, but his deviancy feels like it could reach straight through if I let it.

During my first set of checks, I notice that several of the prisoners have pulled their mattresses on to the floor and are sleeping there instead. When I ask why, they tell me it's because the floor is closer to the heating pipes at the back of the cells. These thick metal pipes run through all the cells, fixed to the wall a few inches above the floor, and they're the only heating the cells have. Radiators are considered too big and cumbersome, too easy to smash and create weapons from. So it's pipes instead. They're the perfect size for prisoners to hang their boxers and socks on to dry. But there are downsides to the pipes. It often takes a few days of warm weather before they're all switched off, and cells can get very hot, very quickly. The pipes also provide an often irresistible temptation for those prisoners with a propensity to seriously self-harm. Just enough surface area to press their faces to until the skin starts to blister and peel off. But tonight, thankfully, the prisoners just want to stay warm.

Just before 2am, Mr Button walks on to the wing, but without the gate-slamming. I'm pleased to see him. Hours on end in this office can get lonely. He's a tall, commanding man with friendly eyes and a mesh of grey beard warming his chin.

'Anything from Peter yet?' he asks.

'No, nothing,' I say, 'but I think that's because he knows another prisoner a few doors down from him is still awake.'

'Who?'

'High Risk Bolt.'

'Ah yes.' Mr Button chuckles. 'Well, he isn't gonna want to piss him off, is he?'

I'm not entirely sure why everyone is so wary of Bolt. He's big, but there are bigger guys here who don't get the same reaction. Many of the prisoners here are loud and extroverted, and only wear clothes that show off their muscles. I had sort of expected that; it's a male-dominated environment, and size communicates dominance. But Bolt isn't really like that. He's very calm and softly spoken. I've never heard him raise his voice or get annoyed. He seems to be more of a passive observer of life on the wing, rather than being in the thick of it himself. Or at least, that's the impression he gives. But there's something about him that sets him apart. Whatever it is, his mere existence is enough to restrain Peter.

Peter doesn't press his cell bell that night. But another alarm goes off instead. It's nearly 4am when I hear it. Just as my eyelids are drooping like cheap tents in the rain. Exhausted. Seven nights of this has taken its toll. I've read before that doing night shifts can take years off your life expectancy, and always thought that sounded a bit ridiculous, but one week of being awake at the wrong time feels like it's aged me about a decade.

When the alarm sounds, it's a horrible whining noise that snaps my eyes wide open and makes my blood seem to chase itself round my body. The alarm gets tested early in the morning, around 6am, but no one mentioned a test at 3.58am on Christmas morning. I scramble to a more upright position, grabbing my radio and turning up the volume.

'All outstations, we have an emergency message,' a voice announces briskly.

Emergency message. That means either escape or immediate risk to life. There's no other reason that alert would be called. I've never heard it before. I am suddenly and completely awake, listening to the radio, to the wing, listening out for any tiny noise. Have I missed anything? Is there something I should have spotted and didn't? I leave the office and press the radio to my ear, scanning the spurs for any signs of – I don't know what. Just anything that shouldn't be happening.

'We've got one on the roof,' the voice continues.

One on the roof? Fuck. The last and only escape from Whitemoor was 1994, the IRA. This can't be happening, not tonight, not on my first set of night shifts. My hands start sweating, my mouth silently opening and shutting in shock as I fumble with the key pouch in my pocket. My fingers are falling over themselves, trying to check all the keys are in there. They are. They definitely are. I check three times over, and they're all there. But did I check all the cell doors properly? I thought I had, but now I'm not sure. I know I closed all the windows on the landing when I came on shift because of the cold, but did I flick the catch across? Has someone got out of their cell and then climbed out of the window, and somehow made it to the roof? I am hot and cold and sweaty all at once.

'All outstations, say again, one on the roof. Dressed all in red. Appearance unclear except for a white beard. Seems to have large vehicle behind him on roof, possibly a sleigh. A dozen reindeer also visible.'

I sink back against the wall and exhale for the first time since the alarm sounded.

There is no man on the roof. It's a joke. A terrible, heart-stopping, prison joke. The kind that has very little consideration for the twenty-two-year-old trying to maintain control of a wing of 120 men, on her own, in the plunging darkness.

My nerves are shot. This week of nights has done me in.

***

The fields surrounding the prison are guarded by an army of white wind turbines, dozens of them standing tall in a field that is otherwise featureless. Despite their number, they somehow still seem solitary, their three long fingers lazily scratching the sky as they turn.

Driving home on these twisting river roads leaves no space for complacency, but I'm so exhausted it's hard to keep my eyes open. I turn left, and left again, then take the last exit on the roundabout. I keep going, past the big shop, then the smaller ones – everything's closed at this time. The roads are even quieter than usual, and it takes me a moment to realise why. It's Christmas Day. Of course it is. The thought wakes me up a bit. I'll get home and sleep for a few hours, then drive to my parents'. My brother will already be there, probably still asleep, and when he wakes up we'll drink ice-cold Corona that's been left outside all night because there's no room in the fridge. We'll snack on sausage rolls and mince pies until it's time for dinner, then after we'll sit by the tree like we did when we were kids, and find the presents with our names on. They'll be the same as always. Books and moisturiser and socks. And it'll be perfect. Because we're all together. The way it's meant to be.

I think of my colleagues turning up for their shifts soon. The start time is an hour later on Christmas Day, except for those relieving the night staff. But the rest will be making their way in now. They'll walk on to the wing and into the briefing room, arguing over whose turn it is to make the first round of coffee and putting their order in with the officer who's agreed to make bacon sandwiches to celebrate. And they'll remind each other that next year, they won't have to work Christmas Day, because they're doing it today. It'll be someone else's turn then. Mine, probably.

At eight-thirty sharp, they'll stand up, straighten their belts and smooth their shirts, check their keys are secure and head out on to the landings. The SO will call unlock and out the prisoners will come. Merry Christmas. And it'll be a better day than usual, because there's no work on Christmas Day. No work, no activities, no freeflow. Or maybe that's worse. Maybe the men could do with the distraction. Instead, they'll have association all day, rounds of *FIFA* and games of pool until an officer calls for lunch on the tannoy. It's a good lunch today: turkey and roast potatoes and little cakes with marzipan wreaths printed on the top. After lunch, they'll go back to the landings for more association; they'll negotiate their place in the phone queue to speak to wives and kids and brothers and sisters and everyone else gathered around the tree at home, the way it should be, laughing and opening presents, but always listening out for the phone.

I'm nearly home now. I go slower on this road, which has fat ditches on either side. Frost sparkles on the road surface. Keep going, left again. I force my eyes wide, and finally I'm in my little town, the flu posters and mince-pie deals welcoming me home.

I step out of the car and up to my flat. I'm finally home. Hannah's snoring so loudly it's worth recording, because she'll only deny it later, but I'm too tired. I see the mince pie she's left out for me. I smile, but I'm too tired to eat it. Too tired to do anything but take my boots off, coat off, everything off, brush my teeth, make a hot-water bottle and fall into bed, covers all the way up, my head so comfy on this pillow. I'm done, done,

done. I close my eyes and I think of men on plastic mattresses on hard floors, curled up near heating pipes. I think of CDs scratched into skin, slamming doors, rustling shell suits, bright lights, darkness, salivating dogs, grey prison socks, silent tears of violated women, light and dark and paper warnings. I think of cold rivers that take lives and show you life reflected, and then take lives again.

I think of Aaron, grateful that he didn't try to kill himself last night.

I think of Peter.

I think of every emotion that lives and dies in that place. And then I fall asleep.

***

Aaron died two months later. It happened at what I now know is statistically the most likely time for a prisoner to hang themself – between midnight and 2am. The officer who found him described the rising panic he felt when he looked into Aaron's cell and he wasn't there: not on the bed, the chair, the toilet.

Then he saw his feet dangling beneath the curtain.

3

The Yard

No one really knows why prisoners always walk in the same direction around the yard. One officer tells me it's because it used to be a way of telling the sex offenders apart. General population prisoners would walk anticlockwise around the perimeter of the yard, while sex offenders would walk in an inside circle, clockwise.

I don't know if that's true. It doesn't seem true. Sex offenders have been housed separately to the general population for decades. It also doesn't explain why the men here, many of whom weren't even alive in the eighties, still walk anticlockwise today.

One hour a day of pacing around a grey concrete square with a single bench in the middle that no one ever sits on.

The exercise yard is one of the more vulnerable locations for prison security. The men are out in the open air, and the officers don't patrol. Instead, we stay by the gate, within touching distance of the alarm bell. The gate is our entry point – and, crucially, our exit too. If something were to happen and we needed to get out quickly, it's no use being halfway across the yard.

Bernard and I have been out here for ten minutes already. Before the prisoners come out, the yard must be checked for contraband. We look under the bench, kick loose stones and shake the metal fencing to make sure it's secure. One wall of Red Spur looks out on to the yard. The cell windows all have cages, so it would be hard for a weapon to be dropped out.

Hard, but not impossible, so we check the ground beneath the windows anyway.

Prison disorder often takes place on exercise yards: things like sit-down protests in the summer. Partly a protest and partly a sunbathing opportunity. But there's little chance of that today, in the grip of a freezing February.

I kick the white gates at the far end of the yard and rattle the cold iron bolt holding them in place. Just in case. Rafik watches me from his cell on the threes landing. His is one of the cells that looks out on to the yard.

'How cold is it, Alex?' he calls.

'Cold, Rafik. Very cold.'

He nods and turns away, his decision made. He won't be coming out for exercise.

Only a few will. They're already lining up on the ones landing of their spurs, ready to be searched by the waiting staff. The spur gates lead into an open area with the hotplate at the far end, a small treatment room to the left, where the nurse hands out medication each morning, and the entrance to the yard on the right. It's quiet at this time. The nurse has been and gone, and the officer in charge of lunch still has another half-hour or so before he needs to collect the food from the main kitchens. But in an hour's time, the prisoners will line up again in a much noisier queue. Eight at a time to the hotplate. The table that's pushed against the wall, currently bare except for a few crumbs and a couple of stray teabags, will be piled high with loaves of bread and hastily arranged cereal packs for an officer to hand out. Soon, this area will be a hive of activity, a flurry of staff and prisoners, and stale baguettes being swapped for dried noodles, or coronation chicken for tuna mayonnaise and pots of yogurt so small you can swallow the whole thing in one mouthful. But now, there's just the bleep of the wand and the sound of Sammy asking the officer how cold it is outside, will just a jumper be OK?

Abdul is first out, wearing an athletics top and neon trainers, ready to do shuttle runs down the middle of the yard like he does every day. He's one of the few that break the anti-clockwise rule. He looks faintly annoyed when I tell him I still haven't managed to shave a couple of seconds off my 5k despite his advice. No carbs after 4pm. Then comes Sammy, hands thrust into the pockets of an oversized coat that I suspect belongs to Bolt. He comes out most days, too. The yard is one of the only times when prisoners from different spurs can associate, and Sammy's good friends with a Scouser from Green Spur. Malcolm is next, a stocky prisoner with the scar of an old knife wound just visible above his collar. He shivers as the fresh air hits him and pauses next to me until I've found his name on the list, then heads to the fence on the left side of the yard and waits. He's got there first today.

The fence separates the yard from an external walkway that leads towards the main kitchens and C and D Wings. Directly on the other side of the walkway, separated by another metal fence, is B Wing exercise yard. It's a mirror image of the A Wing yard; a big square with a lonely-looking bench and two cold staff in the corner. In a few moments, the handful of B Wing prisoners prepared to brave the cold will make their way on to the yard. One of them will go straight to the fence where Malcolm stands opposite, only a few feet apart, but separated by two thick metal grates. They're brothers.

Malcolm never causes any trouble on A Wing, nor does his brother on B Wing, but they have a history of being disruptive when located together. So they're allowed to be in the same prison, but not the same wing. The yard is as close as they get. Like so many of the men here, they're serving life sentences for a gang-related murder. The case is more complex than most, though. Malcolm was already in prison when it happened, but mobile phone analysis showed that calls made in the minutes before and after the shooting could be traced to an illicit phone found hidden in his cell. He was convicted on the basis that he had ordered the shooting from behind bars.

Davis and Ahmet come out next, dressed in matching burgundy tracksuits. These are prison-issue tracksuits, and not the kind someone wears by choice. There are three tiers of status in prison: Basic, Standard and Enhanced. All inmates enter on Standard, and many will stay there for the duration of their sentence. Some work their way up to Enhanced by demonstrating a positive attitude and willingness to comply with the prison regime. They offer support to the other prisoners and help staff where possible. Enhanced status comes with more privileges, such as the right to own a PlayStation, if they can afford to buy it. Enhanced prisoners also get a slightly higher weekly wage from the prison, and can receive more visits. But Basic is the opposite. Prisoners on Basic lose their TVs, their personal clothing and their association time, too. And that's the reason Davis and Ahmet are on the yard now, wearing the uniform that marks them out as serving yet another stint on Basic. They'll be banged up during evening association later, but they're entitled to an hour on the yard every day. This is their one chance to spend time with the other prisoners, to see something other than the four walls of their cells.

Over the next couple of years, I'll see the two of them dressed in burgundy tracksuits more times than I can count.

When the last of the prisoners have filtered out, Bernard and I check our numbers match and radio the total through to the control room. Fourteen prisoners in total: ten Category As and four Category Bs. Then we lean back against the wall and watch. A prison officer's work is made up of lots of moments like this: counting and checking, checking again, then watching.

We watch Davis and Ahmet as they stand with Malcolm, chatting animatedly to his brother and pretending to throw punches. They're almost definitely acting out the assault that put them on Basic. Bernard coughs loudly and they stop. No play-fighting allowed. Not on the yard, not on the landings, not anywhere. Play fights quickly turn into the real thing.

We watch Bolt and Ben circling the yard together, deep in conversation. Sammy is standing by the fence, speaking to a B Wing prisoner with red hair known rather predictably as 'Ginge'. They shout across to each other and then double over with laughter. We watch Romario, a cleaner from Red Spur, muttering to himself as he paces round the yard, overtaking a prisoner convicted of torturing his boss with a blowtorch, and a tattooed man serving life for shooting a toddler in the back. Romario's mood swings are erratic and unpredictable. The tiniest thing can set him off. A certain sound, a bad night's sleep, even staff that he thinks are too heavy-footed. For him, those triggers are very specific. Occasionally, he'll talk about his time in children's homes. How he went from one to the next, again and again, and how footsteps slowing outside his door meant something very different there.

Romario is angry all the time. He was angry at school, angry when he got kicked out, angry when he finally turned eighteen and left the care of the state, angry when he started robbing people, angry when he went to jail, angry when he carried on robbing people – at knifepoint, then gunpoint – angry when he went to jail again. And now he's pacing round this yard, still angry. Most prisoners give him a wide berth.

***

I've been in the job over six months now. I've passed my three-monthly performance reviews and completed the projects I was assigned at each one. It's standard procedure here for officers in probation to take on additional projects during their first twelve months, though Whitemoor is something of a rarity in that respect. I've compiled a detailed dossier on all the electrical appliances on A Wing: the serial codes, working order, age and condition of every fridge, freezer, washing machine and micro-wave. In retrospect, I doubt the custodial manager really cared what models of microwave there were on Blue Spur. The point was more that it would be difficult to complete this task alone; I would need the help of the prisoners to do so. And they did help me. On each spur, they pulled out the freezers and looked for labels on the fridges, calling out the details while I jotted them down. Forming positive relationships is easily the most impor-tant part of being a prison officer, and projects like this provide opportunities for staff and prisoners to work together.

After passing my six-month review, I was cleared to become a personal officer. The personal officer scheme is a big part of life at Whitemoor, and is integral to relationships between staff and prisoners. All officers are assigned between three and five prisoners to work with. The selection process is mostly ran-dom, though the custodial managers use common sense. A female officer would not typically be assigned a sex offender with a known dislike of women, for example. The prisoners are encouraged to see their personal officer as the first port of call for any concerns or queries, anything from booking an extra visit to sorting out canteen refunds.

I've been given four personal prisoners: Jamal, a heroin addict serving life for murder; Harpal, a well-built man in his twenties who's already served one sentence for man-slaughter and is now back in for murder; Max, a pensioner who's almost blind and rarely leaves his cell, also serving life for murder; and Ben. Ben is the only one of my personal prisoners who isn't in for murder. In fact, he isn't even the type of prisoner who would typically be housed at White-moor. His index offence was violent, but in the end no one was physically hurt. His custodial record is pretty terrible, but poor behaviour alone is rarely enough to get someone put in a high-security dispersal. The reason he's here is that he keeps escaping.

It's the height of summer now and the yard is full. I'm pushing the lunch trolley into the hotplate area when I hear him.
Raised voices can split the air in a place like Whitemoor. For
years, this hypervigilance around sudden noise will stay with
me. Pubs, crowds, nightclubs, even an unexpected tannoy
announcement in Tesco, all spark that rush of adrenaline in me.

Neither Ben nor the officer see me as I round the corner, past the table where the loaves of bread are stacked. I see
Officer Stevens's tall frame first, slightly hunched as he leans
into his argument. Ben is directly opposite him, with his back
to the gate that leads on to the yard.

'Get out of my way. I'm going on the yard. Move,' says Ben.

'No, Ben. Go back on the spur,' says Officer Stevens.

'I'm going on the yard. Now move out of my way.'

It's not until I'm face to face with Ben that he seems to
register I'm there.

'What's going on?' I ask.

But before I get an answer, I'm pretty sure I know what
the issue is. I've clocked the black Adidas sliders on Ben's feet.
Prisoners aren't allowed to wear sliders on the yard. Proper
shoes are the only footwear allowed outside. And Officer Eddy
Stevens is not one to turn a blind eye.

'He won't let me on the yard because I've got sliders on.'
Ben's eyes are fixed coldly on Eddy. 'Everyone else lets me do
it. I'm walking ten feet off the fucking spur, and it's boiling
outside. It's just him that's got a problem with it.'

'It's the rules, Ben,' says Eddy. 'This is a pointless argument.
You could have gone upstairs and got changed by now. The
yard is closed, anyway, but I don't mind letting you out, even
though you're late, because it's so hot. But you have to wear the
correct footwear, same as everyone else.'

Eddy is in the right, but I can see this would be an unhelpful
statement to make, and I'm already feeling concerned about
which way this altercation is going to go. Ben has a bad record.

He came to A Wing from the segregation unit, and I doubt he has any qualms about going back. And he has made a good point. Although the majority of staff would ask him to go back and change his shoes, there are some that wouldn't bother. Inconsistency among officers has created the situation that Eddy is in now. Turning a blind eye might have made life easier in the moment for the officers who let the sliders slide, but it has made Eddy's life considerably harder right now.

The footwear rule is minor. The spur is only a few steps away, and there's no immediate damage done by allowing a prisoner to come off the spur wearing sliders. Insisting that he return to his cell makes everything take longer and runs the risk of a fight starting over something that is arguably very petty. But Eddy is right: those are the rules. And if he lets Ben take one more step past him, he will have allowed him to break those rules, and will have lost his authority in the process.

More to the point, though, before I heard raised voices and came to see what was going on, Eddy was on his own in an isolated area of the wing with a man who looks like he is getting tired of talking. There is one alarm bell right in front of me that I could get to in a couple of seconds, and another by the hotplate – but that would mean turning my back on Ben. There are staff on the yard, but they're behind two heavy locked gates – and anyway, the officers supervising the yard can't leave their posts. The custodial manager's office is directly above us and there are staff on the spurs to our right, but there are gates and stairs in the way, and a lot can happen in the time it takes to unlock gates with shaking hands.

I've worked with Eddy long enough to know that he won't back down, but I know the same about Ben.

'It isn't the same as everyone else,' he insists now. 'You gave me a warning yesterday for something stupid. You want me to lose my TV, and you're getting all excited now because you've seen your chance. You have a fucking problem with me, so let's sort it.' Ben clenches his jaw. And his fists. 'Do you think I'm worried, Stevens? One punch and you're down. You're an old man. You won't get back up again.'

I step into the space between him and Eddy and close my hands around Ben's forearms. I can see the way this is going. I don't doubt that he would hit Eddy, but I don't think he'll hit me. 'That's enough, Ben,' I say. 'This isn't a good idea. You've made your point. If you go any further, you'll regret it. Forget the yard. I'm asking you to go back on the spur.'

I can feel his muscles tense under my hands. I've never seen him this angry. It's inflating his whole body, his puffed-out cheeks, puffed-out chest and balled-up fists.

'It's a joke Alex. This guy is a joke.'

'I'm asking you to walk away.'

He drops his eyes and growls in frustration. He walks away. Slowly, with each step taking forever, but he goes. Eddy and I are silent until Ben is back on the spur. Until the gate is locked behind him and he's out of earshot.

'Thank you. I thought I was gonna get a smack there,' Eddy says.

I notice the slight tremble in Eddy's hands. And then in mine. Adrenaline slowly drains out of me.

'It isn't personal,' Eddy says. 'I don't let anyone come out here with flip-flops on. I did give him a warning last night, which definitely hasn't helped, but he was passing in between spurs! He thinks I'm targeting him, but I'm not. It's just bad luck that I'm the person who caught him both times.'

***

Ten minutes later, Ben's on the yard. Wearing trainers. He's walking around with Bolt, who catches my eye and gives me a subtle but knowing nod. If anyone can calm Ben down right now, it's probably him. They know each other from a different jail. Strangeways, I think.

Another lap, and then Ben pauses beside me. 'I would have hit him, you know.'

'I'm very glad you didn't,' I say.

'He's a prick. He's got it in for me. He always has to say something. He's on me for everything.'

'He's the same with everyone, Ben. It feels like it's just you, but it could be any prisoner who'd come out wearing sliders. There's no way he would've ignored it. You know that.'

The prisoners call Officer Stevens 'Robocop'. They might moan about how strict he is, but a lot of them respect him for it, too. He's consistent and fair. They know exactly where they stand.

'Other officers don't mind. It's not that big a deal.'

'Well, he's not one of those officers, is he? There are going to be some officers you get on with and others you don't, but you can't go around smacking people.'

'Why, in case I end up in prison?'

I look pointedly at him. 'You know what I mean. He's a good officer, Ben. I'm glad you walked away. I think you would have regretted it.'

He shrugs. 'It would have felt good, to see him on the floor. He talks to us like shit.'

I don't think Eddy talks down to the prisoners. I think he's blunt and straight to the point. But maybe I'm only trying to see it from his perspective as the officer, rather than Ben's as the prisoner. Maybe someone telling you what shoes you can and can't wear is always going to feel as if you're being spoken to like shit.

'Do you think I'm mad?' Ben asks.

'What? No, of course not. Why would you say that?'

'They wanted me to go on the DSPD when I came here.'

D Wing is known as the 'Fens Unit'. It's one of three 'Dangerous and Severe Personality Disorder' units in the country. HMP Frankland has one, as does Rampton Hospital. DSPD units focus on a psychological model of treatment for prisoners who have been diagnosed with a personality disorder, though to this day there is contention over what constitutes a personality disorder and how treatable such disorders really are.

I didn't know that Ben had been considered for a placement on the DSPD. I knew a bit about his history, but there was never any mention of his mental health on the sections of his record that I've seen. He tells me that when he was transferred to Whitemoor, he was taken straight to the segregation unit. He was given an E List suit to wear, but instead of putting it on he ripped it into pieces and threatened to fight the seg staff. Perhaps this was the catalyst for considering him for the DSPD unit, but it doesn't seem enough on its own.

'E List' stands for 'Escape List', and is essentially just a list of prisoners with intelligence to indicate they're planning an escape. Or, in Ben's case, those who already have escaped, which is the reason he went straight to the seg rather than the wings. E List prisoners wear bright green-and-yellow boiler suits. All day, every day. They're accompanied everywhere they go. Even on freeflow, when the corridor fills with prisoners watched by a handful of staff stationed at different points, the E List prisoners are escorted by at least one officer. Ben is no stranger to these suits, but he didn't want to be in a high-security prison, and, now that he was here, he didn't want to stand out. In this kind of prison with these kinds of men, drawing attention to yourself isn't always a good idea. At least until you've settled in. So he put off wearing the E List suit for as long as possible – until he got too cold. It's that suit or nothing. These different-coloured suits – Basic, E List – create an almost class-like system in prison, highlighting who's the most dangerous, the worst behaved, the most trusted.

After two weeks of good behaviour in the seg, Ben was relocated to A Wing. And after several months of good behaviour on the wing, he was removed from the E List and allowed to wear his own clothes. Since then, he's mostly kept his head down. But something got to him today.

'If I don't get my next parole, it'll be ten years I'm inside for. Ten years.'

Ben received the results of his latest parole hearing a few days ago. An officer from the Offender Management Unit gave me the heads-up before giving Ben the news in person. His situation isn't unique in Whitemoor, but it's not common either. He's one of several prisoners here serving an IPP sentence.

'IPP' means 'Indeterminate for Public Protection'. And these sentences are exactly that: indeterminate. Ben doesn't have a release date. It's difficult for him to make any plans or to set himself realistic goals, because he doesn't know whereabouts he is in his own sentence. His index offence is, compared with most of the prisoners here, fairly minor. He threatened someone with a weapon, but he didn't use it. He did steal, but only to the value of £50. There are rapists and child sex offenders in here who have set release dates and will end up serving less time than him.

It wasn't Ben's first offence, and the crimes he'd committed before suggested an escalating level of violence and continued disregard for public safety. And so, the judge imposed an IPP sentence with a minimum term of two years. Ben didn't really know what that meant at the time. He thought that he'd be out at the end of his tariff. But that didn't happen. Every two years, his case is reviewed by the parole board. A panel meet to decide if his risk has been reduced sufficiently for him to be released.

If you were to ask him about it, he'd shrug his shoulders and say, 'What's the point in trying?' Every mistake he makes can and will be used against him. Ben doesn't have the luxury of messing up. Getting released from IPP sentences is notoriously hard. *Serving* an IPP sentence is notoriously hard. So much so that, in a few months' time, though neither Ben nor I know it, these sentences will be abolished altogether.

Despite this, Ben will stay in jail. The overwhelming majority of prisoners serving IPP sentences will. The change in law will not be retrospective. In fact, by 2021, over 1,700 prisoners serving an indeterminate sentence for public protection will still be in prison, and more than ninety-five per cent of them will have already completed their initial tariff. Many of them will be way over it, by as much as ten years.

'I can't do ten years, Alex. I'll be institutionalised then, won't I? I'll think all this is normal.'

Until the idea of the DSPD was put to him by a trainee psychologist concerned for his welfare, Ben had never considered himself mad. Now he wonders if he is. Or if he will be, after ten years. Ten years of this. Of walking anticlockwise round a yard. Ten years of balancing cartons of UHT milk on window cages in the winter to keep them cool, and hanging socks out there in the summer, fresh from the laundry, to dry them out. Ten years of talking to someone through a fence. Of wearing sliders and not wearing sliders and arguing about it. Will he be mad then?

Only a handful of prisoners are actually exercising; it's too hot for that. An impromptu rap battle is taking place in one corner of the yard. In another, a group of men angle their faces towards the sun and close their eyes. They might be outside, but they're far from the outside world. Even with your eyes closed, it's hard to forget where you are. Rather than the things you can hear, the static of radios and jangling of keys, it's the things you can't hear. Things that maybe, after ten years, you would forget you'd ever heard.

There's no distant hum of traffic. There are no planes overhead; prisons are no-fly zones. There are no babies crying, horns beeping, phones ringing.

'I haven't killed anyone, Alex. I'm not like these guys. I'm not the type to murder someone.'

But who is? The guy on the other side of the yard, who took revenge when his brother was shot and left paralysed for life?

The guy who stabbed someone in the head after that someone had shot his two-year-old daughter? The terrorist who was planning to detonate a bomb at a public event, but got the date wrong? The university graduate with a genius IQ who buried the body somewhere so obscure that police still haven't found it? The ex-prison officer, the man who grew up in care, the academic, the drug addict, the drug importer, the multi-millionaire, the family man? Who *is* the type?

IPP sentences were meant to act as a kind of middle ground for individuals considered a danger to the public, but not so dangerous that their offence warranted a life sentence. But they ended up being a version of a life sentence anyway, poorly thought out and inconsistently applied. Too many IPP sentences were given out, far more than were initially expected or, crucially, provided for. The Prison Service and parole system were overwhelmed. They were unable to give IPP prisoners access to the courses and resettlement programmes that would demonstrate they were no longer a risk to the public. And yet the prisoners couldn't progress through their sentence without these courses. And on top of that, many IPP prisoners were given relatively short tariffs of eighteen months or less, which makes the suitability of the IPP sentence questionable in itself. The system was inherently unfair.

Ben and I are having this conversation in 2013, in a yard bare of any of the features that will soon be commonplace in prison recreational areas. The yards will improve, but the hopelessness that many IPP prisoners may feel as they pace round them will not. This hopelessness is made up of the familiarity of prison, of being told when you can step outside and being searched before you do, the fear of institutionalisation, the disconnect to the outside world, the pointlessness of making plans. In ten years' time, the impact of IPP sentences will be debated in the House of Lords and described as a form of modern-day torture. Families of deceased IPP prisoners will attribute their loved ones' suicides to the hopelessness they felt, never know-ing when, or if, they would make it home.

Maybe that's why Ben keeps escaping. Maybe that's why he lost his temper when someone asked him to change his shoes.

***

It isn't just the prisoners who want to be on the yard when it's hot. The officers do, too.

There's only ten minutes left of yard time when Eddy comes out. And when he does, the atmosphere changes in a second.

Ben is still standing next to me, right by the gates that lead on to the yard. He wasn't expecting to see Eddy out here, and, despite Eddy saying he didn't mind if Ben was to come on the yard, I don't think he was expecting to see him, either. I see Eddy look down quickly at Ben's feet. Trainers, not sliders.

Before Ben came over to talk, I'd let the other staff on the yard know what had happened. Information sharing among staff is crucial in prison. So when Eddy comes out, a few things happen. Small but perceptible changes that demonstrate the constant state of alertness that characterises this job.

Bernard stubs out his cigarette, even though he hasn't finished it. Brian takes his hands out of his pockets. Roger shifts position ever so slightly, so he's now within reaching distance of the alarm bell. All of us scan the yard, trying to assess the general mood. This is one of the worst places to have to restrain someone: locked on a yard with over a hundred prisoners. And five of us.

I can feel my adrenaline starting to build again. I make eye contact with Bolt, who shakes his head as if to say, 'He won't, don't worry.'

Ben's head is down, eyes fixed to the floor. It's one thing to walk away when a woman he gets on with is asking him to, but there's nowhere to go here. The gates are locked. And all his peers are watching.

Eddy takes a deep breath. 'Things got a little heated earlier, Ben. I didn't want that to happen. I know you think I was picking on you, and if I had singled you out I'd understand your reaction. If it was just you I'd asked, I mean. But you know the way I work. I would have asked any prisoner who came out with sliders on to change.'

Ben says nothing.

Bolt walks past and stops to tie his shoelaces.

'I know I can be very direct in the way I talk,' Eddy continues, 'and I apologise if that comes across as rude. But I was in a difficult position earlier. I'd asked you to do something within the rules, and I can't backtrack on that. I'm not a young man anymore, Ben. I don't want to be rolling around the floor with anyone, much less you. It wasn't personal.'

'He's right,' says Brian, smiling. 'I wouldn't fancy a scrap with you, Ben. You may have little legs, but I've seen you down the gym, and I reckon you're quick with your hands.'

There is no one else in the world who could get away with making a jibe about Ben's height right now, but it cracks the atmosphere just enough to tease a smile out of him. He looks up. 'Do you think I made a mistake, Alex?' he asks me.

'I think you might have done this time, yeah.'

Bolt finishes tying his shoelaces and carries on walking.

'I'm sorry, Mr Stevens.'

'Well, I'm sorry too,' says Eddy. 'I wasn't trying to disrespect you. I think we just got our wires crossed.'

They shake hands, and I notice the slight tremble in my own. I still haven't had my first restraint yet. Ben is probably one of the prisoners I get on with best, but he's told me before how much he struggles to contain his anger. He's often at pains to remind me that he isn't a bad person, that I don't need to worry about him becoming violent, but I was worried today.

Bernard steps forward and shouts, 'That's time then, lads. Let's go back in, please.'

I open the yard gates and put on a pair of blue gloves from my pocket. Roger still has the wand in his. All prisoners are searched on to the yard, and they'll all be searched off the yard, too.

One by one, the prisoners are wanded by Roger, then split into three queues to be searched by me, Bernard and Brian.

Bolt joins my queue. 'All good?' he says, as he raises his arms.

'All good.'

***

This incident marks a turning point in my career and the way I view my role. Although violence is inevitable in prison, there are many instances where it is avoidable – not through physical intervention, but through negotiation, emotional intelligence and quick thinking. These are turning out to be my strengths. I'm starting to see the operational value in them. It's these qualities that are enabling me to develop positive relationships with prisoners, to have sensitive and important conversations with people like Joseph and Bolt. Ultimately, that's what's making me enjoy the job more. Of course, there are times when things become violent regardless, and none of this will work, but there are many more situations where it will. And just as that's a relief for me, I think it is for some of the prisoners, too.

I've spent a lot of time with Ben. He was one of the prisoners who helped me with the white goods project for my three-month probation review. We've talked about his family, his crime, how and why he escaped, and his fixation on ten years being his limit. He can't do any more. I've spent a lot of time listening to him. And today, when it really counted, he listened to me.

Bernard told me that the violence would come, that I wouldn't need to look for it. He also told me that it was one of the least significant aspects of this job, despite the way prisons are typically portrayed. And although I've been pleasantly surprised by how rarely fights and assaults happen, I've also found that being a woman has been a great help rather than a hindrance. There are prisoners here who have a real issue with women in authority, but there are many more who feel more comfortable talking with female staff.

For many of the prisoners at Whitemoor, their self-worth is tied to how physically strong they are and how violent they can be, and it's these attitudes that prevent them from acquiescing to male staff. Ben and Eddy were caught in a stalemate, neither wanting to back down, but for different reasons. Eddy needed to maintain his authority and show that he isn't a pushover. Where Ben comes from, respect is everything, and to back down from a confrontation with another man is a sign of weakness. Even if he didn't really want to fight, even if in the back of his mind were thoughts of his next parole review and the implications of a staff assault, he couldn't back down. Not when he was nose to nose with a man who'd disrespected him. But it doesn't feel like that so much if a female officer intervenes. It gives the prisoner a way out without losing face. Some old-school rules still apply here: don't fight in chapel, don't fight in front of kids in the visits hall, don't hit women.

When I started this job, one of my biggest insecurities was my size and the fact that I'm female. Going up against huge men with a propensity for violence, I didn't know how effective I could be. I worried that I would be considered less capable. But what I thought was my weakness was actually my strength.

4

Education and Workshops

'LIMA ONE, ARE you in position?'
The voice crackles through my radio. I check the call sign taped to the side: 'LIMA 3', in faded black letters. The label is a dirty white, peeling at the edges.

'In position, Lima One out.' The officer in charge of Workshop 1 this morning sounds bored.

'Lima Two?' The OSG from the control room again.

'In position, Lima Two out,' the officer in Workshop 2 answers.

It's 7.50am, and freeflow is about to start. Officers on every wing, in every workshop, are waiting to confirm that they're where they should be. I'm standing at the top of a spiral staircase, my highlighter hovering over a list of the prisoners due to attend education this morning.

'Lima Three?'

I unclip my radio from the pouch on my belt. 'In position, Lima Three out.' I slip my radio back into its pouch. Lima Three is the call sign given to the officer supervising the education department.

This is the daily rhythm of prison life. The way one thing leads to another and then another, the radio sounds and then bodies, bodies, bodies. At the same time each day, down to the minute, the choreography is identical. The officers stand in position, checking left and right to make sure they have a direct line of sight to their nearest fellow officers, the nearest alarm bell, covering any blind spots the cameras don't capture. Everyone knows exactly where they have to be and what to listen out for. It's rare that anyone misses their prompt from the control room. As officers, we're all cogs in a well-oiled machine, and the radio is at the centre. Nothing happens unless the control room calls it first.

Ben will later say to me that he doesn't know how I work in this environment – not because of the danger, but because everything is dictated by a faceless voice coming from the little black box on my hip. He says the officers are controlled just as much as the prisoners, that we can't go anywhere, do anything, without permission first. But it doesn't feel like control to me. It feels safe.

'All outstations in position, you may commence freeflow. Say again, commence freeflow.'

The moment that order is given, the noise starts. The sound of prisoners filling the main corridor, of officers calling after them – 'No running!' – of the metal detectors beeping as men reach the gym, the workshops, the library.

Standing beside me is Bev Callard, the female officer in charge of Whitemoor's library. The prison library is next to the education department. There are bookshelves on wheels neatly lined up in the centre, with laminated labels denoting the genre stuck on each shelf. Thrillers, politics, historical fiction, legal advice. Legal advice is popular. Those books are always taken. The most popular is the *Archbold*, a thick hardback with silver lettering that covers legal precedents, trial protocol, case studies and more. There's always a waiting list for the *Archbold*. The prisoners pore over it, writing notes and folding back the corners of pages relevant to their own cases, searching for something within those pages, some detail or loophole that their legal teams might have overlooked. Other popular books include *The Secret* by Rhonda Byrne, and 50 Cent's *The 50ᵗʰ Law*, books about how to succeed and the power of a positive mental attitude.

Just as there's a list of in-demand books, there's also a list of prohibited ones. Anything involving paedophilia, banned. Anything that features pictures of young children, including clothing catalogues, banned. Certain religious texts deemed to be fundamentalist, banned. Just because something isn't permitted, though, doesn't mean it won't find its way into the prison – and the banned religious texts do. They'll often be smuggled in with different covers, something innocuous that gives no indication of the actual content. The text itself can be in a language other than English, and so harder for officers to identify.

One corner of the library stocks DVDs for those prisoners who have a PlayStation on which to watch them. Despite the fact HMP Whitemoor doesn't accept prisoners under the age of twenty-one, DVDs rated 18 are banned, though these find their way into the jail far more often than banned books. This is because one of the prison workshops recycles old DVDs. Prisoners are employed there to remove the plastic casing and throw away the discs, but the DVDs that come in aren't vetted first, and it's commonplace for some inmates to try to sneak DVDs down their trousers without being seen. The workout DVD *Insanity* is big at the moment. Last week, a group of prisoners were found in the recess room with one of their PlayStations hooked up to the TV on the wall, sweating and panting as the *Insanity* instructor yelled at them from the screen. But not for long. The DVD came from the workshop, not from the library, and the only way it got there is because someone snuck it out. So it was removed. Even among staff, this feels a little excessive, especially as the DVD was going to be binned anyway. But rules are rules, and choosing which ones to break can be a slippery slope.

At the far end of the room, past the books and DVDs, is Bev's desk, piled high with return slips and records of who's borrowing what. From where I'm standing, I can see her desk and the poster for World Book Day stuck to the front of it.

'Here we go again,' she says, smiling at me as she plucks a highlighter from the pen holder clipped to her belt. She's one of the only remaining female staff to have been in the Prison Service when female officers were issued skirts as their official uniform, and the only officer I know to still wear hers.

There are only a few prisoners due to attend the library today, but most of the men on my list pause to say hello to Bev first before going down the stairs. She's been running the library for almost fifteen years, and has been recommending books to some of these men the whole time. The muscles, the scars, the tattoos that cover their limbs and faces and bald heads – she's seen it all before. She doesn't care. She just wants them to read.

I recognise most of the names on my list. Bolt has a meeting with his Open University tutor. Ben has a maths class. Rafik has GCSE English, same as Ahmet. A Londoner from B Wing, Raphael, is down for art class. When he reaches the stairs, he pauses to show Bev some drawings he's carrying in a folder. They're portraits of men on his wing, other prisoners she knows, drawn entirely in biro. Prisoners only have access to one type of pen; small blue plastic biros, like the ones you get in gambling shops. Other inmates commission Raphael to draw their portraits or to copy from photos of their wives and children, so they can send them home as gifts. They pay him in chocolate or soft drinks.

A prisoner from B Wing says good morning and stoops as he goes down the stairs; another, with 'LOVE' and 'HATE' tattooed on his knuckles, does the same, both too tall for the sloping ceiling. Others I don't know but have seen on the news: the man who stuffed his girlfriend's body into a suitcase and threw it in the Thames; the man who killed his own mother, and other people's, too. One of the officers on his wing told me that whenever they search his cell, they find stacks of gossip magazines with all the women's eyes cut out.

Most of the prisoners say hello as they go past me down the stairs, but not him. He grunts his name and keeps walking. But I already knew his name.

I tick each prisoner off as they go, tallying up the totals from each wing. There's one E List prisoner in education today, a chubby man from C Wing with a plait of black hair that hangs limply down his back. A mobile phone was found in his cell last week, hidden inside a can of Coke that wasn't quite what it seemed. The top section of the can twisted off, revealing a compartment just big enough for a phone. It was only the lightness of the can that made the searching officer suspicious. He picked it up and thought the weight felt a bit off. The security department analysed the phone and concluded that there was sufficient intelligence to indicate that it was being used to plan an escape. So now he's on the E List, vibrant in his yellow-and-green suit. He's the last prisoner to go down the stairs to education, accompanied by an officer from his wing.

At the bottom of the stairs is the education department. Paintings and poetry decorate the walls. Sculptures constructed entirely from matchsticks are set out on plastic tables. The display boards outside each classroom are bordered by roses made from toilet paper, each layer of petals folded with painstaking precision. Certificates are stapled to the doors, celebrating exam passes and acceptance on to Open University courses. The whole department is just this one corridor, but it feels packed with creativity and possibility and potential. I see this energy on the wing sometimes, but not in the same way. Prisoners don't have access to the same tools to create artwork on the wing: just biros and determination. And determination can get a little distorted there.

Officer Parry and I are the only disciplinary staff in the education department; the rest of the non-prisoners are teachers dressed in civilian clothing. They don't wear batons and anti-ligature knives attached to their belts; they wear chinos and smart shirts, long dresses and boots with small heels, jewellery and nail polish, too. As a rule, female officers don't wear any jewellery – perhaps a single necklace or studs in our ears, but no more – and never anything on our nails. We don't wear perfume or lipstick, or anything but black boots and black trousers, starched white shirts with every button done up.

I haven't worked with Officer Parry before. He's a slight man who prefers the blue V-neck prison jumper to the black fleece most officers wear. We swap clipboards to check our numbers match. While I counted the prisoners from the top of the stairs, he counted from the bottom. He studies my clipboard with narrowed eyes, chewing the end of his pen as he checks, making a point of getting out his highlighter and going over my own, then lowers himself into one of the two seats in the corridor.

'All looks fine,' he says finally.

I wait until all the prisoners have disappeared into their classrooms, then take my seat next to him. There's a circular wooden table between us, empty except for a telephone and a laminated list of the extension numbers for every department in the jail, decorated with the doodles of bored officers. Officer Parry and I will stay here for the whole session, patrolling occasionally and peering into the classrooms, but very rarely going in. The classrooms are the domain of the teachers and their learners. The two officers on duty are there in case anything goes wrong.

There are benefits to not having officers inside the classrooms. I think it probably allows some prisoners to feel a bit freer, to feel less observed, and maybe even less like a prisoner at all. Some of the men here never finished their GCSEs, and others haven't learned to read or write, so the education department can be an intimidating place – and that's without someone with a uniform and a baton watching over you.

But there are downsides to us sitting outside, namely that we don't know what's going on in those rooms.

Maybe this is what's going through Officer Parry's mind when he says what he says. He asks me how I'm finding the job, and I tell him that it's going well so far, but I'm still getting used to everything. Which is true, because there's a lot to get used to. The place, the people, the protocols. It's a lot to take in.

'That's good,' he says. 'Although – no offence, Alex – I don't think women should work here.'

It's impossible for me not to be offended by this.

'All that carry-on with Abdullah certainly wouldn't have happened, would it?' Parry continues. 'There wouldn't be any of that if women didn't work in prisons.'

Abdullah. He's the focus of a lot of attention at the moment. He's the subject of every briefing, his picture on the front of every security memo. And he's only been back at Whitemoor for a few months. The last time he was here, he was found in the cleaning cupboard at the far end of the education department with a female teacher. They weren't cleaning. He went to the seg, she went to jail. He was shipped to another prison and lost his Enhanced status. She gained a criminal record and lost her career, reputation and kids while she was inside. And yet in spite of that, she continued to write to Abdullah and send him photos. Hoping that the relationship meant something, I suppose. In prison, all incoming and outgoing mail is monitored. Abdullah never replied.

He did well out of it, though. She brought in phones and drugs for him, which he sold on to other prisoners, making him a lot of money. She, on the other hand, was convicted of supplying Class A and misconduct in public office. Abdullah wasn't charged with any additional offences, as it wasn't deemed in the public interest to proceed. He's already serving life.

If you were to take one look at Abdullah's record, though, you wouldn't be able to escape his status as a staff corruptor. It's all there, printed in bold red lettering. Alert after alert after alert. Notes in capitals warning that he's over-friendly with female staff, that he brushes past them when there's plenty of space and asks personal questions. I avoid talking to him and cut off any attempt he makes at conversation. If sex offenders and snitches are considered the lowest of the low among prisoners, then bent staff are the lowest of the low among officers.

But that was one female teacher, not all female staff. Officer Parry's comment is baseless, sexist and antiquated. Not least because male prison officers have inappropriate relationships too. There's more than one reported case of male officers impregnating female prisoners in UK jails. Staff corruption isn't limited to women.

But this doesn't feel worth saying out loud. Officer Parry keeps talking, and I find myself drifting off a bit. Whitemoor is a male-dominated environment, but it's never felt like a misogynistic one to me. I'm taken aback by his rudeness more than anything, not least because I know how wrong he is. My short time in the job has shown me that. People like Jade and Bev are invaluable here. Women might be in the minority when it comes to prison officers, but Officer Parry is very much in the minority with his views. In fact, I will never meet another officer who says anything like this to me. Female staff make an important and necessary contribution to prison life, from OSGs to teachers, dog handlers to governors. The reasons why are everywhere. I see examples of them every day.

There will always be more male officers than female officers in men's prisons, and rightly so. Full searches can only be conducted by staff of the same gender, so it makes sense that the majority of staff are able to carry these out. This is an irrefutable part of intercepting contraband and reducing violence. But contraband does get in, and violence does happen. There will always be those incidents involving particularly violent prisoners where male staff are able to gain control faster and more effectively than the female staff on shift. In those situations, such as planned removals, safety is always the priority. A prolonged physical fight increases risk of injury to both staff and prisoner, so, if male officers are able to bring it to a conclusion faster than the women on shift, no one would suggest doing otherwise. In my experience, though, those instances are few and far between. Restraint techniques are about control, choreography and knowledge, not brute strength.

Thankfully, strip-searching and violence are only two parts of prison life.

Keeping prisons safe is not just about searching prisoners, but about developing relationships between staff and prisoners that humanise the people on both sides. Relationships that, in turn, make people feel safe enough to talk openly and disclose information that can prevent incidents before they happen. For some, those conversations are easier to have with women. And, as we've seen, female officers are often able to defuse tense situations by removing the element of 'losing face' that can drive so many acts of violence.

It's also important to remember that, while Whitemoor is populated largely by lifers, that term is misleading. They all have a release date. A life sentence doesn't mean spending your life in custody. People sentenced to life serve a tariff set by the courts: fifteen years, thirty years, maybe more. Then they are released, and spend the rest of their life on licence. Their time in prison is determinate. It ends. They are getting out. And the society they're being released into isn't made up solely of men. An environment with no women isn't reflective of the world they're expected to integrate into.

Some of the men I meet are very comfortable talking with women, while others aren't. Some of them have poor social skills, particularly when talking to women, perhaps because they've entered the system so young. They haven't matured in the way that the rest of us do, learning how to talk to people, how to form healthy relationships, making mistakes and growing from them. Working with female staff is a way of trying to fill that gap.

There are also some prisoners who believe that women shouldn't be in positions of authority, or even employment. To put these men in a prison with no women would only strengthen that view, reinforcing the idea that these are 'men-only' spaces where women don't belong.

Female prison officers bring skills that are indispensable, but our role is so much more than that. It's symbolic. Women *belong*. Here and in society, in uniforms and boardrooms and sports stadiums and the Houses of Parliament. For those prisoners and officers who think otherwise, our presence challenges their views in a way that being *told* women are equal cannot.

It's a shame that all of this seems to have passed Officer Parry by.

He keeps talking, but I don't hear much of it. I'm distracted by the laughter coming from one classroom, the buzz of what sounds like lively debate from another. The sculpture of the London skyline by the doorway catches my eye, and I see that it was made by a prisoner on A Wing, a young guy, barely out of his teens, who never really talks to anyone. It was never proven whether his victim was alive or dead when he set his body alight. I can see Bolt nodding at his Open University tutor in the room in front of me, and Raph in the art classroom to my right. He's straddling the workbench in front of his canvas, two brushes in one hand.

The radio sounds. Mini-freeflow.

Officer Parry grabs the wand and I put on a pair of searching gloves. I don't often find anything in these searches: perhaps a biro that's easier to write with than the blue pens issued on the wings, or sometimes a handful of coffee granules wrapped in tissue paper, but that's about it.

But you never know. Complacency is dangerous. What might look fairly innocuous can sometimes be much more than it seems. A few weeks ago, one of my colleagues found a scrunched-up ball of paper in one prisoner's pocket as he searched him off the wing. It looked like rubbish. Like something he'd forgotten to put in the bin. But the officer unravelled the paper, just in case, and found a list of names with numbers written beside them. To the untrained eye, this might not have looked like much, but the officer realised the list showed the names of prisoners in debt, and the figures beside them were the amounts they owed. That piece of paper was a crucial piece of evidence. It would tell us who's involved in the prison subculture, who's taking drugs and renting phones, which cells to search and which prisoners to watch. It would be a significant find for the staff, and a serious loss for the prisoner. One that would make him very unpopular. So he needed to get it back. He waited a couple of seconds, acting relaxed, as if it was no big deal that they'd found this small, screwed-up, messy bit of paper. Then he snatched it back from the officer's hand. And ate it. For the staff, this was annoying, but at least no one was dead. There has been more than one case of prisoners in UK jails eating wraps of drugs rather than allow officers to have them – wraps that can then burst inside them and poison them.

So searching is important, and continued vigilance is too. In the same way that all the prisoners were searched before they entered the education department, Officer Churchill and I search them again as they leave. Pockets, collars, waistbands, books and folders. Just in case.

Mini-freeflow is also breaktime. The classroom doors open and the prisoners spill out. They queue for the water cooler or slap Raph's back as they look at the painting freshly stuck to the wall. Bolt stretches as he leaves his tutorial and grins at me. He was a bit nervous before today, unsure if his recent work was heading in the right direction. But clearly it's gone well.

The maths teacher hands me an enormous Sports Direct mug of coffee. Education is one of the only departments where the staff mugs are made of china and not plastic. The rules changed after a prisoner with a beard that reached almost to his knees smashed a china mug over an officer's head. It happened at HMP Frankland in the north, but it's not uncommon for an incident in one dispersal to affect protocol in all of them.

Ben wanders over, downing a paper cup of water. 'Are you on the wing later?' he asks.

'All day. I finish at seven tonight.'

'You know the photos thing? Will you have time?'

Ben's friend posted him some photos last week, but the censors team sent a note explaining that they would only be issuing nine of the ten photos. They're withholding one for security reasons, because the photo shows a man in a balaclava holding a gun to someone's head. It's not surprising that Ben isn't allowed to be in possession of it. But he's curious. He wants me to go to the censors team and look at the photo, to see if it really is a gun, if his friend really is doing what they say he is.

'I'll have to ask the SO. If there's enough staff, I'm sure he'll let me go for half an hour. But Ben, I'm not going to know if it's a real gun or not. I don't know the difference.'

The censors team probably don't either, but that's not the point. Imitation firearm or the real thing, that's not something they can ignore. During my career, I'll come across lots of photos or letters that the censors team will withhold. Anything featuring criminality is an obvious one, though the criminality itself isn't always obvious. Sometimes children's drawings are prohibited, if they test positive for drugs. It's the same with greetings cards, photos and writing paper. They can all be laced with synthetic drugs, soaked in illicit substances including opioids, that can be smoked once dry.

'Do you think the prison will have called the police? To say there was a gun in the photo?' Ben asks.

'Probably. I don't think they'll have had much choice.'

'He's such a fucking idiot. I don't know why he's done that.'

We talk about his friends a lot. His friends, his hometown, his family. He's the eldest of five brothers. The younger two are still in school and have never been to prison. But he knows they're getting into trouble already. He's worried they'll end up in a place like this. He doesn't want this life for them.

From what Ben tells me, he doesn't think the person in the photo was actually being threatened. He doesn't think the gun was even real. As far as he's concerned, the photo would have been staged, something to post on social media, a show of power to demonstrate how much control and influence his friend has. Or wants people to think he has. But the ripple effects of what he's done are vast. Of course the police will have been informed. Probably social services, too. Ben knows just as well as I do that a security report will have been submitted the moment that photo came into the jail, and that's the sort of thing that will stay on his record forever, even if he had nothing to do with it. So many potential red flags will come from that. If he were to be released, would he have access to guns? Are his friends involved in organised crime? Is there a welfare issue at home? But this isn't organised crime, and they aren't gangsters. His friend has been stupid and reckless, and I can tell Ben is embarrassed by it all. I've suggested he phone the friend who sent the photos in, but we both know that the call would be listened to, and he feels like he wouldn't be able to say the things he wants to.

Not all phone calls are monitored, though. Staff aren't permitted to listen in on certain calls, for example those made to a prisoner's legal team or solicitor. The majority of calls are listened to on a random basis, something like fifteen per cent of all calls made that day. Only Category A prisoners have all their phone calls listened to. Ben is a Category A prisoner, so the call will be monitored. And with his IPP status, and the constant uncertainty of his release date looming over him, an angry phone call about a photo of a gun isn't something he wants on his record.

His friend isn't completely new to all this; he's done time in jail himself, but only once and not in a prison like Whitemoor. So maybe he didn't know the mail gets checked, or didn't think the photo would be looked at. Or maybe he thought it was obvious that it's not an actual gun. But no one takes any chances here.

There are too many people in Whitemoor who do know the difference between a real gun and a fake one. Who know the difference between handguns and sawn-off shotguns and Skorpion submachine guns and Uzi submachine guns and AK-47 assault rifles. Who know what it's like to have a gun held to their head, and to be the one holding it, too. To be the one who pulls the trigger. What might have seemed funny to Ben's friend is not funny here.

A teacher comes out of the staffroom. 'End of breaktime, then, gentlemen!'

Ben crushes the plastic water cup in his hand and drops it in the bin. 'Such a fucking idiot,' he says. 'See you at lunch, Alex.'

***

I never go to see the photo. There never seem to be any surplus staff on the wing. Staffing is getting tighter around the jail. On the days we do have an extra officer on the wing, they're soon deployed to workshops or education. A few days later turns out to be one of those days, and I'm that officer. This time I've been assigned to the workshops department rather than education.

Having some time off the wing can feel like a nice break, but workshops is a bit of a gamble. There are nine different workshops to which officers can be assigned, and I won't know which one I'm going to until I get to the activity manager's office on the main corridor. I'm hoping for Workshop 8, the music room. The prisoners here can learn to read and write music, to produce it, too, and even record their own. There are recording booths, keyboards, an upright piano, and state-of-the-art Mac computers for prisoners learning how to use the music-production software. The room itself is bright and colourful, with posters on the walls and a vibrant energy.

Workshop 4 feels very different.

Workshop 4 is a huge room with no windows and industrial-sized pipes that snake across the ceiling. Four wide conveyor belts fill the room with a constant rumbling noise. The prisoners employed here are the ones tasked with recycling CDs and DVDs that have been collected at local supermarkets. The CDs and DVDs pass along the belt with prisoners stationed at various points, removing the sleeve and discs from the cases and flinging them into boxes at their feet. The empty plastic cases clatter into bins at the end of the belt. The room is filled with rumble, clatter, rumble, clatter, rumble, clatter. A solid two hours of that. The more the prisoners get through, the more they get paid, so it's a popular workshop, but not because the work is interesting. Often, the prisoners flip open the cases without even looking, tossing the discs into one bin, the sleeves into another, over and over again with a glazed-over look on their faces. It's mind-numbing work. Boring for them and boring for the officer overseeing them.

Workshop 6 is where the prisoners practise for their BICSc exam. BICSc stands for British Institute of Cleaning Science. All the prisoners with cleaning jobs on the wing have to have passed their BICSc test before they can become cleaners. Workshop 6 has four separate squares of flooring: wood, carpet, linoleum and laminate. The prisoners take it in turns to practise cleaning the different floors with different mop heads and different-coloured buckets and different detergents, guiding the buffing machine in figures of eight as the instructor looks on. Whitemoor is big on health and safety; putting the wrong mop head in the wrong bucket is an instant fail. There's an advanced version of the BICSc exam for prisoners interested in becoming biohazard cleaners. These are the guys called to incidents involving bodily fluids. They turn up with hazmat suits and grim expressions, to deal with shit, piss, vomit and blood. Normally blood. Unsurprisingly, it's one of the least popular jobs, despite being one of the best paid. The workshop where they practise is quiet and never too busy.

Most of the workshops are located on either side of a long corridor at the opposite end of the jail to the education department. As with education, a spiral staircase leads to it. Far more prisoners attend workshops than education, and the stairs are well-worn, with flaking strips of anti-slip tape on each step. This staircase is one of the few areas in the prison not covered by CCTV, which hasn't gone unnoticed by the inmates.

Part of an officer's job is to be observant, but we're matched in that regard by the prisoners. They don't miss a thing. A couple of prisoners will mention this particular staircase to me, well aware that it's one of the prison's blind spots. It's not uncommon for stairs to be without cameras. There's no specific reason for this, other than money perhaps. CCTV coverage is expensive. It makes sense to have cameras in the more obvious areas where prisoners spend a lot of their time, such as the wings and the gym. Staircases take a couple of seconds to pass through. So it's not surprising that, if somewhere has to be without CCTV, the stairs tend to be that place. But the consequences of this are that a serious assault takes place in a staircase at every prison I work in: an attempted slashing at Whitemoor, a successful one at Belmarsh, and at Scrubs a particularly sinister incident, when the stairwell lights will suddenly be switched off and an officer will be injected with something unknown from a syringe later found discarded on the floor.

I've heard a staircase at Whitemoor described as 'a slit throat waiting to happen'; years later, a prisoner will tell me that he only ever walked down it when his two friends from other wings had joined him first. We're discussing this years later, when we're both at HMP Belmarsh, reminiscing about a safer time, when jail didn't seem quite so volatile. Or at least, that's what I thought. I didn't know it back then, but he was under mounting pressure to convert to Islam at Whitemoor, and his consistent refusal saw him threatened with violence. It was just a staircase to me, but to him it was a place where his palms started to sweat and his heart rate quickened, where it looked cowardly to rush but it was foolish not to, where he felt a mixture of gratitude and guilt that his friends walked there with him, taking each step in tandem, all of them knowing that their show of solidarity meant they could all become targets, all of them knowing that hours in the gym won't stand up to a knife, all of them reaching that last step and, each time, feeling like they'd dodged a bullet. Or a shank.

But they're just stairs to me, and I take them two at a time, with no idea that a prisoner I see and talk to every day is currently praying that his request to transfer gets approved so he doesn't ever have to walk these steps again.

I head into the corridor with workshops lining either side. I'm lucky today; I've been given Workshop 8. Officer Callard is there too. Not Bev, but her husband Anthony, who's done even longer in the job than she has. In fact, he's been at Whitemoor since it opened, a time he describes to me as 'like being in a warzone. All the other jails just sent us the prisoners they didn't want, just emptied their segs. Alarm bells all day, every day.'

Anthony taps a small pot of coffee granules against the edge of the wooden podium. All the workshops have these podiums at the back of the room for the officers to sit in, raised just enough for them to give an elevated view of the room.

'Nothing like this.' He looks out at the prisoners milling about in front of us.

I can imagine he's right. There aren't any seg prisoners down here. Workshop 8 is in demand; there's a lengthy waiting list and prisoners don't get a spot on it by behaving badly.

I can see Malcolm in the recording booth at the far end of the room, with black headphones clamped over his ears. A couple of his friends are huddled round the booth, nodding their heads in time to the music. More prisoners are in the production area opposite. They sit in front of computers so large that they look like windows, their vast screens showing rows of soundwaves lit up in bright colours. Most of the prisoners are seated just in front of the officers' podium. This is where they compile their music on to CDs. As well as the music programmes, the computers have basic software installed, like Word and PowerPoint, which some of the older prisoners use to practise their IT skills.

'Coffee?' Anthony asks me.

'Yes, white and none please. I'll do a quick patrol while you're making them.'

Officers are required to patrol their workshops multiple times throughout the session. I weave through the IT area, and pause next to Sammy. He's learning PowerPoint with the help of another prisoner who studied Computer Engineering at university and is employed in the workshop to help tutor prisoners.

'What does anyone even use this for?' I hear Sammy mutter.

Beside Sammy is Ginge, his friend from B Wing. They met in the chapel one Sunday and have been friends ever since.

'Got myself a space down the kitchens,' Ginge tells me with a grin. He's lucky. The waiting list for a job in the prison kitchens is even longer than the one for Workshop 8.

I glance at all the screens as I pass. The computers are donated by local businesses and should all be stripped of their internet connectivity. The only computers with access to the internet are those used solely by staff, and even then the sites that staff can reach are heavily restricted. Today, it's all as it should be: Word, PowerPoint and music software.

Malcolm is exiting the sound booth as I walk into the recording area. It's darker in here, with padded walls on one side and a wooden partition on the other to separate it from the rest of the workshop. He looks hyped up. Sweat glistens above his upper lip.

'I'll play you it when it's done, Alex,' he says and winks. 'It's all clean, don't worry.'

Prisoners aren't allowed to make music about their crime or any kind of violence. Most of them record songs about their lives before prison, and, for many of them, violence was such an integral part of that that it's hard to omit entirely. During cell searches, I regularly come across journals or lyrics that document their lives on the outside. Officers have to check everything as part of a search – only legal paperwork is exempt, and even that has to be rifled through in the prisoner's presence to ensure no contraband is concealed within it. In the past, officers have gone through letters and diaries to find confessions to unsolved crimes, or even poorly codified notes revealing detailed plans for terrorist attacks with the potential to obliterate entire shopping centres. But more often than not, the words I read are a window into their lives before prison. They're the same words I hear in Workshop 8, in this tiny recording booth with its one aged microphone. A lot of these men feel a real and urgent need to tell their stories about life before Whitemoor, before they're forgotten or the newspaper versions become the only account out there. The challenge is how to do that without graphic depictions of violence to make their point.

I pass through into the production area. There are only two men in here. One who recently changed his name by deed poll to David Bowie – your guess is as good as mine – and another so massive that he doesn't fit in the normal workshop chairs.

The instructor has given him one of the staff chairs instead. He's not fat; it's all muscle. His nickname is 'Shoulders'.

By the time I'm back at the podium, my coffee is waiting for me, in a tall, stainless-steel cup Anthony found in the makeshift kitchen at the back of the room.

There's something about the atmosphere in Workshop 8 that feels different from the rest of the jail, maybe because it's one of the few places in prison the prisoners want to be. It's not relaxed, exactly, because to relax in prison is a dangerous thing, but there's less of the tension that hums like constant background noise everywhere else. And there's something humbling about seeing people make soundtracks to their lives right in front of you.

Many of the prison officers here have been in the job all their adult lives. They joined up in their early twenties and are still here thirty, even forty years later. They've developed their own ways of coping with that background noise, and the violence that crescendos from it every now and again.

'The early nineties were rough here. It settled down after a few years. You don't see so much of it now, that kind of violence. But it's more than that; it's the never knowing what's coming next, being alert to everything all the time. That's what you need to look out for, Alex. Make sure you have your time to relax and spend time with people who have nothing to do with prison. Take your annual leave, and don't do too much overtime. This job will change you without you even realising.'

A few of the older officers have said this to me. That the job changes you. That you become desensitised to the horrors you see. Otherwise, how do you cope? But I don't feel changed. And I haven't really seen that much. If I am different, then it's for the better. I'm more confident, more knowledgeable. I don't hate coming into work anymore. I've started to enjoy it, just like Jade said I would. And I feel as if I know a little more about the real world, about what's actually out there. The older officers say it's this knowledge that has made them wary and distrustful, but I find it hard to relate to that. And anyway, they've worked through a different era in Whitemoor's history, a time when there were no cameras and every prisoner had come from a seg somewhere. It isn't like that anymore.

'My wife noticed differences in me before I did,' Anthony says. 'Things like, I'd only sit at a table that faced the door in the pub, with my back to the wall, so I could see everything that was going on. And I stopped taking care of myself as much, or doing the things I used to enjoy, like being in the garden. I let everything get overgrown. Weeds up to here.' He smiles and slaps the side of the podium. He pauses for a few moments, and I wonder if he's going to carry on.

'Then one day, I turned up for my shift, parked the car, and I just couldn't get out. I couldn't get my legs to work. So I just sat there. For ages.' He stares into his coffee.

I feel privileged that he's telling me this, this well-respected and experienced officer who acts as if nothing and no one fazes him. I'm struck, too, by the strangeness of having such a vulnerable conversation in this setting. Even if it's only the two of us who can hear.

In fact, a version of this is going on all around the workshop. The men are doing the same. Telling their stories. Talking about the things that have shaped them.

'I never thought I was scared of this place. But my body was telling me I was. I was frozen. Bev had to come pick me up.'

'How did you—?'

'Get better? I went to the GP after that. Ended up on meds for a while, which I wasn't sure about, but they got me out of that hole. The prison also paid for me to have some counselling. Now I just try to take better care of myself, not drink too much, that kind of thing. But this job is a lot to take on, even if you don't realise it. It can weigh you down if you're not careful.'

He's interrupted by the prisoner who tutors other inmates, asking for a pen. Anthony is his personal officer and has been for almost four years. I'm sure that during that time they've had plenty of disagreements, but they've figured them out and stuck with each other. Their dynamic is friendly and almost playful, but it's hard won. The respect the prisoner has for Anthony is obvious.

'Make sure I get it back, young man,' says Anthony. 'I keep dishing these out and forgetting who I've given them to. Right, I'll do the next patrol.'

He strides towards the production area, patrolling in the opposite direction to the one that I went in. That's jailcraft. Take a different route, at irregular times; stay alert to everything. But I'm starting to realise how much more there is to it. It's the way you treat people and the commitment you show.

***

Senior management at Whitemoor encourage meaningful interactions with the prisoners at every turn, some of whom have never had any real consistency with the people in their lives, or have never had a positive relationship with someone in authority. Ben is one of these inmates. He's told me before that I'm the first prison officer he's ever properly spoken to. But while that approach is framed as being solely of benefit to the prisoners, I'm beginning to see that it really works both ways. I see it in the way Ant talks to prisoners in the workshop, the way Bernard talks to everyone, the way Bev gets to know the men who visit her library before recommending a book to them, the time and resources the education staff have put into supporting Bolt through his degree. To do something for someone else is to do something for yourself.

Admittedly, I don't feel that way about all the prisoners here. Though I would never say it in front of my managers, there are plenty of men here whom I would happily see locked up forever, with the key thrown away. Men so narcissistic and cold and devoid of empathy that you won't find much about them in these pages. Just enough to say that yes, they're here. Because they are the ones you already know about. There is already so much written about them. And maybe that's the problem. I thought there would be so much more of that in prison than there is. I came here wanting to help, but I wasn't expecting to develop such a rapport with the men I was trying to help. I wasn't expecting to find them so normal, so likeable.

These kinds of interactions between staff and prisoners make me feel more confident in my role as a prison officer, and, ultimately, they make Whitemoor feel like a safer place to me. I'm not being *told* about the value of developing positive relationships, I'm *experiencing* it. It takes a kind of vulnerability for a prisoner to tell me about his life, and a kind of stoicism from me to listen to it. But we both benefit. The walls of 'them and us' are broken down a bit, and I'm left with more of an understanding of what it is to be him. It makes me more socially conscious, too. I read the papers in a different way, watch the news differently. I become more aware of the way that prison shines a light on the wider societal issues. Politics, public health problems and the state of the economy: all of it filters down into people's homes.

Consequently, I feel even more committed to helping prisoners change. Some of them have already done the hard work for me. I don't have to try to convince them to stay away from drugs, or make the case for a crime-free life, because they already want that for themselves. Others, like Bolt and Ben, often seem as if they have a foot in both worlds, enthralled by the idea of change and what a different life might look like, but steadied by what they know. I can be a positive role model, a sounding board and someone to talk to, but it isn't up to me to change anyone. The battle is within them. I'm slowly learning this.

Whitemoor might be closed off to the outside, but the people inside are teaching me about the world far beyond it: about tower blocks in Deptford, drugs dens in White City, gun caches in Manchester, and terror-filled homes in Peterborough. They are teaching me about the corners of society that, this time eighteen months ago, I was happy to ignore.

The radio sounds and lets us know it's time for freeflow. The prisoners hear it, too, and gather their things. Ant rubs down, I wand. 'Shoulders' doesn't bat an eyelid when I wand his arms twice to make sure I cover the entire surface area.

When all the prisoners have gone, Ant and I check the workshop, just as we did before the session began. I never find anything hidden in a workshop, but I know better than to skip a check.

We look under tables, chairs and keyboards; we rifle through paperwork, stationery and sheets of music; we peer behind computers and wires and boxes. Then we part ways, Ant to the gym and me back to the wing. It'll be bang-up soon.

'You take care,' Ant says and strolls off.

As I walk back to the wing, Ant's words are running through my mind. How fear had engulfed him and he couldn't leave his car. And it strikes me that, although there is so much in place to support prisoners' mental health, there is very little for the staff. Quite rightly, the prisoners here have access to a GP, to counsellors and pastoral support, to forensic psychiatrists, individual sessions and group therapy, courses and workshops. For those living on the DSPD, there is also an intensive and targeted programme of therapeutic support. But we have very little: an employee support helpline and peer support. Many of the inmates come to Whitemoor already marked by trauma, while the officers accumulate it along the way. It's human nature to run from danger, but prison officers are paid to run to it. It's what we signed up for. And that's fine, as long as you have a way of coping with the walk back, once the alarm bells have stopped, the biohazards team have been and gone, the blood is cleared and the doors all locked. As long as you have a way of dealing with what you've seen. You need to be able to go home and be a father, husband, wife, mother or friend, and not still hear the alarm bell ringing in your head. You need to be able to come back in the next day. But I think I'm doing fine. I've got the balance right. I'm close to my friends and family, I don't drink much, I work hard but I rarely do overtime. Even though I'm based on a wing, supposedly the toughest place to work, I still have time away from there every now and again. I still get to come to the workshops or education. Having time to do something different is important for the staff, just as it is for the prisoners. The same thing every day can become boring, and boredom is problematic in prison. The long-term nature of Whitemoor's population means I'll never know if attending a workshop makes a difference to their risk of reoffending, but it's still a significant part of life here. It takes them off the wing and gives them something to focus on. It distracts them, maybe even ignites a passion. For music or education, I mean. No one feels passionate about the CD-recycling workshop.

***

I turn into A Wing, that familiar space with its usual sounds and smells, the officers and prisoners whom I see every day. I say hello to Brian, his head bowed as he tries to figure out how to type something without the letter 'B'. That key on the keyboard has been broken for a while now. He checks his watch and tells me it's two minutes to lock-up, and all the spurs are fully staffed, so I can go on whichever one I want. I pick Red Spur, and feel in my pocket for my key.

And then suddenly, he's right there.

Ben.

He's right opposite me, pressed up to the bars of the one gate that separates us. His hands grip the bars so tightly they could crush them like slender necks; his face is so angry and red with rage that it poisons his tongue. He shouts and shouts, calling me names neither of us will remember, swollen words that spill one into the next, that don't make sense, that don't mean anything, that are out of context. And where has all this come from? And I'm just standing there, so confused that I can't do anything but stand and look and think *who the hell is this man and why are his fists so clenched and what have I done that has made him do this and he can't be the Ben I thought I knew and I don't know this man and what do I do to make him stop and thank god thank God THANK GOD that gate isn't open.*

Rafik pulls him away. He appears from one of the cells, craning his neck round the door frame to see what all the noise is about. He sees Ben and he sees me, and then he moves so fast it's like he flies from the cell door to the gate where Ben stands. He grabs him round the waist and lifts him, physically moves him away, yelling at him to stop, and that's enough, and calm the fuck down, just leave it, leave it. Ben is so angry he doesn't even fight him, just keeps screaming at me as he's dragged away.

Rafik moved so fast it was like he flew. I wonder if he thought the gate was open.

He knows something I don't.

5

The Kitchens

'Y OU KNOW I would never hurt you, Alex. You know that.' He stares at the ground, his arms dangling over the railings. He can't look at me.

It's been two days since Ben tried to get at me from behind the gate. He was locked in his cell after it happened. His food was brought to him for the rest of the day. He had a sit-down with Gavin the SO, never a good sign. But the main decision regarding the course of action is on me. It's my call. Gavin has made it clear to me that if I want Ben off the wing, he's gone.

'He'll be on B Wing by the end of the day, Alex,' he told me, and snapped his fingers.

But I don't think that's what I want. I still don't really under-stand what happened, and Ben isn't giving much away. He says that it wasn't about me, that he was just having a bad day. That it wasn't personal.

It certainly felt personal.

I know that the relationship between personal officer and prisoner can be a tenuous one, and I don't want to throw away all the progress he's made. Sending him to another wing doesn't feel like the right thing to do. It's not just me he gets on with; he's close with Bernard and he trusts Jade and Brian, too. Bernard has told me that sometimes things like this hap-pen, arguments and outbursts and changes in mood, and we as officers will never know why. He's reminded me that things are rarely as they seem. There's so much going on behind the scenes that the prisoners keep hidden from officers. It could be a bad phone call or the anniversary of a crime or tension with another prisoner – and sometimes all three – and we'll never know how close things came to imploding. It's like two worlds co-existing, in the same place, at the same time. But the officers only have access to one.

I know that out of all the personal prisoners assigned to me, Ben is the only one with a really poor custodial record. Hostage-taking, escape, assaults, phones, drugs. But by his own admission, Whitemoor has been the first and only prison where he's changed that. He's off Basic, off the E List, out of the seg and into education. He's thriving here. It was a bad day, that's all. A blip. A bump in the road. We can get things back on track. When he's in a good mood, Ben is funny and engaging and insightful. He's introspective about why he's here, one of the few prisoners who doesn't try to deny his offence or claim it wasn't him. I'm focusing on all of this, because if I don't I will remember how I felt in that moment.

Ben says he was rattling the gate out of frustration, but I saw a man trying to rip it off its hinges. He hasn't behaved in that way to anyone else, though, so maybe I've exaggerated it in my head. I don't want my colleagues to think I can't handle this. I passed probation with flying colours; I'm being put forward for courses in hostage negotiation and mental health support. For all my initial anxieties, people think I'm good at this job. If I admit that I was scared, will they still think that? If I admit that I think he could have hurt me, what will they say?

Because he doesn't act like this with anyone else.

My strength is talking. So we talk.

We talk about the reason he came to prison in the first place, why he did it and how it happened. He tells me about the embarrassment he feels at the way it derailed his life so dramatically. When I ask about what it was like to go to jail for the first time as a teenager, he describes the apprehension he felt, and a kind of nervous excitement, too, at finally going to the place almost every young man in his area had been already. Ben doesn't drink or take drugs. He isn't part of a gang. His journey to prison was different to a lot of the others I've heard so far. There was no Pupil Referral Unit, no assaults on teachers. After a certain point, he stopped going to school. There were no real consequences, so he just didn't go. But the anger he then saw played out on the streets wasn't new to him. We don't talk about it much, but I get the impression his home was not an easy place to be.

We've also talked about the pressure he feels at being the eldest child, the weight of trying to be a role model to his family when he has no template to copy from. And how is he supposed to do that from here, anyway? Is there any point? I can read between the lines well enough to know that there was no role model for him.

He's talked and I've listened. I've seen so much good in him, and I'm choosing to believe that that's the real Ben. Not the one I saw beating his fists against the gate.

He can do this. And so can I. I don't want to give up on him.

Bernard says that consistency is one of an officer's greatest tools in prison. A prisoner's circumstances may change, his moods may fluctuate, and everything in his life could fall apart, but we must stay the same. We must show up, be steady and reliable and always present, every time we're on shift.

So I do. And Ben stays.

***

Ben and Bolt are at the gates when I go to pick up the food, their heads lowered in conversation. I've been cleaning officer for the last two shifts, doing bin runs, handing out cleaning equipment, dropping off laundry and serving the meals with the four prisoners who make up the hotplate workers. Some staff hate being cleaning officer, but I enjoy it. You can be as busy or as lazy as you want. Your time is your own. Other than making sure lunch and dinner are on time, the cleaning officer isn't really bound by the regime in the same way as the landing officers are.

Today is a Thursday, which means apple crumble for dessert tonight. That's everyone's favourite. Lunch is less exciting. A recently thawed baguette with a little plastic tub of cheese, tuna mayo or coronation chicken. The menu at Whitemoor rotates every two weeks. Lunch is generally the same, baguettes or jacket potatoes, with crisps and fruit for dessert. Dinner consists of a meat or vegetarian option, with rice or potatoes, and a warm dessert like rice pudding. There are a few staples that everyone looks forward to. Chicken and chips on Fridays, a full English on Saturdays, and apple crumble on Thursdays.

If you've ever seen the kitchen in a restaurant or hotel, then prison kitchens are very similar to that. Whitemoor's is an expanse of grey metal. There are silver food trolleys parked next to laminated signs for the area they belong to, stainless-steel shelves topped with pans and trays, enormous pots that slow-cook stews and casseroles for 400 men, so big they look like cauldrons, and ladles and spatulas – and knives, too. The knives are, obviously, a risk. But it's impossible to run a kitchen without them. They're referred to as 'tools', and all tools are kept inside a small office. Only the staff have access to the office, and each individual tool is signed in and out when it's required. The prisoners employed in the kitchens have gone through a rigorous vetting process beforehand. If their crime involved a knife, then there's no chance they're getting a job down here. If they've used ever a makeshift weapon in prison, they're out. In fact, any history of custodial violence is normally an immediate no.

Normally.

Attwood slaps a plastic carrier bag full of chocolate bourbons and custard creams on top of the A Wing trolley.

Attwood is new to A Wing, and he's the only prisoner working in the kitchens who lives there. The rest are all on another
wing. The kitchen staff pick them up early, before morning
freeflow even starts, and they're not back on the wing until late
afternoon, so it's easier for the kitchen staff if all the prisoners
who work in the kitchen are from the same wing. Attwood
was on that wing with them, but then a pillowcase was found
cut in half, with two eye holes cut out of it. Like a kind of a
makeshift hood. One you might use if you were planning to
take someone hostage. It's only been a couple of months since
an officer was taken hostage by two radical Islamist prisoners
in HMP Frankland, and we've all felt a change in atmosphere
since then. If it can happen there, it can happen here. The pillowcase hasn't helped. There's no direct evidence to indicate
that it was Attwood's, but he's suspected to have been involved
in some way, or at least known about it. There's no question
that he's an influential prisoner. He's the kind of man the other
prisoners defer to. He's older, with a long time in prison already
behind him, and a record so violent that it garners him a kind
of respect. Or wariness.

The security department directed that he be moved to
A Wing. It isn't uncommon for prisoners thought to have some
involvement in the subculture to be moved around the jail to
disrupt their activity. Attwood didn't complain. He just packed
his things and left. He's a well-liked prisoner and has friends all
over the jail, A Wing included. But I was nervous when I heard
that he would be coming. And I wasn't the only one. He has a
reputation. The kind of reputation that has followed him from
jail to jail, seg to seg.

He looks intimidating, too. He's covered in tattoos, on his
arms and legs and the tips of his ears, that look like tiny spiders
crawling over his body. But the more I get to know him, the
less intimidating he becomes. In fact, he's good company. He's
the kind of guy who could tell the most boring story and make

it sound interesting. And that's a good skill to have in here. Prison can get tedious.

Not that any of the stories he's told me so far have been boring. He once told me he knocked someone out with a frozen chicken.

And yet here he is, employed in the kitchens, surrounded by frozen meat. And knives.

'No Jammie Dodgers today, Alex,' he says.

'Great,' I say, anticipating the complaints I'll get later. There haven't been any Jammie Dodgers for a week. They're everyone's favourite. Sammy's especially.

Attwood disappears and returns with 120 plastic cartons of UHT milk on a cardboard tray. Ginge appears and precariously balances a plastic carrier bag full of crisp packets on top of my trolley. 'Did Attwood tell you we've run out of Jammie Dodgers?'

If Attwood looks intimidating, then Ginge, well, doesn't. He looks like someone's stuck a boy's head on a man's body. He's got chubby round cheeks with dimples that slice into them when he smiles, which is a lot, and bright red hair. But it's his height that makes him stand out. He's so tall that you'd look twice if you saw him in the street. His feet are so big that the prison have to order in shoes especially for him. And he styles his hair in spikes, frozen stiff by too much gel, like little turrets on top of his head. He's funny, always smiling, always cracking jokes. I like him.

More officers are coming in now. The cleaning officers from B Wing, C Wing and the seg are all here, checking their trolleys and making sure they've got everything. I do the same, ticking everything off against a hastily scrawled list I've got in my pocket.

One hundred and eighteen yogurts, tick. One hundred and eighteen baguettes, tick. Coronation chicken, tuna mayo, cheese – tick, tick, tick. One box of salad for the prisoner who has Crohn's disease. Crisps, biscuits, Jammie Dodgers – tick,

tick, cross. I'm good to go. The cleaning officers can't leave the kitchen until all the tools have been accounted for, but this doesn't take long. The majority of tools are used for the evening meal, not for a cold lunch. I wave to Attwood and Ginge and push my trolley to the gate, being careful not to knock the worktops. The trolleys are heavy and cumbersome, and there's a real knack to getting them round corners. And unfortunately for me, the route is past the exercise yard. Which is now full of men.

I put the brakes on just the right distance before the gates, so the gates don't swing into the trolley when I unlock them. I start turning as soon as I go through the gate, angling the trolley just slightly, and then push all my weight against the right-hand side – and I'm through. The prisoners cheer as I narrowly avoid hitting the gate.

As I walk back on to the ground floor of the wing, Brian spots me from the twos landing. Seconds later, I hear his voice over the tannoy. 'Hotplate workers to the hotplate, please, hotplate workers to the hotplate.'

The hotplate workers are a good team. Four men who help me prepare the hotplate, serve the food and clean up after. We don't have knives on the wing, there's no need for them. But there are ladles and spatulas, heavy metal trays and, during dinner, an urn of custard that's hot to the touch: all things that could be used as weapons. Being a hotplate worker is a trusted role. And a relatively easy one, too. So once prisoners get the job, they tend to stay in it for a while. I've had the same four prisoners on the hotplate for a few months now.

Harpal is out first. He's one of my personal prisoners, in the early years of his murder sentence. Before his murder conviction, he'd only been out eighteen months after serving a ten-year stretch for manslaughter. He flings on a white jacket hanging on the hook next to the tools cabinet. There are five jackets there, in a variety of sizes, all but one of them too small for the men who wear them. And Harpal's got the well-fitting one. He kicks off his trainers and replaces them with brown workman's boots. It's one of the conditions of working behind the hotplate. You can't wear your own shoes; it has to be the boots. And you have to wear the white jackets, as ridiculous as they look. None more so than mine. I've picked the smallest one, but it's still way too big for me. The shoulders slide off my own like a lazy coat hanger. The sleeves are too wide and splattered with remnants of yesterday's custard. Harpal starts setting everything out straight away. Baguettes to one corner, crisps and yogurts to another.

Harpal is joined by Phil, a slim prisoner with drooping circles in his earlobes where earrings used to be. He's part of a well-known organised crime family, and once told me that his father first took him out on an armed robbery when he was twelve. He grumbles at missing out on the best jacket and starts organising the milk cartons.

The next hotplate worker to come out is a thin prisoner with a Charlie Chaplin-style moustache and bushy eyebrows. Wojcik is serving a long sentence for drug importation; almost £100 million's worth of cocaine was found on his yacht. He's hoping to be extradited back to Poland and serve the rest of his time there.

And finally, along comes Matthew, who's always the last one out. He takes his place by the baguettes and puts on a pair of blue gloves, pretending he hasn't seen the hat I've left there.

'Hat please, Matthew,' I say. He rolls his eyes and makes a big show of folding the paper into a hat and placing it on his head.

The four of them work well together. They share a kind of camaraderie that's interesting to see, because they're all very different characters. I'm not sure that Phil would ordinarily hang out with someone like Wojcik, and equally I don't think I'd ever seen Harpal speak to Matthew before they got this job. But now they've got it, they don't want to lose it. This is the job everyone wants. First pick of the food – and any extras – and the dynamics between staff and prisoner are different behind the hotplate. I'm not just standing there watching them, or searching them, or locking gates behind them. I'm navigating the same sort of issues they are, the same sort of routine problems that come with mealtimes. There's always someone unhappy with their menu choice, unhappy with the portion size, demanding extras. This kind of thing is easier for me to deal with than it is for the hotplate workers, who are negotiating with their peers and their friends, people to whom they might not necessarily want to say no. Mealtimes can be fractious, but we're all working towards the same goal. Make sure everyone gets their food, and does so with no alarm bells pressed. Working behind the hotplate is also the only time we're not set apart by uniform. We're all wearing the same ill-fitting, custard-stained whites.

The prisoners gather by the gates that open onto the central ones area. Roger and Jade are on gate duty today. When I give them the nod, they'll unlock the spur gates, one spur at a time, letting out eight prisoners at a time. It doesn't sound like a particularly testing job, and most of the time it isn't, but things can go wrong quickly. There are 119 men waiting by those gates, and mealtimes in prison can be volatile. Hunger can do that to you. The queues are meant to impose order, but some prisoners jump in and shove the more vulnerable men out the way, and some ignore the queue altogether. They ignore the tannoy, the officers calling for them, the bellowed warning that 'This is your last chance!'

And if they miss their turn, then that's it. They've missed lunch. The regime won't wait. The prisoners know this, and most aren't interested in confrontation; they just want their baguette and crisps.

Roger gives me a thumbs-up and I nod back. We're ready to go. Jade unlocks the gate to Red Spur and stands aside as the first eight men come out.

On my clipboard is a list of the names of every man on the wing, and the food choice they selected a week in advance.

'Alastair, cheese. Romario, cheese. Mustafa, tuna. Griff, salad. Davis, cheese. Ahmet, tuna. Ben, cheese.'

Some hold blue plastic plates, the ones issued by the prison when they first arrive, but most don't bother. They stuff the baguettes into their trouser pockets instead. Ben playfully tries to grab an extra carton of milk when he reaches me, but I move it out of his way just in time. He winks and smiles. Everything's back to normal. It was just a blip. A bump in the road.

The last eight prisoners return to the spur and the next eight come out. Five times over, until Red Spur are done.

'You ready for Blue, Alex?' Jade calls to me, her keys already in the lock of Blue Spur gate.

'Send on Blue Spur,' I call back.

And out they come. Eight at a time. Bolt is one of the first ones out; he always is. Sammy is close behind him, shouting to anyone who'll listen that the lack of Jammie Dodgers is against his human rights. He's only half joking. The milk pile goes down, the bag of baguettes empties, the biscuits are rifled through and moaned about. By the time Green Spur come out, there's only a handful of custard creams left, and the rest are plain.

The whole thing only takes about twenty-five minutes. It's a cold meal, and no one gets that excited about a cheese sandwich. There's not much to hang around for, or seconds worth bargaining for, and certainly not anything worth fighting over. But dinner will be different. Dinner is burgers and chips.

And apple crumble.

***

When I get to the kitchen to collect the evening meal, Ginge is already sliding a tray of burgers into the A Wing trolley.

The air is heavy with the smell of too much food in one place: burgers and chips and fish and curry, all crammed into one trolley. It's noisy, too. The clattering and slamming and sloshing of trays being put in and taken out and counted and put in again. The cleaning officer from D Wing is already here, looking slightly panicked.

'I'm missing a whole tray of apple crumble,' he says, staring at the piece of paper in his hand and then into the trolley. 'Ginge, I'm missing a tray of crumble!'

'On it, boss,' Ginge calls back, pressing his back to the worktop to let Attwood through. Attwood is pushing his own trolley, carrying steaming urns of custard.

'Have you got everything?' he asks me, and lifts one of the urns on to my trolley.

'I'm just counting the burgers, but yes, I think so.'

'We haven't got any more chips, so don't let them give out too much. But we're keeping a spare tray of apple crumble here in case any of the wings run out. I made extra.'

'You're on dessert today?' I ask. Attwood doesn't look like the kind of guy who enjoys making puddings.

'I always am. I just finished tomorrow's coffee cake,' he says. 'It's my speciality. I'll make sure you get some.'

'I'm not in tomorrow. But remember me for next time.'

Ginge speeds past us, tray of crumble in hand.

'Thank god for that,' the D Wing officer says. 'We'd have had a bloody riot.'

'Tools please, lads!' the kitchen SO calls from somewhere near the back. 'I'm missing a ladle!'

'Attwood, have you seen the ladle?' Ginge shouts.

'No. I've been on dessert. What would I be using a ladle for?'

'No one's going anywhere until I'm holding that ladle!' the SO shouts again.

Attwood slopes off to help look for it.

By now, all the cleaning officers are here. We've finished checking the crumble and burgers, and we're all now checking our watches. The D Wing officer leans over to me.

'If they don't find it soon, we're going to be late. It's always the bloody ladle.'

He's right. This is frustrating, and we're all thinking it. Until all tools are accounted for, no one can leave the kitchen. So we wait. But the frustration is building. The kitchen workers come back to our trolleys, they open the doors and pull out the trays, checking the ladle hasn't sunk into the curry. They check that it isn't behind the pile of chopping boards, or in one of the walk-in fridges, or in the cupboard at the back where the cereal is kept.

I glance at my watch again. Dinner can be tight as it is without losing precious minutes here. I switched on the hotplate before I left the wing, so at least it'll be warm by the time I get back. Still, the prisoners will notice if dinner is late, even if only by ten minutes. Mealtimes are like mini events in prison, something that breaks up the day and takes people off their spurs, giving them somewhere to go and something to do, even if that's just a quick trip to the hotplate. Once they've collected their food, it's straight back to their cells.

The prisoners don't eat together. There are no tables and chairs in the communal space for them to sit and eat at, and bang-up is scheduled for immediately after lunch and dinner, so they can't eat in each other's cells, either. Despite this, the prisoners plan their meals meticulously. Most of the men on A Wing are in tea boats together, in groups of three or four. They plan in advance who will cook, who will wash up, and whose turn it is to buy any extra ingredients necessary from the prison canteen. These might be herbs and spices, or extra vegetables to combine with food collected from the hotplate. If the prison menu is serving chicken that evening, the prisoners might plan to have a chicken curry, and spend their association time cooking the sauce and dividing it between them before getting the meat from the hotplate. They don't get to eat the food together, but the time spent planning and preparing it lends a sense of community to mealtimes. This kind of community can only exist on the wings, though. In the segregation unit, prisoners still leave their cells to collect their food from the hotplate on the unit, but they do so one at a time, with an officer on either side of them, and the person behind the hotplate is another officer, not a prisoner.

'I've got it!' yells Ginge. 'It was in the curry pot!'

He's grinning so much his dimples look like little ladles of their own.

'Thank fuck for that,' says the kitchen SO. 'Tools are in!'

He picks up the phone to let the control room know.

'Alex, take this.' Attwood reaches over the worktop and hands me a small foil container with a cardboard lid. I put it on the trolley without looking at it. It's probably some extra crumble.

I flick off the brakes on my trolley and wait for the familiar clicking sound that means the electronic lock has been taken off. And when it comes, we're off. We're out the gate and scattering like ants. With a flurry of goodbyes and 'Good luck with the crumble!', the wing officers head in one direction, the seg and healthcare officers in another.

***

'Where've you been? It's crumble day!' Harpal's gold tooth glints when he smiles.

'I got held up. They couldn't get tools correct in the kitchen,' I say. I pull the trolley in through the archway to the hotplate. Harpal comes over and takes it from me, pushing it with ease into its usual spot at the back.

All the hotplate workers are here, even Matthew, though he pretends to look surprised when I point at his shoes, as if he'd forgotten he wasn't wearing boots. And they've done me a big favour. Everything is ready. Each alcove on the hotplate is labelled with the name of the dish it'll hold, written in capital letters with blue marker pen. It looks like Wojcik's handwriting; the 'g's are looped and swing into the other letters. Even my clipboard is set out where I normally stand, the list changed from lunch to dinner.

While I put on my jacket and ridiculous hat, the prisoners unload the trolley for me.

'We just need the tools, Alex,' Harpal says.

I unlock the cabinet and let them grab what they need. A spatula for the burgers and another one for the fish, a scoop for the chips, a big ladle for the curry and a little one for the custard. Matthew stands next to me at the cabinet, perusing what's on offer as if we've got all the time in the world. He's stepped up and agreed to give out the crumble, despite the arguments that normally come with the job, and I'm glad he has. He can be lazy and careless – the last time he did the washing-up he forgot to turn off the tap and nearly flooded the whole floor – but he won't back down for anything. If he says that's all you're getting, then that's all you're getting.

'That one, please.' He points to a flat server. 'Crumble, boys?' He cuts four generous slices of crumble and puts them into separate blue bowls, then hides them underneath the hotplate. The hotplate workers are meant to do their own food after everyone else's has been given out, but that's a rule that rarely gets followed. They work hard, they inevitably get abuse from prisoners displeased with their portion sizes, and they have less association time because they spend their evenings scrubbing trays blackened by burned food and grime. So most cleaning officers turn a blind eye to them getting first pick of the food. And tonight, it's thanks to them that we're ready to go within ten minutes of me being back on the wing.

Most of the prisoners try to negotiate a few extra chips, and those having burgers spend a few moments selecting the one they think looks best from the tray. But we're still making good time. Matthew is a champion with the crumble. He talks to everyone, making jokes and acting like he's picking out the best pieces and doing people a favour when he's already cut the crumble into almost identical portions. But in between spurs, he's on his knees, checking the remaining trays underneath the hotplate. Checking he hasn't given out too much, and that we've got enough. Wojcik stands next to him, spooning custard into the bowls the prisoners hand him. Wojcik is quiet and diligent. He doesn't say much to the other prisoners and keeps himself to himself. But he's got his eye on the crumble, too. When his co-defendant from Green Spur comes out, he nudges Matthew to make sure he gets a good portion. The best bits are in the middle. No one wants the corners. Those portions are never quite as big, and are too much crumble and not enough apple.

But by the end of dinner, one corner of crumble is all we've got left. All the chips are gone. Two portions of unwanted fish are left in their tray, the white sauce congealed and thick. The heat from the hotplate has cracked Wojcik's writing. The metal beneath the ink shows through the blue like little silver bubbles. I check my list. There's only one name left unticked. Miller.

I don't like Miller.

He's rude. Obnoxious. His lips are upturned in a permanent snarl, as if his features are carved from spite. It can be hard to imagine some of the men here doing the things for which they were imprisoned, but not Miller. His attitude matches his crime. And he acts like he doesn't want to be separate from it, anyway. He wants you to remember what he did, who he is, who he could still be if you dropped your guard enough. His is the crime that led to a government inquiry. Public outrage. An overhaul of the entire probation system. His is the crime that caused headlines dominated by questions: how could this be allowed to happen, why was he let out, why wasn't he recalled?

back, closer to the door that leads out of the hotplate area and into the space where Miller and Attwood are standing.

Miller picks up his plate and throws it into the bin pressed up against the wall. Jade's hand drops from the alarm bell to the keys in her pocket. She unlocks the gate to Green Spur, and Miller walks silently through it.

'Did you open the box?' Attwood asks me, as if nothing has just happened.

The box. The little foil container he gave me just before I left the main kitchens. I'd forgotten about it. I reach for the container, still where I left it on top of the trolley. Scrawled on the cardboard lid is 'ALEX'.

'Is this for me?'

Attwood grins. I peel back the lid to see a slice of coffee cake inside.

'You said you weren't in tomorrow. So I cut you some.'

Roger peers over the hotplate. 'What's this? Coffee cake? And you didn't do me any, Attwood? That's my favourite.'

'You look like you've had enough cake in your time, Rog.' Attwood laughs his loud, booming laugh.

'I'll do you some tomorrow if you're in.' He turns to me. 'You owe me one, Alex.'

'For the coffee cake?' I ask.

'No. Because there's loads of crumble down the kitchens.'

***

One of the things that makes Whitemoor unique is the access prisoners have to the mini kitchens on each spur. The main kitchens are broadly the same as any other I'll come across in the different prisons I'll go on to work at: loud, busy, and churning out a lot of potatoes and rice and questionable-looking meat. At Belmarsh, I'll find fillets of mackerel with the fins still attached.

But the mini kitchens are specific to Whitemoor. And from the perspective of an officer, they're one of the best things about prison life there. They make things easier. Arguments at the hotplate are normally about portion sizes, and this is less of an issue when prisoners can add to their meals with food they've cooked themselves. The act of cooking your own food is important: it gives back a little of the control that's taken away when prisoners are handed life sentences. The prisoners can decide what to eat and when. They can make it themselves and share it with others. They can microwave porridge in the morning and make toast; they can concoct elaborate meals that take a week to plan, ordering the ingredients from the canteen, and an hour to cook during evening association.

These mini kitchens are certainly mini. Only six or seven men can fit comfortably in there at one time. But there are never any fights. If disagreements do arise, they're quickly taken out of the kitchen and on to the landing, or into cells with the doors pulled to. The kitchen is too precious a thing to lose. It's about more than just the food, it's what the food symbolises. Birthday cakes, roasts at Christmas, biryani for Eid and plates piled with cardamom biscuits. A little bit of everything for Whitemoor's annual celebration of diversity event, when prisoners of different cultures are encouraged to cook dishes for each other to try. And then there's Pancake Day. Pancake Day is a big one.

I'm on Blue Spur with Roger this particular Pancake Day, slyly checking my watch. I like a pancake as much as anyone. I'm ready for this shift to end.

It's evening association, the time when things seem to both slow down and speed up. Bang-up is less than an hour away, and that'll be it for the day. Most officers will be finished then, including me. Almost all of our daily checks are done, personal prisoner reports are completed, paperwork is filed.

For the prisoners, evening association is the one time of day when they can do what they want, and they make the most of it. There are men in the spur gyms. *FIFA* is inevitably taking place on the threes landing. And it's library night, so there's a handful of prisoners queueing by the gates. The rule for library night is one for one. When one man makes his way back on to the wing with a stack of books or DVDs under his arm, another gets let off the wing.

The kitchen is busier than usual. The normal curries or chicken are forgotten tonight. It's all about the pancakes. Who can make the best one, who can flip theirs the highest. There's a lot of soggy batter flying about, a lot of laughter and jibes about pan-handling abilities.

Roger and I keep an eye on what's going on in there from our position on the other side of the netting. We're not expecting any issues tonight. And then Sammy trots up to us.

'I think you guys need to go in there, you know,' he says.

'Why?' asks Roger.

'Wallace is acting proper weird.'

'Wallace?' I say, surprised.

Sammy nods. 'Proper weird.'

That's strange. Wallace is so quiet, it's often easy to forget he's even here. He wears glasses with thick rims and trousers that never quite reach his ankles. And he's always polite. I've taken him to Healthcare a few times for check-ups with the GP. He's diabetic, and the prison nurses keep a close eye on him for that reason. I've heard that he can become aggressive if his blood sugar dips. But I've never seen it.

The nearer we get to the kitchen, the more it empties. Prisoners slip into cells or press their backs against the wall to let us pass. They know where we're going. Where they've just left.

I peer inside. Wallace is bent over the hob with his back to me. He's the only prisoner in there now.

'You OK, Wallace?'

But he doesn't reply. He doesn't move either. He stays in exactly the same position, frozen. Smoke rises from the pan in his left hand.

I step inside. 'Wallace?' I say again.

He wheels round, pan in hand, and faces me. His face is dripping with sweat. The collar of his jumper is stained with it. He stands with his feet planted shoulder-width apart and stares blankly at me.

Roger is beside me. It's so hot in here. I can hear prisoners behind us, their whispers floating around me like the smoke, and I know without looking that they're gathering on the landing outside the kitchen. They're calling him a nutjob, a weirdo, who gave him that pan in the first place. This kitchen, small and cramped anyway, suddenly feels tiny. It's so hot.

'You need to put that pan down, Wallace,' Roger says.

'I haven't. Finished. Making. My. Pancake.' He hisses the words at us in a voice that doesn't sound like his own.

I've never seen Wallace as much of a threat before. Not in the obvious way that some of the prisoners are. He's placid. Meek, even. He's one of the prisoners who can almost disappear into the chaos and noise of the wing. But I see him now.

I see that heavy metal pan, too. 'Put the pan down, Wallace.' I try again.

Situations like this are precarious, like balancing on a tightrope. Things can go either way; the right person or the right choice of words can defuse a situation just as quickly as getting it wrong can cause everything to escalate. One wrong move or phrase or gesture, something that Wallace might take as provocation in his confused state, and that pan could become a weapon.

By now, the prisoners' whispers will have spread. Someone will have noticed the growing crowd outside the kitchen, and that Roger and I aren't visible on the landing. It's likely that one of the prisoners has discreetly mentioned to the other staff that there is an issue in the kitchen. That they should probably have a look.

But if more officers were to suddenly rush in here now, that could make things a lot worse. It's a delicate balance. No one wants to inflame the situation. We need Wallace to put the pan down of his own accord. Not because we're wrestling it out of his hands.

He isn't thinking straight, I can see that. There's a tremble in his hands and his glasses are now so steamed up I'm not sure how much he can actually see.

'Wallace, that pancake is looking a bit burned. There's more batter on the side. Leave that one for now and make another one later,' I say.

Wallace looks at the pan, then back at me.

'I think the pan needs cleaning before you make a fresh one,' I continue. 'I'll ask Sammy to wash it while you go back to your cell for a minute.' I look back at Sammy, who's standing on the landing outside the kitchen. He gives me a sarcastic thumbs-up and mouths 'Cheers' at me.

'Why do I need to go back to my cell?' says Wallace. He sounds drunk.

'Are you hungry?' I ask. 'You've spent ages making that pancake. Go and get a snack or something while Sammy washes all the pans.'

Sammy throws his hands up behind me.

'We'll come with you, Wallace,' says Roger. 'You're diabetic, aren't you? One of us can make you a tea. Have you had enough sugar today?'

'A snack,' says Wallace. 'A snack. I don't know if I've had enough, Roger.'

'Can you take your sugar readings in your cell?' asks Roger.

Wallace nods. 'And I have Kit Kats in there.' Slowly, he places the pan on the worktop. 'How long do I need to go to my cell for?'

'Just until you've had a snack and the nurse has had a chat with you,' says Roger. 'You know they like to keep an eye on your sugar levels.'

'But then I won't get my pancake,' Wallace says. 'It'll be bang-up soon, and I haven't had a pancake.'

Griff, one of the prisoners who has been standing outside watching, pops his head into the kitchen. 'I'll make you one, Wallace. Go sort out your sugar levels, and I'll make you a pancake.'

Gavin is standing on the centre landing, watching as Roger and I walk with Wallace back to his cell. By the time we get there, the wing nurse is already waiting outside with Brian, who claps Wallace on his shoulder and says, 'You gave us all a fright there! Got to keep an eye on those sugar levels.'

'Sorry, guv,' Wallace says.

Roger and I have only been in the cell for a couple of minutes when Gavin appears in the doorway.

'Get off the landing for a bit, you two. Go make a drink.'

When we pass the kitchen, it's full again. Sammy's in a frenzy by the sink, drenched in soapy water. Griff is flipping the perfect pancake. A couple of other prisoners are cracking eggs and measuring flour. The kitchen is the last room before the gates that lead off the spur. I'm relieved to get off the landing for a moment. To lock that gate behind me and know everyone is safe.

Things can change in a second here.

It's then that I see Ben. He's at the gates to Red Spur, in the spot where he normally chats to Bolt through the bars. But he isn't waiting for Bolt.

He's waiting for me.

He doesn't say anything. His face does, though. He looks at me with disgust. Revulsion. He is sickened by me. Roger doesn't notice. He's through the gates and off the spur, and up the stairs to the breakroom. He doesn't see Ben.

But I do. I see him.

He was waiting for me. I have no idea why, but he was waiting for me.

6

Escorts

'**Y**OU'RE ON AN escort this morning, love,' Gavin says, as I walk into the briefing room.

Escorts are trips out of the prison: taking prisoners to hospital appointments, or transferring them to another jail, or even bringing them to family events like funerals. There's no distinction between male and female officers when it comes to escorts. Female staff take prisoners out just as often.

'OK, do you know who I'm taking?' I reply.

I'm expecting it to be one of the guys from A Wing. Ideally, prisoners are escorted by staff they know.

'Curtis Franks, off C Wing.'

'She's taking Curtis?' Roger looks up from his coffee, eyebrows raised.

***

Curtis is big. Much bigger than me. The security custodial manager slides Curtis's photo across the table. I recognise him. Maybe he's been in Workshop 8 when I've been on duty in there.

Officer Price and Senior Officer Forster sit on either side of me. They're both from C Wing and know Curtis well. The room we're in is one of three private offices that line the security department. Wooden plaques affixed to the doors state the role of the person inside: senior officer, custodial manager, governor of security. Briefings before escorts routinely happen in the offices of the senior officer or the custodial manager, but I've never been inside the governor's.

Outside is a larger office where civilian staff work. Civilian staff in prison are essentially those without a uniform. They aren't trained in control and restraint, and their contact with prisoners is limited, if they have any at all. But the work they do, so often behind the scenes, is invaluable. In the security department, civilian staff review intelligence reports as they're submitted and listen to prisoners' phone calls. Some of these are monitored in real time, such as those made by men on the E List. The E List prisoners know this. They have to pre-arrange their telephone calls forty-eight hours in advance to ensure a member of staff will be present, ready to listen in. Other calls are listened to as and when.

The CM's office, where we're sitting, is small and minimally furnished. Lever-arch files stand on the bookshelves, with things like 'Management of Category A prisoners' and 'PSI 1600' written on the labels. 'PSI' stands for 'Prison Service Instructions', and relates to prison operational policies. There's a framed A4 certificate of commendation acting as a bookend, bearing the CM's name and the governing governor's signature. Two years ago, the CM saved a prisoner from a cell fire. The prisoner had set the cell on fire himself, while locked inside.

There are noticeboards on the walls with mugshots pinned to them, showing current prisoners of interest. Men suspected of involvement in drugs trafficking or extortion, bullying or staff corruption, and one believed to have a mole within the police force giving him information on people within the witness protection scheme.

But none of the mugshots show Curtis's face.

'There's no escape intel on him,' the security manager says. 'But he's a lifer, so that's an incentive as it is. He has previous for violence, including against staff, and he's a known gang member with numerous affiliates – but this should be a simple escort,' he explains. 'In and out. The hospital security team know he's coming. There shouldn't be too much waiting around.'

The hospital security team might know he's coming, but Curtis doesn't. His appointment has been booked months in advance, but the confirmation letter doesn't go to him. The prisoners cannot know the dates of any appointments that take them outside of the prison. These include hospital visits, police interviews and transfers to other jails or mental health facilities. If prisoners know where they're going and when, there is an increased possibility that they could use those details to orchestrate an escape.

The security manager talks us through the paperwork. We discuss the hospital we're going to, the different entry and exit points, the department Curtis is visiting and the various consultation rooms he could be seen in. Where are the windows? How far do the windows open? The only time Curtis would be without an officer beside him is if he goes to the toilet, but even then the door would be ajar and he would be cuffed to an escort chain, a long metal chain with an officer on the other end. The escort chain means Curtis has privacy, but is still attached to one of us at all times.

Previous escapes have shown toilets to be particularly vulnerable places. On one occasion, the first indication of something amiss was when the officer waiting outside the toilet felt the chain go limp. The prisoner's associate had planted a pair of bolt cutters underneath the bin. Hospital staff can be tricked into revealing the date of an appointment by someone calling and pretending to be the prisoner or a family member. If the person taking the call isn't sure of the protocol surrounding prisoner appointments, they might unthinkingly give away those details. Or it might be less innocent. They could be bribed, threatened or paid. Or the prisoner himself might realise the appointment he's been waiting for is happening today, right now, as soon as staff come to escort him.

A nod to another prisoner to make a phone call on his behalf is sometimes all it takes. Maybe he even has a mobile phone plugged and can make the call himself if he requests a quick visit to the toilet before getting on the van.

A prisoner once told me how he had one of his friends deliberately break his arm by dropping weights on it in the prison gym, just so he could get to hospital. On the way there, he faked a medical emergency, pretending not to breathe so the staff would open the cell door. Prison vans are similar to mini-buses, except there's a small cell on one side instead of a row of seats. When the staff came to his aid and removed his cuffs to administer CPR, the prisoner threw a few punches with his good arm and made a run for it. He was caught shortly after. More recently, a convicted murderer escaped during a hospital escort after his transport was ambushed by armed accomplices who were ready and waiting for him.

So, hospital escorts can be especially vulnerable. There are only so many hospitals in a local area, and this number decreases if the prisoner's condition requires specialist treatment, making it easier for someone to predict which one they will be going to. And hospitals are busy places, with members of the public everywhere and various routes in and out.

All of this means that even though all three of us have been to this hospital before and done countless escorts between us, we listen carefully during the briefing.

And even when we're done listening, when we've gone over the paperwork page by page, added our signatures and gone over it again, there's still more to do before we get going.

***

I finally meet Curtis in the reception department.

Reception is where prisoners are admitted to and discharged from prison. It looks like a bit like a hotel foyer, albeit a very dated one. There's a reception desk as soon as you come in, staffed by a mixture of officers and OSGs. Their duties range from processing prisoners in and out of the jail, to searching staff going out on escorts, to organising prisoner property. At the back of the room, behind the desk, is an area lined with floor-to-ceiling metal racks, each of them filled with neatly labelled boxes.

This is where prisoner property is kept. Every single prisoner in the jail has a space here. Most of the property a prisoner arrives with at Whitemoor is stored in this room. Only a comparatively small amount actually goes with him to the wing. This system, known as volumetric control, is one of the outcomes of Sir John Woodcock's extensive report into the IRA escape of 1994. One of the recommendations of the Woodcock Enquiry was to limit prisoners to having a small amount of property allowed in their possession. Two large rectangular boxes' worth, to be specific. It makes the cells easier to search. It means there's less to rummage through, less to check inside and turn over, fewer clothes, books, papers, photos, shoes, toiletries and stationery. There's less for officers to miss.

Like Semtex. Or a gun.

At Whitemoor, reception is one of the quietest departments in the entire jail. The staff sometimes only see one prisoner a week.

On the other side are two holding cells for prisoners waiting to be searched. Next is an X-ray machine for property and shoes, and an X-ray portal for the prisoners themselves.

Curtis is squeezing himself through the X-ray portal, dipping his head under the arch. He giggles and does a little dance when he's through. 'Like doing the limbo, eh Forster?'

'*Mr* Forster, please Curtis,' SO Forster says. He passes a pair of prison-issue trainers through the X-ray machine and hands them to Curtis.

Curtis is dressed in one of the E List suits, a green-and-yellow boiler suit that barely fits him. There's no escape intel on him, but he's wearing it anyway, because he's a Category A prisoner. Cat A prisoners are assessed as being a high risk to the public, so anytime they leave the prison it's in one of these suits.

I see straight away what Roger was talking about. Curtis is enormous. He's over six feet tall, with arms to rival Shoulders'. That boiler suit has got to be an XXL at least, and it looks like a second skin on him.

'The sun is shining and I'm ready for a day out.' He stretches his arms above his head. The fabric makes a ripping noise. 'This the biggest you got, Forster?' he asks.

'Yes, Curtis,' SO Forster says, lifting a black leather holdall on to the table by the X-ray machine. 'And it's Mr Forster, please.'

Inside the holdall is everything we should need. A mobile phone to maintain contact with the prison, handcuffs, an escort chain, paperwork and more paperwork.

I give Curtis a rubdown search. I go over his arms, his collar, the cuffs of his sleeves, his waistband, his legs, and make sure his trousers aren't tucked into his socks. Officer Price searches his trainers by hand, even though they just went through the X-ray machine. And then Officer Price, SO Forster and I are all searched as well. We take it in turns to walk through the portal as an OSG watches the screen. Then, one by one, she pats us down. Our arms, collars, sleeves, trousers and boots. Because it isn't just prisoners who break the law. And it isn't just smuggling contraband into prison that is dangerous, but the potential harm caused by taking things out.

I'm the one handcuffed to Curtis. The handcuffs rub and are just as uncomfortable as you would think they'd be. Trying to manoeuvre through gates and into elevators and up and down stairs when there's so little space between you isn't easy. SO Forster is in charge of paperwork, because he's the most senior of the three of us, and I'm the one being cuffed because I'm the most junior. Officer Price has the best deal. No paperwork and no cuffs.

As horrible as the stories of prison vans being ambushed are, I know the chances of anything going wrong are slim. The size difference between me and Curtis is a bit comical, but I don't feel particularly vulnerable being cuffed to him. That's what all this preparation is for – the briefings and checks and protocol. And although it can be awkward being locked in such close proximity to someone you don't know, that isn't the case with Curtis. He's friendly and chatty, and none of this is new to him. He knew that he would be double-cuffed, which means both his wrists are cuffed together as well as being cuffed to me. And he knew he'd be in the E List suit. He's just happy to be getting out of prison for a few hours.

'How's A Wing?' he asks me, as we wait in the doorway of reception.

'It's really good on there at the moment,' I say.

I've been at Whitemoor over two years now, and A Wing is probably the most settled I've known it – except for Ben and his moods, although they only seem to apply to me. There hasn't been a violent incident for months. Even giving someone a written warning is big news at the moment.

'How's C Wing?' I ask.

'Boring. Everyone's old. Do you think they'd have me on A Wing?'

C Wing has an over-fifties spur and is generally the quietest wing in the jail. It's not an accident that Curtis has been located there. History has shown that he's easily influenced by others and likes attention. There's not much bad behaviour to bounce off on C Wing.

'No, Curtis. You're staying on C Wing,' SO Forster shouts from the van.

The prison van is parked as close to the reception doorway as possible, six feet away at most. Despite that, there's a dog handler and his Alsatian waiting for us. It will take a matter of seconds for me and Curtis to walk from reception to the van, but the fact remains that during that time, Curtis will be outside and in the prison grounds. Once he's seated in the van, my cuffs will be removed, but his will stay on. The cell door will be locked shut and checked. The van door will be locked shut. Only then will the dog go. The staff in the control room will be watching the whole thing on the cameras. They'll note the exact time he left reception and the exact time he was secured in the van. Everything is meticulous and diligent and by the book.

'Hurry up, Forster,' Curtis shouts.

Officer Price and SO Forster are checking the van. These checks have already been done by OSGs, but nothing is ever checked just once in prison. The driver's cabin, the footwells, the glove compartment, the seats, the fabric of the seats, the headrests, the safety hatch in the roof and the cell that looks even tinier than usual once Curtis is filling it: everything has to be checked and checked again.

And even when we're all in the van, there's still more to be done. The van passes through several sets of double gates, each one at least six feet high and made of solid metal. When we reach the vehicle compound, the security manager's office window is visible to my left. To my right are several prison vans, neatly parked alongside one another. A couple of OSGs are testing the emergency lights, sparking streaks of blue on the asphalt.

Emergency lighting on prison vehicles is the same as the blue flashing lights on police cars or ambulances. The lights aren't often used, unless a high-risk Category A prisoner is being escorted somewhere. These are the most high-risk prisoners in the country, the ones who pose the greatest risk to the public and who have the means and resources to stage an escape. For them, the lights flash the whole way. A convoy of police cars leads from the front and follows from behind. The police inside them are armed. On those escorts, there is no stopping. The convoy goes straight through red lights, straight across junctions. A police helicopter escorts from the sky. High-risk escorts are massive operations that take weeks of planning. They don't happen often, but when they do, every possible contingency is thought through. The man onboard cannot escape.

But Curtis is not that man. And today is not one of those days.

He's in a good mood, excited for 'a day out', as he keeps calling it. The OSG behind the wheel steers us out of the vehicle compound and comes to a stop at the entrance to the vehicle lock. This is the final checkpoint before we leave the prison. The vehicle lock is part of the prison gate-house, the same area I pass through each day when I walk into work, and it's the entry and exit point for all vehicles. Most of the time, the only vehicles to come through are the prison's own, like the one we're in now. But sometimes fire engines, ambulances or coroner's vans will pass through.

The seven-metre-high, bombproof gate rises up, and we're driven inside the vehicle lock. It's called a lock for good reason. Four solid walls with no natural daylight. The only way in or out is via the gates set into the brickwork at either end. The gates are electronically operated by OSGs, who sit inside the gatehouse and watch from behind bulletproof glass.

Once we're inside, the driver switches off the engine. The lock is quiet except for the mechanical hum of the gate as it lowers behind us. It's excruciatingly slow. There's a slamming noise as it locks into the purpose-built groove in the concrete. Next come the sounds of boots and chains and bleeps, as OSGs swarm around us like a crew at a pit stop, wielding torches and mirrors fixed to the ends of extendable poles. They're on their hands and knees, checking under the van, then the tyres, the rims, the bodywork, the bonnet and the engine. When they've finished checking the exterior of the van, two OSGs board the van itself and repeat many of the checks that my colleagues performed only moments before.

If this all seems excessive, it isn't. It's time-consuming and repetitive for the OSGs, who search vehicles day in, day out, but it's worth doing properly. Only three years before I started work, a prisoner escaped from a London jail by clinging to the underside of a van as it drove out.

One of the OSGs peers into the cell to verify that Curtis's face matches the picture they have of him, checking that we've got the right prisoner onboard.

'Chains, please,' calls the other OSG.

The three of us stand in unison and dangle the chains hanging from our belts, to show that there's nothing attached. We've already handed in our keys. Taking a set of prison keys outside of the actual prison is a huge security breach. Even if it was only for a couple of seconds, even if they went no further than the car park, taking your keys outside the prison means that every single set of keys would then need to be replaced. It also means that you've probably lost your job.

This is prison. Checks, checks and more checks. Contingency plans, preparation, procedures and policy and paperwork. Coming up with checks, doing the checks and checking the checks, then recording them and checking they've been recorded properly. It's monotonous. Boring. Maybe even the worst part of the job. But none of us question it, and nor would we ever. Because to not do the checks, to miss something, or someone, is inconceivable.

So when the OSGs on the van ask to see our staff IDs, we show them without argument, even though these are the same men and women who searched us into the jail this morning. We swing our empty chains even though the sensors would have gone off by now if we'd still had keys on us. And we move aside so they can see Curtis's face, although it's us who collected him from his cell, and we haven't left his side since. And we'd do it again and again. No one wants to be on an escort where something goes wrong.

But not today. Today is going to be a good day.

***

The van pulls into a lay-by outside the main hospital entrance. SO Forster unlocks the cell door and Curtis holds out his arms. I stand and hold out my right wrist. The metal is cold against my skin. The cuffs click as SO Forster locks them. He moves them roughly against our wrists, checking they don't slide beyond the wrist bone. They don't. If Curtis runs now, I'm running with him.

'I'm a bit nervous, you know, Alex,' Curtis says quietly.

'Why?' I ask.

'Everyone's gonna stare at me when I walk in.'

Curtis is so big that it's hard to imagine a time when people haven't stared at him. But I know what he means. It's been the same for every escort I've ever done. Prison officers, chains and batons, cuffs – and the man at the end of them. People are going to stare.

The reason the driver has pulled up right outside the entrance is so that we don't have a long walk in. We want to get in, get seen and get out. Just like the security manager said. And it makes things a bit less intense for the prisoner. Despite what people may think, I've never been around a prisoner who enjoyed this kind of attention on an escort.

But avoiding it is impossible. Everything and everyone seems to stop as soon as we're off the van. We sidestep together through the revolving doors, trying to keep in step with each other. I can feel the heat from his body as we pause and SO Forster stares up at a sign giving directions to different departments.

Everyone turns and stares. They're about as discreet as Curtis's E List suit. Eyes stay locked on us as they nudge, point and whisper. I feel his wrist tense.

'You think they've never seen a Black guy before?' he mutters.

'Probably more the outfit, Curtis,' I say.

'I fuckin' hate these stripes.'

Our bodies press awkwardly together when we step on to the elevator. We're on our way to the ear, nose and throat department, and I'm grateful that SO Forster seems to know where that is. He strides purposefully ahead while we follow behind.

***

It turns out the purposeful strides were a ruse. SO Forster has no idea where the ENT department is.

'Forster, you giving me a fucking tour?' Curtis says as we walk down the same corridor for the fourth time.

'Language, Curtis!'

Curtis rolls his eyes. He's doing well to contain it, but he's getting agitated.

I'm relieved when we finally see that band of blue above two double doors: 'ENT Suite'. SO Forster goes first and holds the door open for us. Curtis and I enter sideways. The waiting room is about half full. There are women and children, a man in a wheelchair, a teenager on his phone by the window. Plenty of free chairs, but no two next to each other. Officer Price grabs an empty chair from next to the teenager and carries it back to where we're standing. He puts it down next to another empty one. Curtis and I thank him and sink into the two chairs.

The teenager gawks at Curtis, his phone in hand.

'Do you want a magazine or something, mate?' Officer Price asks Curtis. He's careful not to use his name. Curtis is uncomfortable, visibly so. The confident man who limboed underneath the X-ray portal is gone. He does not want to be in this waiting room.

'No thank you, Mr Price. I thought you said we would have a private room to wait in?'

'SO Forster's on it.'

SO Forster is standing at the front desk, talking to the receptionist. We need a private room. Not this waiting room.

Curtis isn't in prison for petty crime. He's in prison for something serious. The wounds from what he did run deep, and they carry on to this day. These people might not recognise him, but others would. He has friends, but plenty of enemies, too. The people sitting among us have phones with cameras, internet access, Google. *Get in, get seen, get out.* But we are getting seen far too much at the moment.

Ahead of us, SO Forster continues his tense exchange with the receptionist. She asks the name of the patient. SO Forster passes her a sheet of paper. It's the confirmation letter. He will not say Curtis's name aloud. Not with so many people around.

It feels like an age before the door to the waiting room swings open. This time, two security guards walk in. One of them looks straight at us and mouths, 'Whitemoor?'

The security guards show us to a private waiting room. We're not in here for long. Soon, we're being escorted down a sunlit corridor to the consultant's examination room. There's only one chair, so Curtis and I sit together on the bed. With the door closed, away from the waiting room and the fog of judgement that fills it, away from the chaos of the main entrance, the stream of people in every corridor and around every corner, away from the whispers and stares and double-takes, Curtis relaxes. He chats easily with the consultant. He asks about the diagrams of ears on the wall, and about which part of his own is damaged.

'So how did this happen, Curtis?' the consultant asks, as she examines his ear.

It happened last year, in the prison gym. He was lying on his back on the exercise bench when another prisoner came up behind him and clapped two 10kg dumb-bells on either side of his head like a pair of cymbals.

'Well, I think we should do a basic hearing test. I can give you eardrops to help with the swelling, but generally this kind of trauma is hard to reverse. So it may be that you need hearing aids.'

'Hearing aids?' he says. 'No way. I can't have them. I'm twenty-eight.'

For Curtis, hearing aids are not an option. Image is everything to him. Outside, he had a reputation. The guy who would fight anyone, over anything, and win. Who would face a murder trial and beat it. He'd rather have a scar on his face than a lump of metal in his ear. His release date should come when he's in his early thirties. He's getting out, he's going home. There's still time to pick up where he left off. A hearing aid doesn't fit in with that.

So when it comes to the test, he focuses so hard that he barely takes a breath. The consultant has shown us to a sound-proof room and given him a pair of headphones to wear. There's a button on the table in front of us for Curtis to press each time he hears a bleep. I hear the first few, but soon they fade away. I watch Curtis as he listens. His hand hovers above the button. He grimaces, leans in closer to the table, as if that's where the noise is coming from, closes his eyes, tilts his head, presses the button. Again, again, again.

No hearing aids – not today, at least. Just more drops and a follow-up appointment in six months' time.

'Can I come when it's less busy next time?' Curtis asks.

'I'll speak to the booking team.' The consultant smiles and shakes his cuffed hand.

***

It's late afternoon when I walk back on to A Wing, after dropping Curtis off on C Wing. He shook my hand and disappeared on to his spur. C wing looks the same as A Wing. It's just the people who fill it who are different. And it's a bit cleaner, too.

I was ready for a break from A Wing. It's been a strange few weeks with Ben. Some days he talks to me, some days he makes thinly veiled insults, and other days he completely ignores me. Which would be fine if I wasn't his personal officer. But I am, and part of my job is to write a weekly report on him. It's a record of his behaviour, how he's doing in himself, anything that's worrying him. It's a hard report to write if he won't talk to me.

So, I climb the steps to his cell on the threes landing. His door, painted the same bright red as all the others on this spur, is ajar. Association time. Most prisoners are either on the yard or wandering the landings, but I've checked on the yard and I can't see him. There are men chatting, playing cards, cooking. A few are in the downstairs gym; I can hear Matthew shouting something about *FIFA*. The same as any other day. But none of them are Ben.

I put my head round his cell door, a little tentatively. I never really know what to expect.

He's sitting at the table facing the wall, writing something. There are sheets of A4 paper in front of him, pages and pages of blue ink. I knock on the door. 'You busy?' I ask.

He looks up and shoves the paper to one side. 'No.'

He leaves his cell and we lean over the railings together. From here, you can just about see the centre office on the twos landing. Bolt is standing outside it, chatting to the officer behind the desk. He looks up and waves.

'Bolt's a dangerous guy, Alex. You know that, don't you?' Ben says.

It strikes me as a strange thing to say. But I'm conscious of some of the little comments like this he's made recently. He's always aware of who I'm talking to, who I'm around.

'Isn't everyone in here dangerous? I'm sure people would say the same about you.'

'I'm not in for murder.'

'You're in a high-security prison. That's not for no reason.'

'I'm here because I escaped, not because of what I did.'

He's right. His offence isn't serious enough to warrant placement in a high-security prison, but escaping from custody is. I knew that he'd escaped from his previous jail, but I don't know the details, so I ask. It turns out that there was no elaborate plan, just a freak accident that presented an opportunity. He was on an escort and the van crashed. One of the roof panels was damaged, and he was able to lever it open and crawl through. He wasn't cuffed; prisoners in lower-security jails often aren't when they're onboard escort vehicles. But once he was out, a little concussed and more than a little shocked at what had just happened, he realised he had no idea where he was. So, in the absence of any mastermind plan, he ran to the nearest tree and hid behind it. Not surprisingly, he was found within a few minutes.

We stand in silence.

Moments like this remind me that no matter how much time I spend with Ben, or any other man in here, I don't know how they feel. I don't know what any of this feels like. What I do know is that more than a few of them have tried to escape, and Ben isn't the only one here who's actually managed it. Whitemoor isn't intimidating to me anymore. I don't feel nervous walking on to the wing. This is a good prison, the best I'll ever work at. Most of my time is spent talking to these men, and I'm glad of it. The quality of the relationships between staff and prisoners here is something I will never experience again, and already I know without question that that's why Whitemoor is as safe as it is. But for all its strengths, all the games of *FIFA* and home-cooked meals, this is still prison. These men don't want to be here. They will break their own arms to get out.

'Is everything OK, Ben? You haven't seemed yourself the last few weeks.'

He glances at the kitchen below us. Someone is cooking chicken curry. 'How have I seemed?'

'Up and down. Sometimes you talk, other times you don't. And on Pancake Day, when I came off the spur, you were angry.'

He closes his eyes tightly. 'I wasn't angry. I didn't do anything. I just looked at you.' But he knows what I mean.

Eventually, he concedes that he was angry with me, but doesn't say what for. He also admits that he purposefully ignores me sometimes, though his reasons for this are just as obscure. He says he finds it easier to cut people out rather than talk to them, that he's always handled things this way.

I'm not exactly sure what he's saying, or what point he's trying to make, but I know I don't want an argument. He's a difficult person to argue with, and it never gets us anywhere. So I tell him that if that's what he's looking for, some kind of confrontation, then he won't get it with me. I wait for him to respond, but he doesn't. He scratches at the railing. Red flakes of paint flutter on to my boots. Someone scores at *FIFA*, and a loud cheer rises from the recess.

He drops his head and groans.

'I don't know what I want.'

***

Ginge started having chest pains at 9am.

He was in the kitchen at the time. Prepping the casserole for tonight. The kitchen staff know his history, and they moved fast, taking him to Healthcare, where he had an ECG. But something was off. The results were enough for them to call an ambulance.

So now, barely an hour later, that's where we are. Ginge, me and two other officers from C Wing whom he knows well. Officer Cullen and Officer Wilmslow. Squeezed into the back of an ambulance, with Ginge lying on the bed fixed to the back wall.

I'm on an early shift, due to finish at 12.30pm. In fact, all three of us are. The prison is well staffed today, and all three of us are surplus. So I supervised morning meds and helped search the prisoners off to work, and now I'm trying unsuccessfully to move out of the way of the paramedics as they monitor Ginge. Officer Cullen and Officer Wilmslow have both been in the job for over ten years, so I'm the one cuffed to him.

This is considered an emergency escort. The process is largely the same as any other, just quicker. There's a sense of urgency underscoring each check, each search, each tick box and scribbled signature on the paperwork. The prison has shrunk into the distance. The yellow and green of the fields rush by. Cars slow down and pull over to let us past. I can see the reflection of the flashing blue lights in shop windows as we speed along.

Ginge is quiet. The pains have eased off now, but he has a heart condition and he knows that none of this is good. Officer Cullen is his personal officer, and has been for years. He leans forward to talk to Ginge about anything other than what's happening right now. He met his parents recently in the visits hall; how are they doing? Football scores, the kitchens, the Whitemoor strongman competition that's coming up. And even though I'm sure Ginge knows that Officer Cullen is trying to take his mind off things, it seems to work. They chat like old friends.

It's a thirty-minute journey to Peterborough City Hospital, but we make it in twenty. A blur of countryside and concrete and swerving cars. When we arrive, the ramp is lowered and we're taken into the Accident and Emergency department, where there are more tests. More wires and machines and bleeps. The staff ascertain that Ginge has had a heart attack.

I'm not sure what any of us were expecting the diagnosis to be, but it wasn't that. Ginge describes back pain, a tightening in his chest, dizziness. The doctor makes notes and reviews his medical history. Ginge looks the same as he always does, perhaps a bit paler. The longer we spend in this bay, with the blue curtain swept around us, the more he seems to relax. The worst is surely over by now. He cracks jokes with us about how the nurses definitely get paid more than we do, and is almost back to his normal self. But I notice the way he sinks into himself when the nurse returns. He's scared.

The nurses are brilliant. If they're intimidated by the cuffs and chains, the three prison officers and the batons we carry, or the reality of who this man is and what he's done, then they don't show it. They are compassionate and sensitive. So are the doctors who visit him. The consultant. And the next set of paramedics and ambulance drivers. More of them this time.

It's been decided that Ginge needs to go to a specialist heart hospital not far from here. And he needs to go now. After he has been wheeled out of A&E, through the corridor leading to an ambulance bay and up the ramp into the ambulance itself, the paramedics load up containers of medical equipment. Mini suitcases like the ones you're allowed to take for carry-on luggage, only these ones are red with yellow lining and 'MEDICAL EQUIPMENT' printed on the side. There are also blue boxes labelled 'BLOOD'.

'In case his condition deteriorates on the way,' a paramedic tells me, when he sees me staring.

Everyone does everything they can to keep Ginge calm. We chat about the cars people are driving and the weird decisions they make when they hear an ambulance siren. How they just slow down when there is nowhere to pull in, despite this meaning the ambulance has to slow down, too. Ginge cracks more jokes. What the hell is the casserole going to taste like now? Those guys don't even know what seasoning is.

But he knows, more than any of us do at this point, that this is serious. He knows the hospital he's going to, because it's where he's scheduled to have open-heart surgery at some point in the next five years.

But not today. Today is a normal day. This morning, he was peeling potatoes in the kitchen for the chicken casserole. This morning, he was asking Attwood if he knows how to make meringue. This morning, he was getting things ready for lunch, for dinner, for the rest of today. This morning, he was in the kitchens, where he is every morning. And where his sentence says he will be for years to come.

But now we're on the M25. The traffic peels away around us. I'd never been inside an ambulance before, and now I've been in two in one day, pushed up uncomfortably close to the bars of Ginge's stretcher, my hand leaning over the blankets that cover him, our wrists still cuffed together. Officer Cullen is on the phone to the duty governor. This is protocol for any escort. If there are any unplanned changes, such as moving to a different location, then the governor has to be informed. If there are any requests for the restraints to be altered, such as removing the cuffs, this has to go through the governor first. Officers can only make those decisions themselves in life-or-death situations. Officer Wilmslow is sitting in one of the blue pull-out chairs, making notes in the escort paperwork, chewing the lid of his pen as he jots down the exact timings of everything: when we arrived at Peterborough City, when we left – and now, when we arrive at the specialist heart hospital.

It doesn't look much like a hospital, though. It looks more like a retirement home or a prep school. The building is red brick, with sloping roofs and what looks like a conservatory at the front. The ambulance follows the road round, past the glass-fronted entrance, past ten-miles-an-hour signs and pedestrian crossings. The ground is dappled with sunlight that reaches through the tall trees on either side.

'Here we are then, Ginge!' Officer Cullen squeezes Ginge's shoulder. 'Getting the royal treatment, aren't you?'

Hospital staff are waiting for him as the ambulance reverses towards a back entrance. The ramp is lowered again and Ginge is wheeled out. The paramedics help move him from the ambulance bed to a bed waiting inside the double doors.

'One, two, three, and lift!'

The hospital staff wheel the bed through the corridors, past signs that say things like 'CT Scanner', 'Thoracic Day Care', 'Operating Theatre'. I walk briskly with them, my hand still cuffed to Ginge's.

'Where are we going?' he asks.

'I'm not sure,' I say. 'Maybe somewhere for some more tests.'

'Signal's crap in here,' I hear Officer Cullen say behind me. He's trying to call the prison to let them know we've arrived.

Just as it is when we're in Whitemoor, the prison senior management must know exactly where Ginge is at all times. The hospital itself isn't enough. They need to know the department, the room, which bay, which bed. We pass more signs. 'Physiotherapy', 'Cardiology', 'Operating Theatre'. Through some double doors. 'Cystic Fibrosis Unit', 'Operating Theatre'.

'Where are we going?' Officer Cullen is beside me, whispering.

I don't answer. I don't need to. The signs are more specific now.

'Theatre One', 'Theatre Two', 'Hybrid Theatre'.

***

The surgeon is ready. He's been called in especially. Today is his day off, but he's here, leaning against a polished white worktop, perusing Ginge's notes. He wears blue scrubs and a tight hairnet that covers almost his entire forehead. A few grey hairs escape just below his ears. His breath smells of chewing gum.

The pace of everything. We were in a different hospital less than an hour ago. Before that, we were in the prison grounds, discussing with the paramedics whether Ginge might have had a panic attack, or if he could have taken illicit drugs. Before that, I was watching the A Wing prisoners line up to be searched, drinking bitter instant coffee with Bernard and watching Ahmet try to do a handstand. And now we're in a corridor outside Operating Theatre Three.

The surgeon introduces himself to Ginge and shakes his hand. He explains what is going to happen. He talks about aortic repair and valve replacement. Ginge listens and asks a few questions, but the outline of the operation is already familiar to him. He knew he needed to have this procedure done someday. He's as prepared as he could be – which is to say, not very. He doesn't want to be here. He doesn't like hospitals, or scans or MRIs or X-rays, all the things that he's had done so many times before. Officer Cullen squeezes his shoulder again and says something about this being the best place for him. That we're lucky to have got here so quickly.

'It's time, then. Theatre is through these doors.' I can't place the surgeon's accent. 'My anaesthetist will talk you through what he's going to do. You'll take a few deep breaths, and then you will fall asleep.'

My hand is still cuffed to Ginge's. He squeezes it and looks at me. There's fear in his voice. 'Will I wake up?' he says.

'Yes, of course,' I tell him.

Because of course he will.

We're in one of the best hospitals in the world. This surgeon is one of the best in the world. My own grandmother had open-heart surgery here when she was in her seventies, and she made a full recovery. Ginge is young and fit and brimming with energy. He's in his twenties. Of course he'll be alright. Of course he'll wake up.

'I just need to get permission from our governor to take these cuffs off, sir,' Officer Cullen says to the surgeon, reaching for the little black mobile phone that goes on all escorts.

'We don't have time for that, officer. The handcuffs need to come off. Now.' The surgeon speaks kindly. But there is no questioning what he is saying.

I don't think it's until this moment that the gravity of the situation really hits me. The surgeon doesn't have time for Officer Cullen to find somewhere in this maze of corridors with a phone signal. He doesn't have time to wait for the call to connect, for Officer Cullen to request that he be put through to the governor, for the OSG to radio through to the governor asking for his nearest extension. The surgeon doesn't have time, because Ginge doesn't have time.

'I need to get permission,' Officer Cullen says again, but falteringly.

'Remove the handcuffs, please, officer.'

It is then that all three of us – me, Officer Cullen and Officer Wilmslow – collectively make a silent decision and nod in agreement. This is one of those moments. We will not wait for prior permission. It is the only time in my career when I will experience this kind of situation.

The cuffs come off.

Ginge squeezes my hand again. Looks up at me again and asks me one more time, 'Will I be OK, Alex?'

He's scared. And I'm scared for him.

But I say, 'Yes.'

***

I get changed in a locker room beside the operating theatre. There are scrubs hanging up in almost every locker and some folded on the benches, too. Beneath the benches are rows of Crocs in different sizes. Everyone here wears Crocs.

I pick the smallest set of scrubs I can find, and the cleanest-looking Crocs. I opt to pull the scrubs on over my uniform and just change out of my boots. When I'm done, I almost look the part. Except for my thick black prison belt, complete with chain and baton.

Ginge might be unconscious, but there still needs to be an officer in there with him. It isn't just about his escape potential, but also about his protection. He's serving a life sentence. His victim has a family. It's not just about Ginge wanting to get out, but others who may want to get in. As a Category A prisoner, its standard for an officer to be with Ginge during an operation, even if he's under anaesthetic. It would be the same for prisoners on life support or in an induced coma. Officers would typically still be present.

When I step back into the operating theatre, Officer Wilmslow looks relieved. The operation hasn't started yet, and he doesn't want to be in here when it does. This time, I'm not in here because I'm the newest in service, but because I offered. Officer Wilmslow and Officer Cullen are both a bit squeamish, and watching open-heart surgery doesn't appeal to them. But I don't mind the sight of blood. The nurses have brought me a chair in case I feel faint, but I think I'll be OK.

The operating theatre reminds me a little of the prison kitchens. The glint of metal everywhere; the trays, trolleys and worktops; the perennially bright lights and the matching uniforms. Although here, those uniforms are made up of scrubs, masks and hairnets, rather than ill-fitting chef's whites splattered with stew. And instead of a locked cabinet containing ladles and spatulas, there is a steel trolley at the foot of Ginge's bed, on which various medical instruments have been placed. Differing sizes of scalpels, scissors, a drill and something that looks like a garden saw.

The surgeon stands at the trolley. He looks over everything and then calls out the names of each instrument from a clipboard in front of him. A nurse stands beside him and confirms that everything is there.

'Forceps?'
'Check.'
'Scalpel?'
'Check.'
'Clamp?'

'Check.'

Just as the senior officer does in prison, the surgeon gives a briefing before he begins. The staff stand around him in a half-moon shape. There are nurses and assistants, anaesthetists and a perfusionist, and others whose roles I struggle to remember. The surgeon outlines the operation. What he will be doing, why it is so sudden, what has caused them all to be called in so immediately. Ginge lies asleep on the operating table in the centre of the room. A blue gown covers his body. There is a long, vertical slit in the gown, directly above his chest. Above his heart.

When the surgeon is ready, the operating theatre fills with a quiet action. People take up their positions in different parts of the room. They monitor screens with numbers that fluctuate, they adjust dials and hold tubes in place, they pass medical instruments to the surgeon as he calls for them. This is their arena – their wing. This is where they do what they do. And though I am here as a prison officer and not an observer, it is an enormous privilege to watch them work. It's hard to believe that I am here, that this is actually happening. I started the day in black trousers and a white shirt, watching prisoners as they slung their laundry bags into the trolley and collected their medication. Now, I am wearing blue scrubs that rustle whenever I move, and watching open-heart surgery.

The perfusionist sits at a machine adjacent to the wall. It looks a little like a desk on wheels, with various screens and dials attached. When the operation is underway, he explains to me what he's doing. The machine he operates takes over the pumping action of Ginge's heart and cleans the blood as it is re-routed, so the surgeon can cut open the heart itself. He offers me a chair away from the bed, in case I'm uncomfortable with the sight of blood. And although I'll see far too much blood in my prison career, nothing compares to the things I see in this room. It is a different kind of blood. This isn't blood spilled by a razor blade melted into a toothbrush. This isn't blood spilled at all. It is blood measured and guided through tubes that overlap and resemble a maze to me, but are layered in perfect symmetry to the people around me. Machines take on the role of organs; they mimic the beating of the heart and drop the body temperature to levels no person could normally withstand, but that give Ginge the greatest chance of surviving this operation with no brain damage.

A few hours into the procedure, a tray of mechanical heart valves is wheeled into the theatre. Each one is in transparent packaging. They look like the ventilation fans in cars.

The surgeon sees me looking.

'All different sizes,' he tells me. 'As soon as we open the packet, they're no longer sterile. So if we pick one and it doesn't fit, that's three thousand pounds down the drain.'

As it happens, I don't see whether they pick the right size first time. Ginge is in surgery for ten hours. I'm there for the first six, and then Officer Cullen, Officer Wilmslow and I are relieved by officers working the night shift. It's late evening when we leave. The sky is dark and the air is cold. None of us brought our fleeces. We thought we'd only be out for a couple of hours.

The taxi that brought the night officers to the hospital is waiting to take us back to the prison. We don't talk much on the journey back. We're all tired. A bit in shock, maybe. In our own thoughts.

It felt intimate and almost otherworldly, to see into this man's chest cavity, to see his sternum as they sawed through it, to see his heart.

His heart.

***

Ginge never woke up.

He had held my hand and asked if he would be OK.

And I'd said yes. Because I thought that he would. I was sure of it. Even though I knew the situation was life-threatening, I also knew that there was no better place he could be. Even when the surgeon turned to me, four hours in, and said, 'You know he might not wake up from this, don't you?'

Even then, I was sure that he would.

But he didn't. He never woke up.

For a long time, the emotional weight of what I'd said to him is almost unbearable. Did my words give him comfort? Or were they just a lie? And does it matter?

Should I care?

He did a terrible thing.

Other officers talk to me a bit about this. I confide in Bernard and tell him about the guilt I'm feeling. These are the kinds of moments that my training didn't cover. The moments that I am not prepared for and will never forget. The heaviness of knowing that mine were the last words someone ever heard. And that they were not enough.

That they turned out to be untrue.

7

When the Doors Close

I SPEND A lot of time speaking about what happened at the hospital. How Ginge died, and how I feel. I talk about it a lot with my two best friends. Charlie, by now a qualified midwife, understands as much as a person can, I think. She's seen some pretty devastating stuff herself. And I talk to Hannah, by now a qualified social worker working with the elderly, and familiar with the hospitals I describe to her. The corridors, the medical terms, the sudden change in circumstances: none of this is foreign to her. But the operating theatre is. That's where I stumble over my words a bit. I want to describe what it was like in there, but it never comes out quite right. I'm not really sure how I feel. On some level, at least, articulating that helps. And although their worlds are different to mine, my friends outside the prison are the ones I choose to talk about it with.

And over time, I find that I don't need to talk about it as much. Over time, I start to forget what Ginge's face looked like when he asked me that question, and how his voice sounded when he said it. Only in the back of my mind, I know that I haven't forgotten it at all, because every now and again, something unexpected reminds me – and then, in a second, I am right back there, and his expression is painfully clear, and his voice is too. And perhaps worst of all, so is mine.

But I'm twenty-four years old. I'm twenty-four, and I cannot let myself be burdened by this. Most of the officers I work with are much older, and they seem to me to be as resilient as they come. So I tell myself I can't remember. I tell myself I'm forgetting, and I let the noise of A Wing and the silence of Ben become the things I focus on.

***

Two weeks since Ben last spoke to me. A little longer since Ginge died.

Ben has ignored me every time I've been on shift lately. When I rub him down as he leaves for education, he turns his head the other way. When I call out his name at dinner, when he passes me in the gateway to the yard, when I tick his name off on a clipboard – nothing.

Two weeks of nothing. And I have no idea why.

It's early evening on a Tuesday. There's a gym session in the main gymnasium. Thirty-seven prisoners from A Wing are there. The rest are out on association.

Gavin sent out an email last week reminding us to be prompt with our personal officer reports, so I'm sitting in a side office waiting for the computer to load. Trying to think what I can write for Ben's report.

'No meaningful conversations during this reporting period. Ben is reluctant to engage.'

Something like that, maybe. But that isn't strictly true. Because it's not that Ben is reluctant; he doesn't engage at all. He acts like I don't exist.

The office I'm sitting in is next to the custodial manager's, though it's decidedly less impressive. There are no coffee machines or potted plants in here. There's no Filofax. Instead, there's a beaten-up old filing cabinet next to the desk I'm sitting at. Each drawer is labelled with a different kind of paperwork.

'BASIC review form', 'ENHANCED review form', 'Warnings', 'Adjudications'.

The bottom drawer is stuffed full of plastic evidence bags in sizes small, medium and large, ready to hold any contraband found in cell searches or hidden around the wing. There's a board on the wall with 'Notices to Staff' pinned on it: reminders to get your annual leave booked in, that there's still overtime available for next month, that all male officers must wear their ties on escorts.

The egg timer is still showing on the computer screen. The IT system here is terrible. It can easily take twenty minutes to log on. There are rumours that new computers are being installed in the jail early next year, along with flat-screen TVs for each cell instead of the old box-style ones the prisoners have now. But they're just rumours. It'll probably never happen.

I wonder again what to write on Ben's report.

'Refuses to interact with staff, though socialising well with peers.'

But that isn't strictly true, either. He talks to all the other officers. It's just me he refuses to interact with.

Roger walks past the office. I've left the door wide open, so I can hear if anything untoward happens.

'They'll be coming back from the gym soon any sec now, Alex,' he says.

He strides toward the gates. To my left, I can hear laughter and chatter coming from the spurs; to my right, there's the sound of metal on metal as Roger unlocks the gate and locks it into the wall. And from both sides, the shrill bleep of the radios, that high-pitched double tone that precedes all incoming transmissions.

'All outstations, you may now send on from the gym. I say again, send on from the gym.'

The noise builds like water rushing through a tunnel, then explodes on to the wing. One at a time, prisoners jog past me, still sweating and wearing the blue prison-issue vests they reserve solely for the gym. They carry net bags filled with towels, deodorants or weight-lifting gloves. All prisoners are given one of these bags when they arrive at Whitemoor. They're made of net so the officers can easily see what's inside.

Ben is one of the last to come by. He doesn't jog. He pauses when he sees me in the office. He looks left and right, then steps inside. And closes the door.

It's just me and him. The egg timer is still on the screen. He reaches inside his shorts pocket and pulls out a bundle of paper, folded into a rectangle. Pages and pages of blue ink.

'Read this,' he says.

And then he goes. He opens the door and closes it behind him. Leaving me with the egg timer and all the words he could never say.

It's a letter. Pages and pages of it. Personal and passionate and emotional.

***

I never read the whole thing.

I try to give it back to him. As soon as I realise what it is, I race on to the spur after him. My hands shake when I tell him, 'I don't want this,' and his shake too when he says, 'Just bin it, then.'

But I can't do that. And he knows it.

***

The next time I see the letter is when it's in an evidence bag, laid out on the governor's desk. The governor of security's office is in the same building where escort briefings are held. I walk through the office where the civilian staff are listening to prisoners' phone calls. Past the posters showing prisoners of interest; Ben is now one of them. Past the senior officer's office, past the custodial manager's, coming to a stop outside the governor's.

This is not an office I've ever been in before, or ever wanted to be in. But here I am, with the door firmly closed, the blind across the window in the door pulled down, and the governor looking intently at me from across her desk.

'Take a seat, Alex.'

It's been barely forty-eight hours since Ben gave me the letter, but things have escalated since then. When I handed the letter in, Ben was taken to the segregation unit. He was put on Basic and put back in stripes. He's being held in the seg under 'GOAD', meaning he poses a threat to the 'Good Order and Discipline' of the establishment. The reason for this is that the letter is being viewed as an attempt at corruption, a way to lure me into an inappropriate relationship and then coerce me into bringing in contraband.

Ben has taken things one step further. When he was interviewed yesterday by the same governor sitting across from me now, he told her that he wasn't trying to lure me into a relationship – because we're already in one. That we've been having a physical relationship in his cell. That this wasn't the first letter he'd written, and that I had written back, too. And not only that, he said that I knew the whereabouts of every phone and drugs stash on the wing.

Ben says that I am corrupt. Bent. Another female officer having an inappropriate relationship with a prisoner. And although I hate myself for thinking it, I can't help but imagine the smug look on Officer Parry's face if he could see me now. He said women shouldn't work here. He said all that carry-on wouldn't happen.

But it didn't happen, it hasn't happened, it's all lies, and I'm in this office anyway.

The security governor is a middle-aged woman with sharp cheekbones and her hair whipped into a tight bun. She wears a navy trouser suit and sturdy block heels. We look different: her in her suit, me in my uniform. She's older, a senior manager with years of experience in the Prison Service, whereas I've only ever worked on one wing in one prison. And yet, she's been sitting where I am before. She goes on to tell me that when she was an officer, a prisoner got himself shipped to the same jail she'd transferred to so he could be near her. It helps to hear that. It almost feels as if there is something unsaid between us, a reminder that it will always be slightly different for female officers. There will always be slightly more to look out for, more to keep an eye on, and there will always be more eyes on you.

Actually, those eyes have worked in my favour here. As the governor tells me now, Ben's lies are easy to disprove. The cameras show I never set foot inside his cell. He's unable to produce any of the letters I allegedly wrote. Other prisoners on A Wing have put it in writing that his allegations are false, and the officers I work with are consistently and unfailingly supportive of me. As they have been since the day I started, almost three years ago now.

And yet, as I sit here across from the governor, knowing I should feel relieved, I am just so embarrassed.

She is so kind to me, but the tears are hot behind my eyes. I'm embarrassed by what he's said, the lies he's told and the rumours that will surely start. Embarrassed that, if truth be told, I really did care. I thought I was helping him.

The governor tells me that kindness can be misunderstood in a place like this; it can be misplaced. But I feel like *I'm* the one who is misplaced. I'm not sure I want to do this anymore. This job isn't for me.

'Did you ever have any indication that he may have inappropriate feelings towards you?' the governor asks.

'No,' I say.

Before the letter, Ben never told me he had feelings for me. He never made comments about the way I looked, he never tried to touch me, he never asked me about my personal life, he never made me feel uncomfortable in that way, not once. His turbulent behaviour often suggested he couldn't stand me rather than anything else.

The irony of all this is just how wide of the mark it is. It couldn't be further from the truth. I'm not in a relationship with Ben; I'm not in a relationship with anyone. I don't even date. My friends call me 'the nun'. But I'm happy. I've had boy-friends before this job, and I always ended up feeling stifled after a while, like I needed to get out. I always ended up walking away. Now I have a job I love, friends I love, a life I love. I'm conscious of the way I look. I'm always in jeans and trainers. I don't wear heels; I don't wear dresses. I'm so uncomfortable with anything that might make people look at me in a way I don't want them to. I don't think much about it in general, but now I'm in this situation, I realise just how carefully I've curated this image of myself. As if it would be impossible for someone to accuse me of improper behaviour when I'm so obviously not interested. But all of that is falling apart. It didn't matter.

I wasn't in a relationship because I didn't want to be. I didn't want anything from anyone. And now this.

Relationships between staff and prisoners are only ever one-way, because they have to be. It's a strange way to build a relationship with someone, but it's that distance that keeps us safe and prevents boundaries from getting blurred. It's why I know so much about Ben, his family and his life before prison, but he knows next to nothing about me.

Having said that, there's a lot that prisoners can pick up just by being observant. The officer who's always worn a wedding ring and suddenly isn't, for example. Or even the way an officer carries themselves. If an officer turns up for work every day looking smart, with their shirt ironed and boots polished, it's a sign that they respect the uniform code and the rules of the establishment in general. But if they look untidy or dishevelled, what other rules are they prepared to bend? Or, on the other hand, if an officer wears too much jewellery and heavy make-up, false nails and clouds of per-fume, the same principle applies. Is their attention focused on the right things?

Over time, I come to think that this is perhaps why Ben's words affect me so much. When I started, I was so conscious of how I might be seen by other officers. A twenty-two-year-old woman with no idea of what she was walking into, completely out of her depth. But I have listened and learned, and worked hard. Almost three years later, I'm a trained hostage negotiator. I'm part of the specialist Tornado unit, a team of officers trained to intervene in riots and acts of mass disorder. I know that I've earned my place here, and that the staff think highly of me. But in the end, it didn't matter.

All of this feels deeply personal. It feels like more than words to me. Ben knows how much what he is saying will hurt me, and that's why he's saying it. He knows exactly what kind of officer I am, and, in the end, he has said it all anyway. I can work as hard as possible, volunteer for everything, come in early and stay late. I can be kind, understanding, firm, compassionate, whatever. It doesn't matter. All it takes is for one prisoner to claim I am something that I'm not, and then I'm here. If I was ever going to be sitting in a governor's office, it was meant to be because I'd become one myself, not because a prisoner was saying we'd had sex.

I never see Ben again. The closest I come is a few weeks later, when I'm dropping some paperwork off in the seg and I walk past his cell. Roger was on shift here a couple of days ago. He told me that Ben was down, upset. That he felt bad about everything that had happened.

If I could see through the cold steel of Ben's cell door right now, I imagine what I would see. I imagine him sitting on the edge of his bed, thinking about what a mess he has made of the whole situation. Part of me wants to see him, face to face, and have this conversation.

I stare at the door. At his name scrawled crudely on the plastic card next to his cell. I think of him inside.

I walk away.

***

Ben is shipped out of Whitemoor about a month later. Things go back to normal quite quickly. The prisoners get bored of asking me about it, and other things happen that take over anyway. There's a nasty assault on the yard. Brian takes a punch to the face. Larry the painter hangs himself. He's the third prisoner to die during my time at Whitemoor. The day before he died, I'd stood with him by the radiator as he painted it a pale beige. We'd spoken about something so normal, so ordinary, that I can't even remember what it was. But in the days that follow, after his body has been taken away and his cell cleared, I notice the specks of paint on my boot and think about how casually he'd spoken to me that day, all the while making plans in his head. So there are other things to talk about when the doors close. More pressing issues than what's happened between me and Ben.

And yet, it's all I can think about. The whole thing has tainted Whitemoor for me. It isn't just Ben. Whitemoor can be a very insular place, years of the same people's lives playing out on the same three landings. I'm curious to see what else is out there. I think I'm ready to go.

It's at about this time that I'm called into the SO office on A Wing. I'm getting tired of being in offices with closed doors.

Gavin and CM Barnes are already in there. They tell me that they're impressed with the way I've handled recent events, and in my performance as a prison officer in general. They say that I'm good at my job, and if I wanted to, I could go far. When the next advert for a senior officer at Whitemoor comes out, they want me to apply.

This is unexpected. I've been thinking a lot about what to do next. I'm considering a move to the seg or even out of the Prison Service altogether. But the conversation with Gavin and CM Barnes is what gives me the push I need. So I do apply when a senior officer advert comes out, but not for the one based at Whitemoor.

I've lived in the Fens my whole life. If Whitemoor has taught me anything, it's that the world is a lot bigger than this. I apply for a senior officer position at HMP Wormwood Scrubs, a Category B men's jail in west London.

Instead of holding 400 men, it holds 1,300. Instead of 120 on a wing, there are over 300. Instead of being built in the nineties, Scrubs has been there since 1875.

I get the job.

***

On my last day at Whitemoor, the A Wing officers surprise me with a card and gifts, and a voucher for Westfield White City. Right next to Scrubs. These people have become my friends for life.

I spend the afternoon walking round the jail, saying goodbye to prisoners and officers from other areas. Most of the staff can't understand why I'm leaving. They know how good we've got it at Whitemoor. They shake my hand and wish me luck, 'because you're going to need it at the Scrubs!'.

It feels strange walking these corridors for the last time. Especially on A Wing. I've spent the past three years with these men. I've been with them more than I've been with my own family. A few are keen to give me some words of advice. Davis tells me not to let any prisoners take the piss, seemingly oblivious to the fact that that's what he did to me for the first six months of my career. Harpal tells me to just be myself. Attwood insists I try to lift a bag of his hardback books to build my upper-body strength, warning me to expect plenty of fights. Sammy describes some of his friends from west London to me, saying that they'll probably become prisoners at Scrubs at some point, and I should expect to run into them.

I say goodbye to Bolt in the kitchen on Blue Spur. He asks me how I'm feeling about the move. He says that Scrubs will

be a culture shock, that the prisoners there won't care for consequences or warnings. He tells me not to change. I don't say
it, but I wonder if I already have.

As I turn to leave, he says, 'Ben isn't a bad guy. He messed up.
It can be hard in here sometimes.'

'I know,' I say. It can be hard for the officers, too.

'You know, Alex...' He puts down the potato peeler and
turns to me. 'When the doors close at night, you'd be surprised
by how many of us cry.'

PART 2

8

Du Cane Road

THE WALK FROM my new home to my new prison takes barely five minutes. It's a strange feeling to step out your front door and know that HMP Wormwood Scrubs is just up the road. My shifts at Scrubs start earlier than they did at Whitemoor, mainly because the prison itself wakes up earlier. Court vans start arriving at Scrubs at 5.30am, ready to transport prisoners to the nearby courts. This is the nature of local prisons. They serve the courts local to their area, and hold the men awaiting trial there.

I'm out of the house by 6am. It's still dark. A man wearing a suit and New Balance trainers emerges from one of the houses on my right. He crosses the road on to Erconwald Street and disappears into the square gateway of East Acton tube station. The station backs on to the garden of my new house share. I've moved here for the job. I live with three other people: a restaurant manager, an artist and a paralegal. We're all in the early stages of our careers, paying an extortionate amount in rent and pest control. My bedroom window looks out on to the tube platform. The sounds of swooshing doors and automated voices will become strangely soothing to me over the next couple of years, especially when the Central Line starts running at night.

I turn left on to Du Cane Road. The road is named after Sir Edmund Frederick Du Cane, a military engineer who organised convict labour in Australia in the 1850s before designing

HMP Wormwood Scrubs in 1874. Du Cane Road takes me under the bridge the Central Line crosses. There's a strong smell of stale urine and the brick walls are daubed in neon graffiti. The underside of the bridge is covered in netting and bird shit, and the severed head of a pigeon is caught between mesh and metal. On the other side are a couple of shops, an off-licence and a barber's, and a café, where I pick up my daily cappuccino. Just as I have before every shift since I started last month. Even something as small as that would be impossible at Whitemoor, where the rules state that only empty bottles or those with sealed lids can be brought into the prison. But things are different at Scrubs.

A couple of streets to my left is Braybrook Street, the site of the notorious 'Shepherd's Bush Murders', which saw three police officers shot dead in 1966. One of the perpetrators was released in 2014 after serving forty-eight years in prison. He was lucky not to have been hanged. Capital punishment was abolished the year before his conviction.

This area is steeped in history, from the streets to the architecture to the people. And perhaps nowhere more so than HMP Wormwood Scrubs and those who have lived inside its walls. Ian Brady, Charles Bronson, George Blake. As I approach, the towers that mark each corner of the residential wings rise in front of me, tall and imposing and latticed with white framework. If you're facing the right way and you know when to look, you can see these towers from the Central Line, between East Acton and White City. You can catch a glimpse of the prison wings, studded with hundreds of barred windows that look out over west London like suspicious eyes.

I keep walking, past Wulfstan Street, where one of my new colleagues will soon perform CPR on a teenage stabbing victim he finds lying on the ground. Past the bus stop on my right that takes you to Hammersmith, Shepherd's Bush, Oxford Circus. Past the old prison officer quarters, self-contained flats that, at one time, officers could live in for next to nothing. And then I'm here.

The prison gatehouse is probably the most iconic part of the jail and certainly the most well-known. A pair of symmetrical octagonal towers flank either side of the vehicle lock. The busts of two famous penal reformers are carved into the stone: Elizabeth Fry and John Howard. And stretching out from the towers like an endless arm is the perimeter wall.

Inside the gatehouse, OSGs sit behind panes of glass. They do the same sorts of jobs here as they did at Whitemoor. They monitor mail, watch CCTV, check vehicles and search staff. They operate the airlock and hand out radios as the officers arrive at the prison. But behind the glass is where they stay. No one searches me as I walk through. No one puts my bag through the X-ray machine, because there isn't one. Nor is there a metal detector portal for me to walk under. I press my finger to the biometrics machine and the doors slide open. And just like that, I'm in the prison grounds.

***

The same towers I saw from Du Cane Road are now right in front of me. Up close, they are even more impressive. And intimidating, too. These buildings began as a corrugated iron structure built by a handful of trusted prisoners, and have evolved into what they are now: four storeys high, with their towers higher still, columns of Victorian brick that puncture the London sky. These buildings have seen a lot. They have inspired literature, poetry, music and films. Over the last 200 years, they have housed men, women and even babies. The protagonists of some of the most infamous trials of the nineteenth and twentieth centuries have been held here. Trials that have horrified and enthralled the country in equal measure, and changed its political landscape, too. Trials

of espionage and disgraced celebrity, establishment corruption, and murder after murder after murder. And everything
in between.

The wing I stop in front of is one of the largest in Europe.
It's home to 317 men, and led by two senior officers. I am one
of them.

This is C Wing.

9

C Wing

C WING IS different from what I'm used to. It's bigger, louder, busier.

Scrubs is a very different jail to Whitemoor, housing mostly short-termers rather than lifers, but many of the same rules apply. No flip-flops on the yard, no walking topless to the showers, no smoking on the landings. Despite this, the wing still manages to stink of stale smoke and tobacco. The smell wafts under the doors and trails after me as I walk past the rows of cells towards my new office. Smoke, tobacco, a hint of weed – and maybe something else, too. The prisoners get their tobacco from the prison canteen, but their drugs from the dealers on the fours, or a package thrown over the wall, or a drone hovering over the yard.

With the drugs comes, inevitably, the violence. The prisoners fight more here, just as Attwood said they would. They're in and out more here, just as Sammy said they would be. They argue more and care less, just as Bolt said. There's little incentive to try to get on with each other or sort out your problems. Most prisoners aren't in for long enough. It's a different world here, just like everyone said.

***

- Jasper, cell 1-07, Basic for being found with crack
- Ethan, cell 1-08, Basic for being found with mobile phone × 3

- Harrison, cell 2-01, Basic for being found with a home-made catapult and pile of rocks
- Wagner, cell 2-46, Basic for being found with shank × 2
- Callahan, cell 2-50, Basic for punching Officer Bell
- Estrada, cell 3-13, Basic for hiding in the cleaning cupboard during roll check
- Trevino, cell 4-12, Basic for fighting
- Nguyen, cell 4-26, Basic for catching rats and torturing them in his cell
- Sandoval, cell 4-37, Basic for stabbing a prisoner during freeflow

The list of prisoners on Basic is longer than I ever saw at Whitemoor.

My new office is on the ones landing. The whiteboard I'm looking at is at the far end of the room. It's split into three columns, roughly sketched out with a board pen. Basic prisoners, Rule 53 prisoners and ACCT prisoners.

Rule 53 means that a prisoner is 'pending adjudication', and so must stay in their cell until they've had their hearing with the duty governor, who will declare them guilty or not guilty and decide on any punishment. Punishments are typically things like having your TV removed or losing association time. The more serious offences run the risk of time in the segregation unit. But seg time is less common. As with many prisons, the seg at Scrubs is relatively small. It has eighteen single cells. Considering the prison population is roughly 1,300, the idea that only eighteen of them will be naughty is a bit optimistic.

The prisoners on ACCTs are those considered at risk of suicide and self-harm. ACCT stands for Assessment, Care in Custody and Teamwork. The ACCT process is designed to support prisoners in crisis. These prisoners have regular reviews with the SO to try to put in place a practical support plan. This often includes a list of things considered both achievable and likely to help a prisoner struggling with their mental health. The list would typically look like this:

1. Add Smith to education waiting list.
2. Arrange phone call with immigration case worker.
3. Supply Smith with pen and paper to write home.
4. Schedule appointment with chaplaincy for pastoral support.

I didn't have to write support plans as an officer. But as senior officer, it's part of my job to put this kind of thing in place.

All officers must know which prisoners on their landing are on ACCTs. This is partly good practice, the basic principles of getting to know the men on your landing, but it's also because those men require multiple extra checks throughout the day. It isn't enough just to say you've done the checks, either. The officers must record them in their ACCT paperwork and be specific, too. What exactly did they discuss with the prisoner? Was the prisoner talkative? Who were they socialising with? And so on.

On the desk is a list of today's staff.

Officer Akash runs the fours. He's only been in the job nine months, but it might as well be nine years. He's excellent. The kind of officer who wants to solve problems rather than create them, and who does it with energy and humour. The prisoners love him. But the fours can be a tough landing to work on. Not only is it the highest one (several officers will specifically request that I don't detail them the fours because it gives them vertigo), it's also the IDTS landing. IDTS stands for Intravenous Drug Testing Service. Broadly speaking, this means that the majority of prisoners on the fours are drug addicts, or have been recently, and are currently on a detox programme. They take their medication from the treatment hatch at the end of the landing each morning, normally Subutex or methadone.

There are always two officers per landing during association, and the fours have an extra officer to supervise the queue as it forms outside the treatment hatch, although describing it as a queue gives the false impression that it's orderly. It is anything but. Many of these men have no intention of detoxing. The fours landing is a hive of activity, of pills swapped in sweaty handshakes, sugar sachets with drugs hidden in them, chatter about who's on what and how much they're selling it for.

Officer Akash knows the landing and its prisoners inside out. He knows that Stone will do anything for spice, including selling his meals, his toiletries, even his clothes. He knows that Parker doesn't take Tramadol for pain anymore, but only because he's swapped one addiction for another. He knows to check what days Frasier gets visited by his cousin, because his cousin has a history of bringing him crack that, once it gets to C Wing, spreads through the fours like a virus. Crack, heroin, weed; spice, spice, spice.

Officer Fitzgerald runs the threes. He's in his forties and has been at Scrubs for over twenty years. His boots have patrolled these landings many times, and the prisoners know it. They don't try to pull the wool over his eyes. To a lot of them, he almost becomes a surrogate father. In that way, he reminds me a little of Bernard from Whitemoor. I never once hear him shout or lose his temper. The threes landing has some overspill from the fours landing; there are a few IDTS prisoners located here. But it's mostly a general mix of everyone, from young offenders serving their first sentence, to men in their sixties partway through a murder sentence.

Officer Fran runs the twos. She's one of two female officers working on C Wing. Just as at Whitemoor, the workforce is predominantly male. Less than a third of officers are women. The twos landing is a mix of everybody, though the younger prisoners tend to congregate here. Officer Fran is strict, fiercely so. Bang-up is bang-up, not a minute later. Basic is Basic, and she'll check your cell multiple times a day to make sure you haven't hidden a TV anywhere. As unpopular as her disciplinarian approach makes her, it's consistent. No means no.

The ones landing has a couple more staff than the other landings: the officer in charge of the ones, plus the cleaning officer and the box officer. The box officer is essentially the gatekeeper to the wing. The person in this role must be organised and efficient, which makes Officer Rearden the perfect person for the job. He keeps the box office pristine. The box office is just what it sounds like, a small box at the end of the wing with a window looking out on to the landing, and a small tray at the base of the glass with which prisoners can pass him paperwork. A bit like a post office. From here, Officer Rearden checks prisoners on and off the wing, for court appearances, visits, education or work. It's also where movement between the different wings is negotiated, an issue that never really came up at Whitemoor, but takes up a lot of time at Scrubs.

When prisoners first arrive at Scrubs, they spend the night in the First Night Centre, though this has rather grimly been nicknamed the Last Night Centre by staff after a spate of recent suicides there. The box officer on each wing has to know how many cells he or she has available in order for the FNC staff to know how many prisoners they can send. How many double cells and how many singles? How many doubles currently occupied by only one – and who is that one? A smoker? Because smokers can't share with non-smokers, and the only place prisoners are allowed to smoke is inside their cells. A young offender? Because young offenders can't share with adults. There are far more adults at Scrubs than there are YOs, and so a prisoner's twenty-second birthday is always a momentous occasion for the box officer, because it frees up much-needed cell space.

Scrubs has very few single cells. It's hard to make a cell feel like home when you have a new cellmate every few weeks.

The population here is transient and ever-changing. In fact, the entire population is estimated to turn over in approximately six weeks. This is due to the type of prison Scrubs is. As a local jail taking both remand and sentenced prisoners, Scrubs assesses each man as he comes in and decides if this is an appropriate location for him, or if he would be better suited elsewhere. A man with an upcoming case at the Old Bailey, for example, will need to transfer to HMP Belmarsh before his trial starts. A prisoner from the local area with under twelve months to serve will be better off staying put. And there are the internal prison politics to consider as well. There are numerous gangs in Scrubs. It can be difficult to keep them all apart. The four core London locals – Scrubs, Brixton, Wandsworth and Pentonville – see a lot of this. Prisoners are bounced around between the four jails due to gang issues, unpaid debts and case conflict.

This makes it hard to develop the kind of positive, long-lasting relationships that were such a key part of life at Whitemoor. I find that difficult to wrap my head round at first, because I know how important it is. But the personal officer scheme doesn't exist here.

In short, the box officer's job is a difficult one. It involves a lot of sitting in the same stuffy room all day, answering the phone and shouting reminders and last calls over the tannoy. And, most importantly, directing the officers to the specific location of an alarm bell sounding on the wing.

Near the office is the gateway to the exercise yard, so close it's almost a part of the landing itself. There are no spurs here. Instead, there are cells on either side as soon as you walk on to the wing, on landings that seem to go on forever. The cell doorways are lower than I'm used to, so much so that the taller prisoners have to stoop as they go in. I'm told it's because people were shorter when the prison was originally designed. The number of each cell is stencilled above the door in a disjointed black font, making the paintwork look as if it's never quite finished. There are cards with the name and number of the occupants outside some of the cells, but most are missing. The cards would have all been there at some point, but prisoners use them to slide things under locked doors, like sugar sachets or tobacco, and some of the more desperate men use them as rolling papers when they have none of their own.

In the centre of the landing is the staircase, a narrow set of steps that winds its way to the upper landings like a caged tentacle. The stairs are bordered by steel railings and steel fencing, with gates at each level that are supposed to prevent prisoners from accessing the different landings – but the prisoners just vault the railings and jump the gates. Things like this take me a little while to get used to. At Whitemoor, an officer would know exactly how many men were on their spur at any given time. That's nothing short of impossible here. You can't know how many men are on your landing, because you can't guarantee no one's jumped the gates when your back was turned. It's part of the reason only two landings at a time are unlocked for association.

And to make matters even more confusing, it isn't just the people inside the prison you have to watch; it's the ones standing outside it, too.

***

The perimeter wall at Scrubs is bordered by Hammersmith Hospital and Wormwood Scrubs park, both largely unrestricted areas with public access. The prison is surrounded by normal life: people walking their dogs, catching the bus, going for a run. They pass the jail without a second glance, as if they're so used to seeing it that they've forgotten it's even there. But there are some who skulk around the park by the perimeter wall, waiting for an opportune moment.

Packages are routinely thrown over. They land in the grounds and are collected by prisoners who work in what's known as the 'yards party'. This is a group of supposedly trusted inmates employed to pick up rubbish in the prison grounds, but who often make some secondary income picking up the packages and taking them on to the wings. Staff supervising the yards party either don't notice the package in among all the rubbish that accumulates there, or they choose not to. And sometimes, they are very well disguised. Dead pigeons are thrown over the wall. They've been killed, gutted and filled with drugs, then their stomachs sewn back up. The same happens with rats. Scrubs is infested with rats. *Infested.* They are everywhere. So seeing a member of the yard party sweeping up a dead one is not necessarily going to arouse suspicion.

Drugs have always been a part of prison life, but the what and the how is changing now. Weed is still popular, but it's too obvious, the smell too distinctive. Heroin was more common, but it's a lot of effort, getting the foil and bong and putting it all together, and many prisoners don't want that kind of high, anyway. They don't want to leave jail with an addiction they didn't come in with, and there's no escaping the clutches of heroin once you start. So the drug of choice at the moment is spice. It's still in its infancy, having originated only recently on the streets as a type of synthetic cannabinoid, but it's already alarmingly common in prison. It's supposed to give a similar kind of high to cannabis, but without the obvious smell. The wings here are full of it. The nurses have started carrying oranges in their medical bags to deal with the increasing number of spice-related call-outs they get every day. Apparently, oranges help dilute the effects of the drug. But that's hard to gauge when no one is sure exactly what the drug is. It can be laced with almost anything, so the effects are never the same. Some prisoners can take it and feel relaxed, some vomit or hallucinate or trash their cell, and many seem to develop a kind of superhuman strength and want to fight everyone. I've seen one man so high on spice that he thought he was a lemon and started trying to peel off his own skin. Another was convinced he was a crab, writhing around on the floor and trying to pincer the staff. But those guys are the lucky ones, really. Others die.

Another common method of getting contraband in is making a line to which a package can be attached, then reeling it back in. The lines can be made of anything, bedsheets or blankets or smuggled fishing wire, and slung from a cell window over the wall to someone waiting on the outside. That's how close the wings are to the external wall. At some point, netting was attached from the prison buildings to the perimeter wall, meaning that any packages thrown over would land on the netting rather than the ground. This worked well for a while, but then prisoners started setting mop heads on fire to burn through it. Now there are more holes than there is material, and whatever's left just blows around forlornly.

There are no cages on the cell windows here, because some of these buildings are Grade II listed and therefore protected from modification. The prison is over 200 years old. Except for flashes of modernity, walking around Scrubs is like going back in time. One of the most obvious problems with having no window cages is litter. The cells are small and poorly ventilated, and prisoners want to avoid having mice and cockroaches visit them at night, so they throw their uneaten food out of the windows. Food, sweet wrappers, drinks cartons, canteen bags, old clothes, cigarette butts. And that's where the rats come in. The stretch of ground where the litter lands is where they congregate. Not a single day goes by at Scrubs when I don't see a rat. At night, the ground outside the wings looks like it's moving. Ripples of black fur and long tails that leave tracks in the grass.

It isn't just the rats you try to avoid when walking past the cell windows, but the missiles that sometimes come flying out of them, too. Apples with razor blades stuck in them, that sort of thing.

Just as the lack of cages allows prisoners to throw things out of their windows, it also means they can get things in. Despite my scepticism, the old box TVs have gone, and they've been replaced by new flat-screen models with transparent panels on the back, so officers can easily see if contraband is being hidden there. Before these new TVs came in, they were a popular place to hide phones and drugs. Prisoners would unscrew the backs with a sharpened biro and slot in things they wanted to hide. Or those men who were prescribed in-demand medication would take their pills in front of their nurse, then return to their cells and stick their fingers down their throats until they were sick into a cup. They would then pour the contents on to the motor in the back of the TV and wait for the heat to solidify the vomit into something they could sell on again. Money and addiction can make people do appalling things.

While there are positives to the new TVs, there are negatives, too. The new models are slim enough to fit through the bars if you pass them through sideways. It's not uncommon for me to look back at C Wing as I'm walking out of the jail at the end of my shift, and see a prisoner I've only just placed on Basic being passed a TV through his window from one of the neighbouring cells.

Who cares about TVs, though, when the prisoners pass each other phones, drugs and weapons through the windows? They receive deliveries, too. Drones are commonplace at Scrubs. They hover outside cell windows and drop off packages. Sometimes they don't make it that far, and we'll find them crashed on the exercise yard in the morning.

The kind of contraband I'd seen at Whitemoor was, in retrospect, specific to the environment. There, it was home-made weapons, drugs and the occasional mobile phone. Here, we find real kitchen knives, bottles of Jack Daniels, Amazon Firesticks, and even an iPad. So, it's fair to say that Scrubs has a big contraband problem. As do all the London prisons, in fact. It opens my eyes to the reality of prison in a way that Whitemoor never did.

Scrubs doesn't have cameras during the time I'm there. It all comes down to money. If cameras seem like an obvious requirement in prison, that's because they are. Or at least, they should be. But there isn't enough money in the governor's budget to have them installed, so we don't have them. And everyone – staff and prisoners alike – pays the price for it. Because there are no cameras, there's no way of identifying who's throwing things out of the windows – or bringing things in. No cameras means no consequences. So the grounds remain dirty and strewn with litter, the packages keep coming over the walls, the flaming mop heads keep protruding through windows and burning holes in the external netting, because there is nothing there to stop them. No footage, no proof, no real reason not to treat the prison and its grounds as little more than a cesspit. (Cameras will finally be installed on the wings a few years after I leave.)

Whitemoor had cameras everywhere, but then Whitemoor is a Category A high-security prison, with a population of predominantly high-risk inmates. The irony of this is that so many of the prisoners I now see at Scrubs will go on to join the men serving life sentences at Whitemoor. In this way, the stark differences between the two prisons seem less binary and more interchangeable, symptomatic of a whole system that needs changing, rather than specific establishments.

It's places like Scrubs that lead to places like Whitemoor.

***

Their names are Flaherty and Gonzalez. They're from the local area. They refer to Scrubs as their 'local' in the same way that people talk about pubs. And just as people have their favourite places to sit in their local, these two men are always located on the threes landing.

Their brothers, uncles and nephews come in and out regularly, but Flaherty and Gonzalez are constants on C Wing. They're prolific burglars, but that doesn't really make them stand out in here. Scrubs is full of burglars. We're not talking criminal masterminds. There's Alfred on the ones, who got caught burgling someone's house when he jumped into a water tank to hide from the police, but quickly took his clothes off before he got in and left them in a pile next to the tank. Or Stanley on the twos, who's only eighteen, with yellowed stumps for teeth and sunken cheeks, already in the throes of heroin addiction. He got caught burgling someone's house because he was so pissed that he passed out on their sofa. There are a few men in here who have slightly more lofty theft ambitions, such as the guy who robbed Simon Cowell's house or the group on the twos who robbed a jeweller's in Hatton Garden. But they all got caught. They all ended up here.

Flaherty and Gonzalez will steal anything, from anywhere. They target homes, shops, ATM machines. Outside, they make a living from stealing; in here, they make their money by providing. They run the mobile phone supply for C Wing. No one's under any illusion about that. Little black phones, the same thickness as a lighter but smaller, often with a slightly curved end to make them easier to plug. They cost about £30 on the outside. More on the inside. The buttons are so small you have to squint to see what you're pressing. We find them hidden in the toilet, wrapped in cling film and attached to a piece of string tied to the rim, so it's not always the phone itself you need to keep your eye out for. Or sometimes the string will be tied to the window frame, so officers need to use a handheld mirror on an extendable pole to check if there's anything swinging from the external brickwork. Not a bad place to have a line ready and waiting if any of your neighbours want to borrow the phone at night.

Cell searches are almost always intelligence-led at Scrubs, as opposed to being a routine part of the regime. Something about a prisoner's behaviour arouses suspicion among the staff and a search is carried out, whether it's because of the growing pile of tobacco pouches stacked neatly on their table (a common form of payment), or how little they're seen using the PIN phones on the landing (because if a prisoner isn't using them to call home, then there's only one other way). These are the kind of things that give Flaherty and Gonzalez away. In every other way, they fly under the radar. They're polite to staff during association, and are quick to collect their meals and return to their cell, where they sit quietly, surrounded by the graffiti daubed on the walls. Their cell window was smashed by the previous occupants, leaving jagged shards of glass that let in the rain and cold. But they don't complain. They don't argue with staff, or refuse to return to their cell, or fight with other prisoners.

The mobile phone culture at Scrubs is new to me. At Whitemoor, I can only recall two prisoners being found with a phone the entire time I was there. Both of them ended up in the seg as a result. But here, hardly anyone caught with a phone is segregated. There's not the space. There are men stabbing each other with flick knives during freeflow. They're the ones who get segregated, not the guys with phones.

Flaherty and Gonzalez's cell is at the far end of C Wing. The roof of C Wing is essentially a giant skylight, with slanted beams that cut the sun into diagonal shafts on the landings. It has the effect of turning the wing into a greenhouse when it's hot, and when there's heavy rain the sound is almost apocalyptic. But the skylight doesn't stretch the full length of the roof, so this part of the wing is darker. This makes it a popular living space for the cockroaches. It's quieter, too, away from the wing offices on each landing that attract queues of prisoners during association, and just far away enough from the staircases that clatter with men running up and down them. For Flaherty and Gonzalez, this is ideal. The officers are normally busy in the office or patrolling the main section of the landing, where most prisoners associate. So Flaherty and Gonzalez can make some calls of their own. If it's not yet time to pay a prisoner to assault someone who's falling behind on their debts, then they might instead contact the family of the prisoner who owes them. This is easy enough to do. Almost all prisoners write the contact numbers of their family and friends in the prison diaries given to them by chaplaincy as part of their induction. All it takes is for someone to swipe that little book, and Flaherty and Gonzalez have all the information they need.

Many of the prisoners are regulars in jail; they know Scrubs and the culture of prison life. It's not new to them. But there are still plenty who don't fit the mould. There's Alan on the threes, serving five years for white-collar fraud: first time in, aged fifty-five and father of three. Tye lives on the threes as well, serving seven years for drug smuggling: first time in, aged twenty-four, broke and regretful and scared. Ghulam on the twos, serving six months for stealing from a shop: first time in, mute and profoundly deaf. Lorenzo on the ones, serving six years for death by dangerous driving: first time in, aged seventy-two, father and grandfather. These men, and many more like them, are vulnerable. They're vulnerable to having their lunch and dinner taken, their canteen taken, their cells ransacked to see if they have anything worth selling on. They're vulnerable to people like Flaherty and Gonzalez, who charm them with promises of a free phone call – and then, suddenly, the calls aren't free anymore, and the rate is higher than anything they can realistically pay. Higher than anything their wives and girlfriends and children can pay, too. People say that when someone is sent to prison, their families serve the sentence too, and Scrubs shows me that the reality of that is much closer than it seems.

***

Officer Akash and I are standing out on the exercise yard. He's having a smoke; I'm kicking through some of the rubbish. It's canteen day, and there are plastic bags everywhere, chucked out of the windows after they've been emptied. These bags come labelled with the prisoner's name and cell location when canteen is handed out, and sometimes the men forget to rip off the label before they throw it outside. It's an easy way for staff to rebuke someone for littering. They can't really deny it was them if it's got their name on it. But not tonight. There are no labels. Just empty, anonymous canteen bags rustling in the breeze.

'Can you hear that?' says Officer Akash.

I look up at the cell windows, where most of the noise comes from. The sound of the *Crimewatch* theme tune, always a popular show in prison. Some laughter, a cough, toilets flushing: the low buzz of prison life.

'Hear what?' I say.

'That humming noise.'

The hum gets louder, like a mosquito getting closer.

'Fuck. Look up,' says Officer Akash.

The drone is almost directly above us. It looks like a giant claw, with propellers that flash red and blue as it nears the cells. A white package hangs from the centre of the drone, about the size of a brick and wrapped with brown tape. It rises, then drops a little, goes forwards and backwards a couple of times, as if preparing for a run-up, then advances towards a cell window. No prizes for guessing which one. Officer Akash and I stare. We've both seen remnants of crashed drones, bits of metal and glass scattered over the yard, but neither of us have seen a drop in action.

We watch as Flaherty's pale arm reaches out through the bars. He's holding what looks like a table leg, which he uses to unhook the package from the drone. And then it reverses, and is gone. Straight over our heads, over the yard, across the grounds and into the darkness of Wormwood Scrubs park. The drop takes less than a minute.

Whatever Flaherty and Gonzalez have just had delivered, we need to get our hands on it. Quickly. There was a nasty assault in the showers yesterday, a guy beaten so badly he couldn't open his eyes after. He wouldn't say who'd done it, but he did say it was over a phone. A first-timer was found spitting blood into his sink during lunch today. Again, he wouldn't say who'd attacked him, but his eyes filled with tears when he asked to be moved off the threes. First thing this morning, a young offender took such a strong variant of spice that he ran around the wing naked, yelling, 'You'll never catch me!'

Drugs and phones lead to bullying. They feed the culture of violence and self-harm that is endemic in most jails. And they make people do very stupid things. So we need that package. Now.

We slam the yard gate shut and sprint up the stairs, both of us red-faced and panting by the time we reach the threes. We run to their door, keys in hand, both of us amazed at our luck. We're going to get it before anyone else does. A phone, drugs, maybe both. Officer Akash shoves open the cell door. He shouts something about knowing it's in here, show your hands. I follow him in, my eyes searching the cell. Gonzalez and Flaherty are sitting at the table. Their prison diaries are next to them, the pile of tobacco ever growing.

On the table is the contraband.

A couple of Big Macs, a side of fries and some chicken nuggets.

There's not much point in getting an evidence bag for any of that. We let them pocket a couple of nuggets and bin the rest, taking their TV with us. Officer Akash issues Gonzalez and Flaherty with their nicking paperwork. They can explain themselves to the governor in the morning.

***

This is the kind of story that prison officers retell for weeks after: the time officers found a McDonald's meal in a cell on C Wing; the time officers caught prisoners boiling dead pigeons in their kettles; the time a prisoner on the ones admitted he'd been selling grated apple skins marinated in teabags and saying it was spice.

As we tell these stories, we're partly incredulous, as if we're saying them out loud in order to confirm that they did actually happen, and partly relieved. Relieved that if someone's using a kettle to boil a bird, then at least they're not using it to melt someone's face. If they're getting Big Macs delivered, at least it's burgers and not knives. If they're smoking apple skins, well, that's probably the healthiest thing they've had since coming to Scrubs.

Those early days at Scrubs are some of the best of my career. They are busy, chaotic at times, but fun, too. It couldn't be more different from Whitemoor. The shifts there could feel mentally draining, always keeping alert to something that might happen but mostly never did. At Scrubs, by contrast, the challenges are right in front of us. The regime is tough, but so are the officers. And although we are working with some extremely disruptive men, most prisoners feel invested in maintaining the stability of the wing. They make the most of the activities offered to them: education and the gym, visits and the library. The older career criminals support the staff in looking out for prisoners who are struggling. Inmates are normally out of their cells for between three and four hours a day, and those hours are invaluable. They offer time to socialise and be in the fresh air, to go to staff with queries, even time to argue out on the landings in full view of everyone. Airing disagreements in this way is far more effective than being locked in a cell for hours on end, left to stew on perceived slights that then become bigger than they ever needed to be. Violence and vulnerability are etched into the brickwork at Scrubs long before I arrive here, but somehow it feels manageable – at least for now.

I learn a lot from the officers I work with on C Wing. They teach me how developing positive relationships is even more important in a jail that lacks the security infrastructure of establishments like Whitemoor. They teach me that grey areas can be just as important as black and white. So much of Scrubs at this time is give and take, and the landing officers on C Wing are excellent at it.

But things are changing.

Cuts to public services mean that the government has implemented an extensive benchmarking system that, to the staff walking the landings rather those sitting in offices in Westminster, makes little to no sense. This was happening while I was at Whitemoor, but I didn't notice it in my day-to-day work there. Benchmarking was in its infancy then, and it has taken some time for the impact of the cuts to be felt, particularly in a jail with low staff turnover to begin with.

Put very simply, benchmarking means that if most prisons use four staff to operate a certain process, but one prison is found to use only two, then ministers will consider whether this is replicable in other establishments. It then becomes the 'benchmark' standard. But benchmarking is a rigid, deductive principle. It works on the assertion that prisons are predictable places, that what works in one situation will work in another. It treats people as if they are robots. In addition to benchmarking, the Ministry of Justice introduced a Voluntary Early Departure scheme, also known as VEDs. This allows long-serving officers on higher salaries the opportunity to leave before retirement age. Newly recruited staff enter the job on lower salaries, and so, in theory, this should save money. But these cost-cutting exercises fail to take into account the value of experience in a place like prison, and what that means for some of the most vulnerable people in society, who typically are the ones who end up inside.

At this time, Scrubs is only just starting to feel the impact of VEDs. Experienced staff are leaving, but the prison is coping. The older staff who stay know better, though. They've been through versions of this before. They've seen enough changes happen in the Prison Service, enough swapping of political parties and knee-jerk reactions disguised as penal reform, and they know how it plays out in real time. On the landings, in the cells.

They warn me.

A storm is coming.

10

The Emergency Regime

I T'S ALMOST THE end of my shift when Officer Fran shouts.
All the prisoners are locked up for lunch. Staffing is tight at
the moment, and today is a particularly bad day. We didn't
have enough of our own staff for association, so we had to
borrow from elsewhere in the jail. In principle, this isn't an
issue, but if it happens too often then the consistency and time
invested in getting to know the men is eroded. Different staff
each day makes a wing very difficult to run effectively. And it's
happening too often.

'Code Red on the twos, Code Red!' Code Red means heavy
blood loss. I hear her calling it over the radio as I run up the
stairs. There's panic in her voice.

The prisoners hear it too. They kick their doors and shout as
I run past. 'Who's cut up, miss?'

Cell 2-14. Euan's cell.

I've never seen anything like it. The blood is everywhere. It's
pooling in the uneven grooves in the cell floor, it's painting the
exposed brickwork at the back of the cell, it's gathering in puddles on his mattress, it's dotting the ceiling like little red stars.

Euan is sitting on the bed with his back to the wall. His arms
are resting on his thighs, with his forearms facing up. He's smiling. There's so much blood that it's hard to see exactly where
it's coming from, but his arms are a good place to start. At some
point since entering his cell, I've put on gloves, though I don't
remember doing it. I use my hands to try to stem the bleeding,
and ask Officer Fran to get towels. All the towels she can find.

Because our hands are never going to be enough. There is so much blood.

Euan doesn't even seem to notice I'm there. He just smiles at the wall. His eyes are glazed over.

I hear myself ask, 'Why have you done this, Euan?'

He says, 'Someone told me a bad joke.' And laughs. But his laugh is weak.

Officer Fran is back in seconds, her arms piled with thin blue towels. She presses them to his legs, his inner thighs, where the skin is scored with more cuts. It's just us in here, despite a Code Red being an emergency. Where are the responding staff? I look at Euan. In this cell that is awash with colour, his face is losing his. This Code Red will become a Code Blue soon. Code Blue means a prisoner struggling to breathe. Self-harm that begins as a Code Red very rarely turns into a Code Blue. I've never known it to before. But Euan is losing blood at a quicker rate than I can stop it. I call a Code Blue.

Prisoners sometimes self-harm as a form of stress-release, a way of feeling something, a cry for help. But this is not that. This is to die.

'Code Blue, Charlie Wing. I need an ambulance,' I say into my radio.

I lean down to pick up another towel, and as I do so I hear the chink of metal. It's then that I see the tiny razor blade on the floor. A slim silver blade, not even the length of my thumb, has done all this.

I look at Euan, who is now swaying and falling back against the cell wall. He lifts his neck and looks at the ceiling. And now I see he's cut his own throat. Officer Fran sees it too.

'Jesus Christ.' She abandons his legs to hold a towel to his neck.

A governor is suddenly in the cell with me. Governor Olive is part of the prison graduate scheme, where university graduates are fast-tracked to positions in management. Officers tend to be sceptical of people on the fast-track scheme, but Governor Olive is proactive and well-liked. He's ex-military, too. He starts using the towels to make tourniquets.

'Keep doing what you're doing,' he says to me and Officer Fran.

But the towels we're using are sodden. I'm leaning my elbow on one patch of cuts, my forearm on another, and my other arm is pressed against Euan's. More staff are arriving now, but the reality is that there aren't many of us to respond in the first place. The majority of officers left about forty-five minutes ago. And those who are still on shift are unable to leave their own wings.

Due to staffing shortages, Scrubs is on an emergency regime. This means that prisoners will be allowed out of their cells for the bare minimum of time – and emergency regimes create emergencies of their own.

***

When it's all over, when the paramedics have been and gone, taking a barely conscious Euan with them, I sit in the office. My coffee is still warm. I knew Euan before today. He's been on the wing a little while. He's a prolific self-harmer, and I'd done a couple of his ACCT reviews. But until today, he's gone weeks without hurting himself. We thought he was on the up.

HMP Holloway has recently closed. The staff there have been sent to different London jails. We have about ten of the Holloway officers here. Officer Ronnie is one of them. She sits with me in the office. She responded to the Code Blue. There's blood on our shirts, our trousers, our boots. The other officers have gone to the stores department to get a clean change of clothes. I'll go after this coffee. I just need a minute.

'That was one of the worst I've seen,' Officer Ronnie says.

I'm shocked to hear her say that. She worked at Holloway for twenty-five years. Holloway was notorious for the amount of self-harm that went on there. In general, female prisoners self-harm far more than their male counterparts – and often more severely.

She talks about her experiences at Holloway, and I'm grateful for the distraction. I'm grateful to be in another world for five minutes, even one with its own inimitable horrors.

After our conversation, the image of Euan sitting on the bed becomes blurred with another in my mind: an image of another prisoner, submerged in a different kind of red. Officer Ronnie tells me about the time she responded to a cell fire at Holloway. The prisoner had set herself on fire. Officer Ronnie says that it wasn't the flames that horrified her so much, or even the smell of the prisoner's burning flesh. It was her face. She was smiling. It is August 2016. We have been on an emergency regime for months now.

Experienced staff are leaving in their droves. New staff join, but the retention rate is poor. Most don't see out their probation. I don't blame them. Violence is through the roof.

The situation is dire. Prisoners are so desperate to come out of their cells that they fight each other just so staff will unlock the door to intervene. They cut themselves just to get out and see the nurse. They lie about having toothaches, headaches and back pain, just so they can come out for some paracetamol. The cell bells buzz constantly. Prisoners who have always stayed away from drugs before have started taking them now. There is an almost constant haze of spice and cannabis floating from under the doors. There are so many ambulances arriving at the prison for inmates under the influence of spice, or mamba, as it's often called, that officers start referring to them as 'mambulances'. The fire engines come more often, too. The prisoners are bored. They set their bedsheets on fire and throw them out the windows, where they erupt into the waiting rubbish like little bonfires.

I'm exhausted. We all are. We're in the midst of the storm that the older officers warned me about, and it shows no sign of abating. Staff sickness rates are rising, alongside serious assaults and self-harm. If it felt like there was no time for cell searches before, there certainly isn't now. We can only wonder at what's being hidden. We can only wonder at what we're missing.

***

At first, I think they're dancing.

Khan is bouncing from one foot to the other. His arms are beating the air in front of him. Okowo is opposite him, his head jerking back and forth. It takes a couple of seconds for my vision to focus properly.

They're not dancing. They're fighting.

I've seen hundreds of fights by this point. Hundreds of punches and kicks, swipes and slaps, kettles to the face and belts used as whips and chicken bones as knives and tuna cans in socks. Split lips and black eyes and slashed skin and holes in flesh. But this one feels different. There are too many prisoners gathered on the ones, ready.

I lock the office door behind me and run towards Khan and Okowo, shouting, 'Fight on the ones!' as I go. Someone hits the nearest alarm bell in response. I see Officer Akash running from the opposite direction. He shouts for staff. The lights start flashing and the sound of the alarm bell floods the landings. It's a horrible noise, like a siren. I will never get used to it.

It's common for a crowd to build around fighting prisoners, but this time the crowd itself becomes the fight, and quickly escalates. Within seconds, it's no longer one-on-one. It's four-on-one. It's two-on-two behind the pool table, three-on-three by the showers. People are being thrown down the stairs. Pockets of fighting break out everywhere. The wing explodes in violence, and, even though I know it's happening, I'm almost blinded by tunnel vision, concentrating on Khan and Okowo, because they're the ones I saw first. I grab Okowo, who is the larger of the two. Admittedly, this was a bit ambitious, and he swipes me back as if an insect has landed on his skin. I go again. And he shoves me back again, this time harder, so my head hits the brick wall.

Fights like this are vicious. They are chaotic and feral and extraordinarily violent. There is no fighting fair now. There's no walking away when one of you hits the floor. There's no fighting with just fists. Instead, there are men flinging off their shoes and stuffing pool balls into socks, and there are shanks being pulled out of waistbands.

The staff from all the other landings are on the ones now. Officer Fitzgerald is dragging someone off the stairs. Officer Fran and Officer O'Hare are trying to restrain prisoners single-handedly. Two other officers are clamped on to the arms of a prisoner lying prone on the floor, but his legs are swinging at their heads like he's trying to do a backward somersault. One of them shouts, 'We need a third person,' because a safe restraint is three officers to one prisoner. But there is no one else.

Officer Fran abandons her restraint and punches the alarm bell nearest to her.

Our radios sing in unison. 'All outstations, we have a second alarm bell on Charlie Wing, second alarm bell on Charlie Wing.'

'Are you OK?' Officer Akash calls to me as I get to my feet, wrestling with Khan.

Okowo is slamming someone's head into the pool table. Two prisoners fall to the ground beside me, grappling with each other. Officer Rearden skids to a halt next to me, and together we somehow manage to separate them. But he's the box officer. He shouldn't be here. He's meant to stay at his post and direct responding staff to the source of the alarm bell. The fact that he's here is a sign that we are losing control.

But we aren't losing control.

We've already lost it.

This is a gang fight. This is west London. This is the collision of men from the Mozart Estate, from White City, from Ladbroke Grove, Shepherd's Bush, Stonebridge, South Kilburn and Harrow Road. This is the repercussion of the stabbing last weekend. This is the fallout from murders that are years behind us now, but their impact reverberates still. The man shot in the barber's, the teenager stabbed at a party, the drive-by execution. Those are the murders that put the men I worked with at Whitemoor behind bars, and now the same thing is happening to their sons, their brothers, their nephews.

This is what happens on the streets when you don't have decent housing, employment, role models, opportunities. This is what happens in prison when you have no staff. Eleven officers to 317 prisoners. No staff and no structure. Workshops left empty every day because there's no one to run them. Classroom sizes dwindling to almost zero because there's no one to patrol the corridor.

This is what happens when you spend twenty-three hours a day in your cell, raging at what you've seen on social media on your smuggled mobile phone, the latest attack against your group of friends. The friends you are prepared to die for. This is loyalty and honour and fighting for something that started before you were even born. This is what happens when you have only one hour out of your cell a day. One hour to make it right. To do something. To let them know you're not a pussy. To expel this rage and energy and explosive feeling of being disrespected that consumes your entire body. One hour to get revenge.

This is hell.

Barely discernible under the roar of the alarm bell and the shouting is a patter of tiny clicks. The sound of batons being drawn. I have my baton in one hand, my radio in the other. For the first time in my career, I call an 'all available staff'.

The alarm bell sounds again on the radio, and the OSG in the control room follows with, 'All outstations, we have an all available staff on Charlie Wing. All available staff to Charlie Wing. Batons drawn.'

I spot Khan at the same time as another officer. There is a crowd of four, maybe five teenagers surrounding him. He is on the floor, curled into a ball and burrowing his head into his chest. They throw their arms back behind their heads, grey prison socks wrapped round their hands, bulging with plugs and tuna cans and pool balls, and they smash them into his head. We run towards him and try to pull the prisoners off him.

It's a beautiful day outside. The end of summer. The sun streams in through the broken windows, creating diamond-shaped shafts of light on the floor. Someone's blood glitters on a discarded shank. There's a tiny mound of rat droppings next to me. There is a dead mouse under the hotplate. I've fallen. Someone hit me over the head with something. Horizontal lines of light shoot past my eyes as I lose consciousness.

Everything goes black.

***

I'm only out for a few seconds. When I come round, Ullah, a prisoner I get on well with, is kneeling in front of me, stopping anyone from getting to me. But I'm so vulnerable. My shirt is ripped open and I have a radio on my belt, keys in my pocket, my baton next to me. The fight is still going on. I see a female custodial manager, notorious for her bad temper, taking on a prisoner wielding a pool cue. Her baton is outstretched. She steps forward and smacks the cue out of his hands.

Governors don't normally attend alarm bells. But the wing is full of them now. Men and women in suits who don't normally carry batons, but, after today, will be strongly advised to always have theirs on them. The officers who normally work in the admin buildings away from the main wings are here, too. Steadily, we take back control.

***

Four prisoners end up in hospital after that incident. Khan is one of them. When the incident is over and staff are locking prisoners in their cells, he is found in a cell that isn't his own, having a seizure. He stays in hospital for a few days. When he returns to the prison, he opts to be located in the segregation unit for his own protection.

Another prisoner who goes to hospital wasn't actually involved in the gang fight, but the incident presented an ideal opportunity for another inmate to whom he owed money. While all the staff were on the ones, his creditor sliced his cheek open with a razor blade.

One of the officers who responded hands in their notice the next day.

***

The days that follow that incident are quiet. Even some of the prisoners seem shocked by the brutality of it, by how quickly things got out of hand. Various prisoners are shipped out, or moved around the wings to try to ease the tension on C Wing. For a lot of us, though, staff and prisoners alike, that tension stays wound up within us. I see officers standing by the alarm bells as soon as we unlock, ready and poised, and prisoners who lean against the walls during association rather than walking the landings, wary of who could come up behind them.

First thing in the morning, before the briefing, I get into the habit of drinking my coffee on the yard. The fresh air and relative quiet help me mentally prepare myself before the day starts. Often, another officer will stand with me, having their first smoke of the day. But today, it's just me.

Standing on the yard the way it is right now, at 6.30am, with the London smog giving it a kind of sepia tint, makes me think back to a photograph I saw when I first started at Scrubs. The photograph dates to the 1900s, and shows female prisoners on C Wing exercise yard. The same yard I'm standing on now. The photo has an eerie, almost ghostly quality. The women are dressed in bonnets and ankle-length dresses. The thing that struck me when I saw it was not just the sight of female prisoners from the Victorian age in a yard that remains unchanged today, but what they held tightly to their chests as they walked. Their babies.

The last few weeks have been tough. There isn't much time to think or reflect when we're behind on the regime before it's even begun, when alarm bells are so common they're almost like background noise, when the whole day can feel like one long fight. But something about being on the yard right now forces me to confront some uncomfortable truths. It's foggy this morning, and maybe that's what it is that reminds me of the picture, the way the mist is pinned into the air like the green bedsheets I see hanging across the cell windows above me. Because we don't have curtains to give to the prisoners. The mist makes the yard look the same as it does in the photo. Bleak. Like I'm standing in the past.

How far have we come since then? Since women held their babies and walked equidistant from one another round this very yard? I've visited the mother-and-baby unit at HMP Peterborough. I remember the officers telling me that they take the babies out in their prams for walks round the local estate, just to get them used to the sound of traffic before they leave at eighteen months. That's the longest a baby can stay with their mother in an MBU. In a prison. A baby in a prison. I cannot imagine the agony of having your child taken from you at eighteen months, but I also cannot fathom this society in which we jail babies.

The yard looks the same as in that photo. The wing does, too. The windows with their curved frames and iron bars and the same ones I look up at now. I wonder if the windows were smashed back then. Did the prisoners use Brillo pads to cover up the holes? Did they use towels pressed to the floor against their doors to keep the mice out?

I'm reminded of a quote by John Howard, the same man whose bust is carved into the stone in the gate, when he visited Edinburgh prison: 'The prisoners… were closely confined, being out only one hour a day.'

Just as it is now. One hour a day, in 2016. The quote is dated 1783.

11

SO Office

TRISTAN FIGHTS. HE argues. He spits. He threatens. He trashes his cell. He sneers at Officer Fran and refuses to return to his cell on the twos landing. He ignores Officer Fitzgerald and mocks Officer Rearden. He whips off his yellow polo shirt and flings it on to the netting when his girlfriend is refused entry to the prison for wearing inappropriate clothing: jeans with rips in the thighs. The dress code sent out to visitors is clear: no ripped clothing, no skirts above the knee, no steel-toecapped boots. Some people don't read the dress code before they come, or don't care for it; either way, they turn up inappropriately dressed and are refused entry unless they change. Staff have a box of spare clothes ready for these situations: trousers, leggings, jumpers. But these don't tend to be the most fashionable items, and Tristan's girlfriend has refused the options. So she is turned away and, for the rest of the day, he shouts and swears and punches the wall.

Tristan is what staff sometimes refer to as 'a problem prisoner'. Because he is a problem. He's a headache. He's hard work, frustrating, impossible to understand. He never gets what he wants, no matter how much he acts up. He just stays locked up for longer, with no TV for longer. Nothing works. I can't get through to him. People like Tristan make a hard job harder.

The Basic list is getting longer. Tristan's name is there, of course. His review is due today. This afternoon. Now. I'm dreading it.

I trudge up the stairs. This morning was hectic. There was another fight. In the showers, this time. An officer slipped during the restraint and hit one of the buttons on the wall, and soon we were all rolling around in hot water and blood. There's dried soap and dirt on my trousers. The stores department didn't have any spares in my size for me to change into. I stop outside Tristan's door. His cellmate is on a visit, so it's just him in there. When I look through the observation panel, he's sitting on the bottom bunk, staring at the wall. He barely looks up when I open the door. He knows why I'm here, but he doesn't care.

'It's your Basic review, Tristan,' I say. 'Do you want to come to the office?'

He shrugs, but follows me downstairs anyway.

In the office, he sits opposite my desk and looks at the ceiling, the floor, anywhere but me. I've brought up his prisoner profile on the computer. Officers can add entries here, positive comments for good behaviour and negative ones for the opposite. Tristan's page makes me wonder if the mouse is working. I keep scrolling, but the headings stay the same.

Negative Entry. Negative Entry. Negative Entry.

He doesn't care.

I keep reading his prisoner profile. He was kicked out of Cookham Wood for rioting. Cookham Wood is a young offenders' institution. He was there when he was fifteen. He was moved to Feltham, but got kicked out of there for assaults on staff. He was transferred to Wandsworth, then transferred out again on a 'security move', indicating he was involved in the subculture. Phones and drugs. He's done stints inside for possession of a knife, GBH, possession of a bladed article. He's been out on the streets again, then back inside.

He's twenty-four now, and I'm just another person in uniform who's locked him in a room and taken away his TV. He doesn't care, and why would he? Being on Basic hasn't worked before. Why I am expecting it to suddenly start now?

'Do you want a shower?' I ask.

Basic prisoners aren't permitted to have association with the other men. They are entitled to have a shower, though, so on C Wing we try to facilitate that in the afternoon, when everyone else is locked up. We're still on an emergency regime. It's been almost a year now.

'Yeah, OK.' He shrugs again, but he doesn't get up.

I keep scrolling through his record. The picture taken of him at Cookham Wood shows him with his hair tied in bunches on either side of his head, chubby cheeks and a cheeky grin. At Feltham, he's got a shaved head. At Wandsworth, he's got a scar running through his eyebrow and a hardened stare. The person in front of me looks emotionless.

I don't know how long we sit in the office in silence. There's a pile of blank cell cards in front of me, waiting to be cut out of the big, laminated sheet they've been printed on. Tristan picks up the plastic safety scissors lying next to them, and starts cutting them out slowly. He puts them in a neat pile on my desk. I look up his release date. Four months' time. He's going home in four months. His behaviour makes even less sense now. Doesn't he want to make those last few months as easy as possible? He can see the light at the end of the tunnel now, surely. It's nearly over.

Only it turns out that isn't the case.

I don't know what it is about this office. It's on the landing, surrounded by cells and prisoners and everything else, but, when the door is closed, it could be out of the prison entirely. The Basic list disappears, the mounds of paperwork for the latest restraint, the ACCTs so full of entries that they're now held together by bits of string, they all disappear. Prisoners talk in here.

Over time, Tristan and I get into a little routine. He cuts out the cell cards for me and I catch up on paperwork. Most of the time, we sit in silence. And he stays on Basic. But week by week, as we continue to meet in this office, I'm able to piece together bits of his story.

He's the oldest brother. I've heard this story before, from Ben at Whitemoor. While Tristan has been inside, his younger brother has followed his example and got into fights, defended his area and started carrying a knife. He recounts all this on the phone to his big brother, full of pride. What is Tris supposed to do when he's released? Tell his little brother that that just isn't how we do things anymore? That during his time in jail, he's decided not to live the gang life anymore? With all the people who have hurt him, and whom he has hurt in return, would anyone let him forget it? The answer is no.

In one of our meetings, I ask if he could be relocated to a different area, away from his estate in Camberwell and all the tangled street politics that fester there. He's open to it, but knows that with three different probation officers in the last four years alone, each one with an unmanageable caseload, being moved out of the area is very unlikely. Even if that were to happen, his whole life is there. All his friends are there, all his family. He doesn't know anywhere else. He's never even been to central London, never seen Big Ben or the Eye. His life is that estate. How would he cope in a new place, with his support network gone?

I ask anyway. I email his current probation worker, who says what we thought. It's very unlikely, but she'll try for Leeds. There's a possibility he would be accepted into a hostel there, and the local Greggs hires ex-offenders if he's willing to give it a go. In the meantime, we talk about things that he could do to keep himself occupied in his cell. His behaviour gradually improves, but he still struggles to control his temper and, in particular, to hide his hatred for Officer Fran. So he remains without a TV.

When I ask what subjects he enjoyed in school, he says English. He says his teacher told him he was a good writer.

A few weeks before, I'd found an open letter that the actor and writer Lennie James had written to knife carriers. The next time we sit in the office together, I print it out for Tristan, and ask him what he would say if he had the opportunity to respond to the letter.

This is what he writes.

I would start off by telling Lennie that him and me come from two different generations. He comes from a generation where fist fights were how you dealt with things. If someone got stabbed, it was breaking news. The generation I come from, people getting stabbed is the norm.

The first time I carried a knife, I was ten years old. I carried it for a year until I was arrested. After that, I stopped carrying a knife, in fear of getting arrested again. Three years after this, when I was thirteen years old, I was stabbed on my way home from school. I can't lie – because of my environment, I was involved in gangs from a young age, but no one deserves to be stabbed. Especially not a thirteen-year-old schoolboy.

After this incident, there was not a time that I didn't leave the house without my knife. I even went to the extent of sleeping with it under my pillow. I guess, in a way, being stabbed sealed the deal of my involvement in gang warfare.

A short while after, I stabbed someone for the first time. By the way, they weren't unarmed, like you said. He actually pulled his knife out first. Lennie, some people do say they carry a knife for protection and don't ever end up using it. But some of us really do need protecting, from ourselves and others.

I stopped carrying a knife and started carrying a gun and a knife. That's how heavily involved I was before I came to prison. I want to change my life, I don't wish to continue living the way I'm used to, but then again, that's all I know. I need help. I need guidance. I need a way out. Otherwise, it's just going to continue until something dreadful happens. Either a life sentence or I end up dead. To be honest, prison has helped me stay alive this far.

I'm dreading getting released.

***

The time I was able to spend with prisoners at Whitemoor is a luxury I don't have here. Especially because of the emergency regime. It's made the job less enjoyable for me. In fact, it's changed the job entirely. I feel like I'm part prison officer, part report-writer, part form-filler, part data-inputter. It's tedious, and, if there are any benefits to it, I don't see them on the land-ings of C Wing. None of us joined this job to look at a screen.

It's not often that I am able to spend as much time with a prisoner as I do with Tristan. It works in this instance because he is open to it, despite his initial reticence, and because the mounds of paperwork I have to do mean that I'm sitting in the office for at least an hour after my shift finishes anyway. But there are so many men on this wing who could benefit from having that hour. An hour in a room that isn't their cell, with someone who isn't their cellmate. To talk about everything or nothing at all. Tristan is more than just an angry young man who hates the system, and I am more than just a uniformed representation of that. Our time in the office teaches that to us both.

***

I've never really thought of myself as a political person before, but the more time I spend in prison the more I start to think differently. Politics are everywhere in prison. They're in the decisions made about who gets sent there, what for and for how long. They're in the condition of the cells we put the prisoners in, and how we treat them once they're there. Maybe by now I should be more familiar with the way that political bluster inserts itself into prison life. I can still recall how it felt to go from cell to cell at Whitemoor and remove prisoners' books, after the Justice Secretary declared them an unnecessary perk and imposed a ban. From that point in late 2013 onwards, prisoners had to earn the right to buy books as part of the new 'Incentives and Earned Privilege' scheme. Any that they already had in their possession, outside the slim parameters of this IEP scheme, were removed.

Politics sat uncomfortably at the centre of the feeling that what I was doing wasn't right. It wasn't just, or necessary, nor did it seem to have any real point to it other than to shame. Perhaps the worst thing about the book ban, though, was the quiet acceptance of the prisoners. Most just left their book in a pile outside their door. They didn't bother trying to fight the system. They'd given up. And I felt a growing sense of unease at what I was doing. Especially when I came home and saw my flat, with piles of books in every room.

Although the book ban was overturned a year later, and the prisoners I'm working with at Scrubs do have access to some reading material, it plays on my mind. I've always been a big reader. And especially now that work is so intense, I've needed that time to myself more than ever: that ability to disappear into another world. I imagine that reading probably feels the same for the prisoners, but probably with more urgency. Theirs is a world from which they really do want to escape.

Decisions like the book ban are at best questionable, and at worst dangerous. They are more likely to be a way of coming across to the public as hard-nosed, to win votes by champion-ing the 'tough on crime' policy that we all know doesn't work. But taking away books? That feels painfully close to removing someone's right to have hope, to feel curious or engaged with something, or to feel connected with the outside world – a world that almost every prisoner will eventually rejoin. But what is mandated in Westminster must be carried out on the landings. So we did it. We took the books.

***

I'm sitting at my desk in Scrubs, surrounded by ever-mounting paperwork and the slightly acrid smell of mouse urine, slap bang in the middle of another political maelstrom.

The machinery that powers the Prison Service, the people and processes and policies that are the nuts and bolts of it all, are starting to groan. You can see it in all areas of the criminal justice system, from policing to probation to prisons, all struggling under the weight of expectation and duty. We're all feeling it. The impact of cuts to public services is becoming clearer, as demonstrated by some of the more obvious outcomes, like rising violence and self-harm, but also in the stories of people like Tristan and Wesley.

Wesley is admitted to Scrubs in the winter of 2016, when the view from my office window is a blanket of frost. One side of C Wing looks on to the exercise yard, but the other side, the side where my office is, looks out on to the green between C Wing and B Wing. Well, normally it's green. Today, it's glittering white and silver. Officers trudge up the long path that snakes through the centre of it, wrapped in scarves and knee-length prison-issue coats.

In front of me is Wesley: thick, curly hair, wide eyes and a concerned expression. I was expecting to see him this morning. We haven't met before, but an officer called me last night and explained the situation. He's done his best to keep Wesley safe overnight by putting him in a cell with Osman. Osman is a smart, sensible young man. He's polite to staff and managed to get himself a cleaner's job within a few weeks. He's streetwise, too. Although he won't assign himself to any social group here, he dips in and out of them all. He stays just on the periphery of everything. Osman can handle the landings; he can hold his own. It isn't fair to ask him to do the same for Wesley but, at least with him, Wesley will be safe when the door closes at night.

Wesley is eighteen and has severe learning difficulties. He's been remanded for possession of a firearm, an offence that carries a minimum sentence of five years in prison. The files that have accompanied him all the way from the custody suite in the police station, to the court where he was remanded and finally here, to my desk, are all stamped with a red self-harm warning. Although he doesn't have a history of hurting himself, it's clear to everyone who has met Wesley just how vulnerable he is. He doesn't really understand why he is here. Why he can't go home. Although numerous people have attempted to explain it to him, he just keeps repeating his story.

Yes, he had the gun. It was in a carrier bag underneath his bed. Yes, he was the one who put it there. Yes, he suspected that there was a gun in the bag when it was given to him because it felt heavy, but he never actually looked. He'd heard people in his area talk about guns, and he knew that some of the boys his age knew where to get them. But he'd never looked inside the bag. If he'd known for sure, he would have told his mum. But he didn't look. He just went home as quickly as he could and put it under his bed.

So yes, he had the gun in his possession, and no, this isn't the first time he's hidden carrier bags underneath his bed. But he was told to do it, by someone he's scared of, someone who has beaten him up before, slammed his body against the metal cage where he played football sometimes on the estate, and then shared footage of it on Snapchat. This time, he said he would hurt Wesley's mum. Bricks have already been thrown through their kitchen window. So Wesley took the bag, and put it under his bed.

Wesley has been taught to do the right thing. When questioned, he told the truth. He keeps telling the truth. His story never changes. He hopes that soon he will be allowed to go home to his mum. Wesley doesn't understand the complexity of his situation, nor does he understand why his legal team are recommending he plead guilty. But of course they are. He's admitted a serious criminal offence. The thought of Wesley, who has no prior convictions or even a caution, spending five years in prison is almost unbearable. I don't know how he would cope. I'm not sure he's even coping right now. I can see that he hasn't washed since he's been here, and his grey prison jumper is on back to front.

Although he tells me this story calmly and quietly, I can see he is upset. He asks when he will be able to go home, and telling him I don't know the answer to that feels torturous. The best I can do is offer him an extra phone call to his mum, here in the office, where he won't be pushed out of the queue or overheard. The prisoners can't overhear, but I can. The office is too small not to, and I can't leave him here on his own. His mum answers the phone immediately. In a tearful voice, she tells him to be brave. She says it will all get sorted, but in the meantime he must be brave and do what the officers ask of him. He holds on to the phone tightly with one hand and plays with the cord with the other. Ten minutes. That's all he gets.

When he hangs up, I tell him I will come and see him before the end of my shift. But as it happens, I don't have to wait that long.

Wesley is unlocked in the afternoon to collect his epilepsy medication. My heart sinks as he enters the office, and sinks further still when he says, 'Thank you for your help earlier, Miss South, but I am ready to go home now.'

Every time he says this, I can feel my resolve faltering.

He's carrying a bin bag containing his possessions. He's wearing his jacket. And I can tell from the rigid smile plastered on his face that he doesn't understand this situation or what it means, but he is trying so hard to be brave.

But he would like to go home now.

***

Challenging moments in prison are commonplace. In the last few years, I've met such a wide cross-section of people, many of whom I get on with and genuinely want to help, others who do their time so quietly that I barely notice them. There are some, though, so cold and callous and brutal in their cruelty, and these are the moments when the professionalism of the uniform I'm wearing on the outside feels poisoned by all the stress and exhaustion and judgement I'm feeling inside.

In those moments, with those people, the ones who spew vitriol at staff and terrorise the weaker inmates, the ones who spit and punch and wish cancer on people's families and shout that they hope an officer's daughter gets raped, I struggle to see them in the way I see someone like Tristan. I just see rage and violence. And in those moments, I lock their doors and think, *Good. I'm glad you're locked in there. In that tiny, dirty cell with cockroaches and mice. I'm glad you're locked up in here, rather than free out there. I'm glad.*

Then there are moments like these, when the person in front of me is confused and frightened and asking to go home, and it feels like my heart is breaking.

***

On one of my days off, a prisoner stumbles to the treatment room on the ones landing during association. He knocks on the door. Fortunately for him, there is a nurse inside, who opens the door promptly. She takes one look at the prisoner and presses the alarm bell. His blue T-shirt is red with blood.

He's been stabbed in the stomach eight times. Stab wounds from improvised prison weapons can look quite distinctive, jagged and uneven. But these are very clean. This was not done with a prison shank. He has been stabbed with an actual knife. The initials 'A.J.' have been carved into his forehead.

He's taken to hospital immediately, and Adam Junior is taken to the segregation unit immediately. There are no cameras on the wing, but the initials are a big giveaway, and enough reliable prisoners come forward to put his name in the frame. By the time I'm back in the following day, Adam has been returned to C Wing. There's no room in the seg. Until a cell becomes available, he'll be staying with us.

Adam is another very young prisoner. He's only eighteen, but acts younger. He's not really a problem to staff, though. In fact, he's well-liked. He's cheeky and boisterous, but also has a quick and very extreme propensity for violence. This isn't the first time he's carved his initials into someone's head.

I ask to see him before association. Officer Fitzgerald brings him down from his cell on the threes. He shuffles into the office in a tracksuit that's too big for him, wearing fake Prada trainers with flapping soles.

'Do you want me in here with you, Miss South?' asks Officer Fitzgerald.

'No, thank you,' I say, knowing full well that Officer Fitzgerald will now just stand outside the closed door. He's an old-school officer. He will never leave a female member of staff alone with a prisoner, no matter who the prisoner is, and no matter her rank. He doesn't need to do this. But though I'd never admit it, I'm glad he's there. Having Officer Fitzgerald outside the door feels more reassuring than any alarm button.

Adam sits in the same chair he normally sits in when we talk in the office. The whiteboard is behind him, and his own name is written just above his head.

'What happened yesterday, Adam?'

He plays with the frayed cuff of his jumper. 'You know what happened, Miss,' he says. 'It wasn't just me.'

I already know that. There were four of them. They'd held the victim down while A.J. dragged the knife up and down and across through his forehead.

Adam evades some of my questions, answers others, and in general tries to minimise the seriousness of what he's done. He describes the victim as his enemy, someone from a different area on the outside whose friends have previously robbed his friends. He says all this as if what's happened was inevitable, which I suppose is probably true. It reminds me of something a prisoner at Whitemoor once said to me. He described going to prison as 'an occupational hazard'. If you choose a career in crime, then jail is always a very real possibility. If you choose the gang life, then it's like Tristan said. You either die or end up catching a life sentence.

Adam tells me to stop asking him questions, please, because I'm making him feel bad. I cannot comprehend the fear the victim must have felt, being held down in the dirty showers on the threes, a sweaty hand covering his mouth, a blade puncturing his flesh and opening up his forehead, wondering if these are the last things he would see, wondering if this is where he would die. When I say this to Adam, he looks at me for a few seconds, then breaks down. He cries and cries. So much so that Officer Fitzgerald comes into the office to see if we're OK. Adam is not OK. I've seen him laugh and shout and fight, but I've never seen him cry.

Through his sobs, he eventually asks me if I think he's mad. He's asked me this several times before, normally after a fight. It's his greatest fear. That someone would consider him to have crossed the line from just violent to violent and insane. As far as he's concerned, insane people get locked up in secure hospitals and forgotten about.

I don't think he's mad. But what do I know? Prison officers receive shamefully minimal training in mental health. Adam might not be mad, whatever that means, but he is certainly fragile. He suffers from palpable anxiety and severe lows. It's inconceivable that he has not been segregated after what he's done, but part of me is glad they didn't have space for him. I don't think the segregation unit is a healthy place for him to be. That said, neither is C Wing. Wormwood Scrubs is not rehabilitating Adam; it's making him worse. And I shouldn't be surprised at that. I don't think there are many people who could spend twenty-three hours a day locked in a dirty room for weeks on end, then come out feeling refreshed and ready to contribute to society. Many of the prisoners come into Scrubs angry and leave angrier, shamed by the degrading conditions in which they live and the relentless violence that shapes their days.

Adam has been stabbed himself before. During one of our chats in the office, he told me about the first time it happened, on the top floor of a bus going through Holland Park. He says the main thing he remembers is the heat of the blood as it came out of him. He wasn't expecting it to be so warm. Adam has been stabbed and beaten many times. His parents aren't interested. They haven't visited him once in all the time he's been at Scrubs. His is a life of trauma, and his only way of dealing with it seems to be wreaking it on others. Making them feel the heat of their own blood. Making them see his initials branded on their body every time they look in the mirror. Because he is somebody. He is important. He is worth visiting. He is not dispensable. He is not mad.

***

Unsurprisingly, Adam flatly refuses to tell me anything about how the knife got in here, though he did concede that it was a real knife. When I ask if it's still on the wing, he shakes his head vehemently. It's long gone.

Officer Fitzgerald ended up putting his arms round him as he cried. Afterwards, we stay with Adam for almost an hour. He doesn't want to go back on the landings with red eyes. Once he's gone, Officer Fitzgerald sits in the office with me.

'Real knives now,' he says. 'How is this all going to end? I've never known it be this bad before.'

Neither have I, though I haven't been in the job even half as long as he has.

So what do we do? Strike? I'm not convinced. Because we've already done that. We did that a few months ago, after a female officer was knocked unconscious by a pool ball in a sock and a male officer was threatened with a flick knife. I sat outside in the blistering heat and watched as news crews gathered in the entrance to the prison. I leaned back against the perimeter wall with my colleagues and listened as the reporters interviewed newly released prisoners, as the Prison Officers Association reps made speeches and the local café brought us ice creams. I felt part of something. I felt defiant when the deputy governor came out and asked us to return to work, and I felt proud when, collectively, we refused. This was the moment when things would change. When staff would no longer stand for such a violent work-place with little protection and little support. But the reality is, nothing changed. I lost a day's pay. When I went back in the day after, the wing was still dark and dirty and flooded with phones, drugs and weapons. The prisoners were still angry – more so, in fact, after twenty-four hours of being banged up – and who could blame them? The netting still bounced every time someone jumped on it, the alarm bell still sounded and the packages still flew over the wall. Self-harm was still rife, violence was still constant. There were still no cages on the windows. There were still rolled-up towels outside cell doors to stop the mice getting in. Noth-ing changed.

It takes its toll on all of us, staff and prisoners. For me, it's not so much the big incidents, but rather the cumulative effect of the little ones. It all builds up, the aggression and insults and constant arguments. Every day is starting to feel like a battle.

I'm tired. And even worse, I can feel myself becoming desensitised. The fights are beginning to blur into each other; the cuts are all starting to look the same.

'It's only going to get worse,' Officer Fitzgerald says before he gets up to leave.

He's right.

A few months after I leave Wormwood Scrubs, a prisoner on C Wing is stabbed to death in his own cell.

12

Healthcare

HASHEM LIVES INSIDE his mattress.

He's ripped apart the blue plastic cover and pulled out the material inside. Now it's hollow. And the space inside it is where he sleeps. During the day, he wears it like a boxy all-in-one. He slots himself inside it like someone wearing a sandwich board. Then he spends the day crying, yelling incoherently, and occasionally eating his own faeces.

He hasn't always been like this. The psychiatric nurses are calling it 'drug-induced psychosis', brought on by spice. It's always spice these days. Before now, Hashem lived on C Wing, a broad-shouldered young offender with sharply cropped black hair and a commitment to fashion, even inside. As well as being given standard prison clothing on arrival, prisoners are allowed to wear their own clothes in Scrubs. There are a few exceptions to this: no hoodies, no hats, no white shirts (too similar to an officer's uniform). On the wing, Hashem would wear bright red tracksuits, Christian Louboutin trainers with spikes on the toe that we would all marvel at, wondering, *Are those really OK in here? Could those spikes be used as weapons?* But Hashem was unlikely to turn his prized shoes on anyone. He'd get stressed if they got so much as a speck of dust on them.

But all that was before. Now he's taken spice, and Hashem is unrecognisable. One morning, just before all prisoners were unlocked for association, that precious hour they have in which to shower and make phone calls and go on the yard, Hashem smoked spice. A few minutes after unlock, he started attacking the stairs, kicking and headbutting and punching with such ferocity that it took six officers to get him down, one of whom was knocked out in the process.

I unlock the gates to the Healthcare Inpatients Unit and wave at Adnan, another former C Wing prisoner. He used to only let staff into his cell if they knew the password. Fortunately, the password was always whatever the officer said. Adnan has been admitted to Healthcare after concerns were raised about his mental state deteriorating further. No one wanted to share a cell with him. He wasn't washing or brushing his teeth; he wouldn't call his family or write them letters. Instead, he'd spend the majority of his association period picking up litter from the exercise yard and presenting it to staff as if it were a gift. Now, he waves back to me from his position on the lumpy sofa in the middle of the room. He's doing better here.

The Inpatients Unit is another mini wing. It houses prisoners with physical ailments for whom a general population wing would be considered inappropriate, along with those whose mental health issues are too severe to cope with on a wing.

As well as Hashem and Adnan, there's a burglar with two broken legs. He attempted a rather ambitious escape from the house he was stealing from when the police arrived. He leaped out of a third floor window. There's a teenager with one eye, his face striped with scars after being slashed repeatedly. Another teenager who wears a mask all day after being doused in sulphuric acid. A Syrian man from the Calais immigration camp who has sewn his lips together in protest at ongoing deportation enquiries. A twenty-three-year-old with white-blond hair and a long beard, whose leg is rotting after being injected too many times with too many drugs. It's swollen and stinking and leaking fluids, despite the thick bandages wrapped round it day after day after day. In a few months' time, I'll see him begging outside New Cross station, and I'll notice that he only has one leg, having had the other amputated after being released.

Adnan and Hashem aren't the only ones in here due to their mental health problems. One prisoner believes he is the Messiah and repeatedly tries to crucify himself. Another man has been recently convicted of stalking offences against a famous actress whom he had never met, but with whom he was convinced he was in a long-term relationship. After a relatively stable period, he's become increasingly distressed after seeing her on the front page of a magazine wearing nursing scrubs. He believes this is a message that she knows he's in Wormwood Scrubs and wants to contact him. Some of the men here with mental health issues will go on to secure hospitals, but many will not.

All areas of the criminal justice system are under strain, not just prisons and policing, but forensic mental health services also. Secure hospitals don't have the space to accommodate every mentally ill prisoner. The consultant psychiatrists who visit Healthcare to assess prisoners for a potential bed may acknowledge that they are unwell, but decide that they aren't unwell enough to be admitted. Or they might diagnose their presentation, though concerning, as more behavioural than mental. But even if this is the case, it isn't appropriate or safe to locate prisoners behaving this way on the general population wings.

At the far end of the Healthcare Inpatients Unit is the palliative care suite. There are two cells here, both larger than normal to allow for all the equipment that prisoners receiving end-of-life care might need. There's one man in there at the moment. He's eighty-three, bed-bound, and only ever leaves the cell for hospital appointments with his oncology consultant. Due to longer sentences being given by the courts, and a rise in convictions for historical offences, men of his age group are becoming more and more common in prison. The ageing prison population has led to a growing need for palliative care.

Scrubs is fortunate to have a palliative care suite, because some prisons don't. Those without often develop links with local hospices to enable terminally ill prisoners to receive end-of-life treatment. However, a move to a hospice is still considered a release from custody, and only the Secretary of State for Justice can grant early release, even if it's on compassionate grounds. Early release on compassionate grounds certainly isn't guaranteed, and some prisoners may not even be eligible to apply. Or they might not want to in the first place. Prisoners serving life sentences, who have spent a considerable amount of time in custody and have perhaps lost social connections in the process, sometimes prefer to spend their last weeks in the familiarity of prison.

As well as the palliative care suite, there are also two constant-watch cells with nurses permanently stationed outside, monitoring the men whose risk of suicide is deemed so high that they require constant observation.

Aside from these specialist cells, the accommodation here is the same as on the wings. The cells are standard size, although the view is more expansive. Prisoners here can look out on to Wormwood Scrubs park. They can watch planes as they fly over from Heathrow, see people walking their dogs or going for a run or throwing a parcel over the wall. And the atmosphere here is designed to be pleasant, too. It's bright and well-lit, and, rather than anti-bullying posters, there's prisoner artwork framed on the walls, along with the same kind of picturesque landscapes and motivational quotes I saw at Whitemoor. Quotes about success, determination and teamwork. Teamwork is exemplified here. Healthcare is a small unit, but a challenging one. Working with people weeks from death and others determined to cause their own is not an easy task.

Next to the shower stalls is a mini kitchen for staff, and beside that is a spacious room where prisoners can attend therapy groups or arts and crafts sessions. Hashem doesn't attend any of these, though. He doesn't socialise with anyone. He stays inside his mattress, that cheap polyester becoming a prison all of its own, squeaking as he shuffles round the cell and ignores the repeated attempts of staff to engage with him.

Success, determination and teamwork. These sorts of posters are in all prisons. They're a reminder that people get out, people do better, people make something of themselves. There's no reason that can't be you. Prison doesn't have to be the end.

Right now, though, in Healthcare, in his cell and inside his mattress, it feels a bit like this is the end for Hashem. It is most certainly a low moment in his life, and his is a life that has been chequered by them. Before he took spice, he was a regular in the C Wing SO Office. He has an explosive temper and, by his own admission, he struggles to keep control of it. I once saw him dropkick another prisoner so hard he flew halfway across the landing.

But before the drug-induced psychosis, Hashem was also a typical young man, longing for the freedom and opportunities of his life outside. He'd pop his head round the office door to show me his latest footwear purchase, or to ask what I thought of these shoes with these jeans, or he'd come in and slump down in the chair opposite my desk, run his hands through his hair and shake his head and tell me about his relationship problems. Like the time he gave his girlfriend his Instagram password so she could update his account while he was inside, but she'd taken the initiative and checked his direct messages, which apparently didn't paint him in the best light.

He would say he couldn't wait to be released, but the more we talked, I wasn't so sure. It seemed that he was running from life outside. It hadn't given him much. Prison, at the very least, provided him with the structure and routine that had fallen away as soon as he left care. I think more prisoners feel this way than would admit it. I've never forgotten what Tristan wrote. That prison had kept him alive. And that he was dreading being released. I don't think he's the only one here who feels that way.

For Hashem, institutions, grey and bleak as they are, offered a kind of comfort, or at the very least some familiarity. He was a young boy when his mother passed away. Hashem and his siblings were taken into care. Then, perhaps predictably, he fell in with a gang. It's probably not fair to say that he 'fell in' with them, as if he just tripped up one day and was suddenly robbing people on the street. But it is fair to say that his life has followed the typical trajectory of many young people's lives when fractured by trauma and loss so early on. It sometimes feels too simplistic to reduce the reason that boys join gangs to wanting a sort of surrogate family, something to belong to, but in Hashem's case I think that's spot-on. The men in his gang are constant. They are fiercely, violently loyal to each other. That loyalty is something he can rely on. He's not stupid, though. He knows that the reason numbers are dwindling is because his peers keep getting killed. And he knows that once he's out, it could be him next.

As I make my way through the unit, I pause by the sofa to look at some photographs Adnan wants to show me. His girlfriend sent them in. They show a little girl, his daughter, holding up some paintbrushes proudly. Her toothy grin is the same as his.

'Have you spoken much to Hashem?' I ask.

'Nah, miss,' says Adnan. 'No point. He doesn't recognise me.'

Hashem doesn't recognise anyone. He doesn't even know his own name. The staff here say it's the worst case of drug-induced psychosis they've ever seen. Next week, a team from Rampton secure hospital are coming to assess him with a view to admitting him for treatment when space becomes available. The officers here are glad of that, and hopeful that the Rampton team will agree to take Hashem as soon as possible, but equally they're concerned that he will refuse to attend the meeting wearing actual clothes. It's the mattress or nothing.

I leave Adnan flicking through the music channels and pass the staff office. It's in the centre of the unit, almost as if it's been dropped there as an afterthought, with chairs and computers and mounds of paperwork shielded by glass windows with little squares in the panels. Officers and nursing staff work closely together in Healthcare, and this is where they write up reports, have a quick cup of tea or add written observations to the ACCTs that cover an entire table. I see them piled up by the windows as I go past, mountains of orange cardboard filled with pages and pages of observations, held together by string and Sellotape and clips, or anything else staff can find.

All prisons offer basic mental health provision – ACCTs, Mental Health In-Reach teams and counselling – although some prisons do a better job of running these than others. It's the same old story. Places with more funding, such as those in the Category A estate, are better able to support those inmates who need it. Category A prisons have a forensic psychology team on site, with accredited offending behaviour courses that aren't on offer at Scrubs and other local jails. This is mainly because a lot of the prisoners in local jails are serving sentences shorter than the duration of the courses that might help them. Most forensic support is aimed at long-termers and lifers, such as the therapeutic communities operating at HMP Dovegate and HMP Grendon. These are different environments to a typical prison. Therapeutic communities deliver long-term, accredited therapy to the men who live there. But as impressive as these places are, there are only two of them in the country, and they only accept long-term prisoners. So they don't do much for the drug addicts and gang members and thousands of others I see coming in and out of Scrubs, again and again and again. For those guys, it's the ACCT process, a visit from the In-Reach team, and maybe a stint in Healthcare.

The front cover of a blank ACCT looks smart and professional: bright orange, with neat boxes for prisoner details to be printed in block letters and black ink.

- First Name
- Last Name
- DOB
- Establishment
- Location
- Observation

But the boxes stop looking neat when the details change, over and over again. When it's a new officer filling them in each time, different pens and different handwriting and different issues to add to the care plan. If a prisoner transfers to a different establishment, the ACCT goes with them. And within each establishment, each change in location requires a case review to assess the prisoner's mood. And after each review, a prisoner's frequency of staff observations can go up and down. Typically, this might be written as '3 × 5', meaning three observations during the day and five during the night. But something like a bad day, an argument with staff, a difficult phone call or an incident of self-harm could cause the observations to increase – to five per day and hourly at night, perhaps. Or maybe even hourly, day and night. Or twice hourly. Or every fifteen minutes. Or constant watch. The 'OBSERVATION' box soon gets messy.

Prisoners at Scrubs start in the First Night Centre, often in a dormitory housing four or five other prisoners. Their cell location here might read FNC-02, for example. Maybe they've been put on an ACCT because they had self-harm markers from a previous stint in custody, or maybe they made a comment at the police station suggesting they intended to harm themselves.

After the prison induction in the First Night Centre is complete, they'll be moved to one of the general population wings, providing there's no reason for them to go to a VPU. Vulnerable Prisoner Units house sex offenders, former police officers, bullying victims, prisoners considered to be snitches – anyone who might be at overt risk from other inmates. But most prisoners go to a standard wing, like C Wing. So the location box on an ACCT might now read C2-35.

But C Wing is hard, and I've seen prisoners who come in with no mental health issues leave with plenty. Paranoid, anxious, frightened. I've seen the same happen with staff. The violence, self-harm, the unpredictability of it all. And for the officers, the personal ethics of it can feel like a heavy weight. After all, we are the ones with the keys. But it was never meant to get this bad. None of us signed up for this. In psychology, this is sometimes called a moral injury. It's what happens when the things you witness, or are even complicit in, go against your personal values. And it can chip away at you.

Time on C Wing is enough to mess with anyone's head. So, maybe the prisoner will be moved to E Wing. It's cleaner and smaller, with a roll of only 145, and all the cells are singles. The location box on an ACCT now reads E3-13. E Wing is also the wing for prisoners attending education. Some of the men on other wings attend education too, but the majority are housed on E Wing. So that means more time out of the cell, which – theoretically, at least – is spent doing something productive. This may help with a person's low mood, paranoia, anxiety or fear.

Only sometimes it doesn't. Or it can't, because education doesn't run every day now, or even every other day, and the classes that are available are drastically reduced in size because of staffing issues. So the waiting list gets longer, and the demons in someone's head get angrier. And even if the wing is quieter, there are still cockroaches and rats and fires burning and litter that swirls in the air outside your cell window every time the wind picks up. So maybe that person's low mood drops some more. Maybe all that time spent in their cell plays havoc with their mind, and they start to think strange things, and to say them out loud; to talk to themselves on the landings and survey every passing prisoner or officer with hostility. Maybe they stop washing themselves in their sink (because there's not enough time out of their cell to guarantee a shower), or stop eating properly, or maybe they become suspicious of the food itself and wonder if there are chemicals in it. Maybe it all starts to get a bit much, and they're moved to D Wing. The mental health wing. The location box is crossed out again, and it now reads D4-47.

D Wing is unlike any other wing I will ever see. It is dangerous. It's old and crumbling like everywhere else in this prison, but that's not really the issue. D Wing is all single cells, and it's reserved primarily for prisoners suffering with mental health problems. That's not the case for every D Wing prisoner; there are too many men and not enough cells for each wing to stick to its supposed demographic. C Wing isn't all IDTS prisoners; E Wing isn't all prisoners attending education. And so not all the inhabitants of D Wing are mentally unwell men, but a lot of them are. And they are among the most unwell, the most tormented, I see in my career. They are wild with anger and poisonous in their delusions and gratifications; they are perverted and psychopathic and dangerous.

One man has previous for dragging female staff into his cell and taking them hostage. He pretends to have a limp, to be barely mobile, so that one day a female officer might not have the time or inclination to look up the alerts that redden his prisoner profile; she might not know who he is or what he's done, and, when he beckons her to his door because he says he can't walk, no one will warn her in time, and there will be no experienced staff around familiar with this charade, so she will lean in to hear what he says in that soft, gentle voice that he puts on – and he will grab her.

I'm nice to this man. I give him what he's entitled to, and decline anything he isn't. I do all this because of my uniform.

It's my job. But it jars. I don't want to be nice to him. I'm well aware that, given half the chance, he would not be nice to me. It all feels like such a charade. He wants his record to show a polite man who never slips up. But that's only because he's waiting for one of *us* to slip up.

These men don't scare me. But they do make me angry. Because I know what their victims don't. We don't rehabilitate them. The man with the fake limp doesn't go to any treatment courses or programmes. Nor do we punish him. He's just here. Existing. Until he's let out again. And knowing this makes me feel as if I'm betraying the women he's hurt – of whom there are many. He is a prolific sex offender. Maybe his victims imagine that in prison, he's being rehabilitated in some way, given therapy or something. But he isn't. This feels a bit like moral injury again, or as if I'm taking on someone else's trauma vicariously. Prison officers hear a lot of difficult stories, we see a lot of difficult things. You can mitigate that harm if it feels as if you're making a difference in some way. But we're not. I'm not.

I know what this man has done. I know it, and I do nothing about it.

The staff on D Wing are on another level. They have been in the job for years and years. They know the signs, they are quick and efficient and brave, and they are hyper-vigilant, alert to everything. So maybe they know what's coming, and they recommend an urgent move to Healthcare. And the location box changes yet again. H3-02.

And maybe that's how a prisoner ends up here. There are, of course, many routes, such as Hashem's drug use. But how he got here is irrelevant to him, because he has no understanding of where he is anyway.

I walk to Hashem's cell and pause at the door. I'm hopeful, because the psychologist I spoke to earlier said that there's no harm in trying, and perhaps this will be the time that he recognises me. Deep down, I know he won't. Hashem is somewhere else entirely. I came yesterday, and last week too, and he just stared at me with glazed eyes.

Hashem changes cells daily. His cell is speckled with faeces. So far, he hasn't fought the staff as they relocate him to a different cell or encourage him to use the shower. The potential for violence is there, and so the additional staff are too, but senior management have considered it unnecessary for the officers to be in kit. Hashem doesn't normally fight, but he does tremble with fear. That's why I'm here today. I'm spare, which means I'm getting bounced around the jail doing different jobs as and when they come up. The Healthcare SO is preparing for an ACCT review, so one of today's jobs is supervising Hashem as he is relocated to a shower.

I knock on the door and open his observation panel.

He's standing at the back of the cell, one leg on the heating pipes, talking to an empty yogurt pot. The size and muscle that once made him such an imposing figure is falling away rapidly. He retreats further into his mattress when he sees me.

'Hashem,' I say. 'It's Miss South.'

He stares blankly at me. 'Have you come so we can fly away?' he asks.

'No, Hashem. I've come to help you go to the shower.'

I notice the yellow puddle on the floor by the bed. He scratches his face.

'Do you fly?' he asks.

'No, Hashem.'

'What's the point in your wings?'

I try again to explain why I'm here and what's going to happen. The staff behind me are getting ready. They're not in kit, but they're all wearing gloves. Even on the days when Hashem makes it to the shower room, he very rarely goes in a cubicle to actually wash.

'You're Pegasus, aren't you?' he asks.

Pegasus, the winged horse.

232

I had no idea Hashem knew anything about Greek myth-ology – but then, I didn't know he took spice, either. Much as I try to shake this new identity he's given me, he acts like he's never been more sure of anything. From then on, his eyes widen every time I visit him. He stares for a few moments, shakes his head in wonder and says, 'Pegasus.'

***

I leave Healthcare that day feeling deflated. Two weeks ago, Hashem was so alive, so full of energy. Now he's an empty shell. But on the walk back to the wing, I have an idea. He might not recognise me or any of the officers he knows, but in the grand scheme of things we're just fleeting figures in his life. Unlike Tristan. He's known Tristan since he was five. They went to school together. They lived on neighbouring estates. They were good friends, until the specifics of where they lived made that a bit precarious, but they never became enemies. On the wing, they would stop to talk to each other. Tristan has told me he used to have Hashem and his brother round for dinner sometimes.

A couple of days later, I take Tristan to Healthcare. It's early evening, and Tristan is pleased to be out of his cell at a time when almost no one else is. We cut through the gates on the threes landing that take us in the direction of Healthcare. There are just two weeks to go now until Tristan is released – not to Leeds, sadly – and he's apprehensive.

'I'm going to really give it a go this time,' he says. 'Just gonna stay home with my mum until things get sorted.' By 'things', he means a job. Hopefully one that takes him out of his borough entirely, to somewhere he won't be recognised by people less than pleased to see him.

We pass through the Healthcare Outpatients Unit. The floor here is carpeted. It feels like luxury compared to the rest of the jail. There are rooms on either side of us: a room to see the GP, the optician, the dentist, and a large holding room for prisoners to wait in until their name is called. We walk through another set of gates into the Inpatients Unit. The TV is switched off now. All the prisoners are behind their doors.

I take a seat on the arm of the sofa and watch as Tristan approaches Hashem's door. He knocks first, then shouts who he is, his street name rather than Tristan, and opens the obs panel.

I see from his face how shocked he is. No matter how much I'd tried to prepare him, whatever he was expecting, it wasn't this. I crane my neck to see over his shoulder and into the cell. Hashem is wearing his mattress still. He looks withered, like a plant that's been left in the sun too long. There are tufts of toilet paper in his hair, the skin under his eyes is ringed with black and his lips are chapped and swollen. He looks like a cartoon caricature of himself, his head too big for his shrinking body, his eyes wide and his cheekbones pointed and sharp. In such a short space of time, he's lost so much weight. He looks at Tristan, but doesn't acknowledge him. To Tristan's credit, he sticks with it. He tries every possible shared memory or moment or person to reawaken Hashem. He talks about school, their old English teacher, Hashem's home before he went into care, the time his sister got into a fight in year seven, the trainers Hashem had just bought, the gang fight in Hammersmith with metal poles and machetes that was all over the news a few months ago, even the colour of the school uniform they used to wear. But there's nothing. Hashem laughs a bit, looks up at the ceiling and says he's never been this close to clouds before, and that's it. He looks at Tristan blankly. He doesn't remember a thing.

On the way back to the wing, Tristan keeps shaking his head and muttering under his breath. The change from who Hashem was to who he is now is so stark that it's hard for anyone to get their head round, especially someone he grew up with.

'That's an advert for staying away from rice right there,' says Tristan, as we reach his cell on C Wing. 'Rice' is slang for spice. 'That's what it does to you,' he says. He walks to the back of his cell and looks out the window. 'That's what jail does to you,' he says.

I lock the door behind him.

***

That evening, I read about the story of Pegasus. The ancient myth describes the winged horse, who was captured and ridden by a Greek hero named Bellerophon. Bellerophon attempts to ride Pegasus all the way to heaven, but something goes wrong. Different versions of the myth say different things: that Bellerophon is killed, or wounded, or merely unseated.

And that word sticks with me. It feels like a strangely poetic way to describe what's happened to Hashem. Spice hasn't killed him, but it's certainly changed him. It's unseated him, thrown him off course. Whatever direction his life was heading in, it's going somewhere else entirely now.

Pegasus keeps going. He keeps flying, and transcends physical limitations. I find myself hoping that Hashem does, too. I hope that he's gone somewhere else, and that he can't see himself as he is now, scared and dirty and sick. I hope that if he ever does come back, he never remembers.

13

The Places in Between

WHEN AARON hanged himself at Whitemoor, I considered myself lucky that I hadn't been the one to find him. That he hadn't done it during my week of nights.

At Wormwood Scrubs, five years later, I still feel lucky. But then I cut down three men in one week.

One prisoner is in Healthcare, an ageing man who told the staff everything they wanted to hear. He said he was feeling better, that he'd resumed contact with his wife and an ex-employer had got in touch to say they would give him his job back on release. None of it was true. But he said it convincingly, and each fabricated resolution ticked off issues on the care plan. He seemed to be filled with a certain energy, a certain determination. But as soon as the observations had been sufficiently reduced, he hanged himself with a torn piece of bedsheet. He was still on fifteen-minute observations, but it doesn't take fifteen minutes to kill yourself.

It's early morning when the call comes in over the radio. Not even half six. I am walking past Healthcare on my way to the gym. Moments later, I am hacking at the knotted bedsheets that cut into his neck while another officer holds his body.

We are too late.

He is gone.

***

Two days later, a prisoner on C Wing is found by Officer Fitzgerald. He's slumped on the floor by his bed. He's used his own shoelaces to make a ligature and tied one end round the heating pipes and the other tightly round his neck. Officer Fitzgerald shouts for staff. By chance I'm halfway down that landing as it is, and it takes me seconds to reach the cell.

Together, Officer Fitzgerald and I cut him down. It's not easy, though. The shoelaces are tied so tightly that the folds of skin on his neck overlap them. Prison officers are taught not to cut a ligature by the knot – we're told that preservation of the knot is important for evidential purposes – but it's almost impossible in this case. And we're both very aware that every second counts. We don't have time to isolate the knot and cut neatly around it.

'Can you hear me, Mario?' says Officer Fitzgerald, grabbing his wrist to look for a pulse.

Mario can't hear him. But even if he could, he wouldn't be able to answer. He's stuffed wet toilet paper down his throat, so determined is he to die. Thankfully, removing the toilet paper is much easier than getting the ligature off. Mario starts gurgling, but his eyes never open.

We begin chest compressions, and the noise of the Code Blue alarm sounding through our radios is drowned out by our own voices as we count each compression. Our voices and our heavy breathing, because chest compressions are hard work. Our voices and our breathing and then a sharp popping noise, as Mario's ribs crack under the pressure.

'Come on, Mario,' says Officer Fitzgerald. He kneels against the cell wall as I take over, both of us red-faced and sweating. We take it in turns, thirty compressions then rest, thirty compressions then rest.

I don't know Mario. He's only been on the wing about a week. I don't know his story, why he's here or why he wants to die. Today, this way, in this cell.

By the time the nurses arrive with their grab bags, Officer Fitzgerald and I are exhausted. We move to the back of the cell to give them room. One nurse carries on with the chest compressions while another sets up the defibrillator. The automated voice swells inside the cell, loud and insistent and commanding: 'STAND BACK, SHOCK DELIVERING.'

One of the nurses shouts, 'He's breathing.'

Paramedics run on to the wing. Mario is taken next door to Hammersmith Hospital.

He sustains brain damage, but he survives.

***

On the Friday of that week, I'm redeployed to D Wing for a morning shift. There's a fight between two prisoners on the ones. They circle each other for a few seconds, then go at it, punching and kicking. One of them grabs the bin to launch at his opponent, but falls over as he does so. Neither are natural fighters, and the other prisoners surround them and laugh. But officers intervene quickly, and the show is soon over.

One of the prisoners is taken to see the nurse while the other, Bekim, is locked in his cell to wait his turn. I know Bekim from a brief period he spent on C Wing. He can be a difficult man, erratic and unpredictable in his emotions, full of threats that are never carried out, but still eager for the attention they get him. When the nurse is ready, I go to Bekim's cell to unlock him. I find him hanging. He's still conscious – he can't have been suspended for more than a few seconds before I went in – but, as I shout for staff and slice through the ligature with my fish knife, he screams at me. He screams and splutters and sobs; he claws at his neck and yells at me over and over again, 'Let me die.'

He lives.

***

After that week, I'm OK. I stop myself thinking about it too much, though there are moments when I walk into a cell and notice the bedsheets, that pale sickly green colour that prison bedding is, and think of how perfect they are for making ligatures. Of how neat and precise the knots I've seen in ligatures are. Like a final job done well.

There are a few moments when I meet prisoners in their sixties and seventies, and I think of the man in Healthcare and how cold his skin was, how it looked almost glassy, drained of blood, drained of life. It's Bekim who stays with me the most, though. When I don't have much else to distract me, I think of his bulging eyes and the skin around them, a blotchy purple. He was so desperate to die and yet he was the one who lived, with no brain damage, no physical limitations. I got there just in time but, the way he sees it, I was too early. He didn't want any more time.

I could call the employee assistance helpline, but it's an external service, and I don't feel like talking to someone who has no idea what prison is like. I could ask to see a peer-support worker, but I don't even know who they are. The peer-support programme was well publicised at Whitemoor, a group of officers trained to help others after difficult incidents, but it's not like that here. I don't know if it even exists. And even if it did, when would I have the time to visit a peer supporter? And when would *they* have the time to visit me? They're still officers, working in areas that require a certain number of staff to operate. Officers who are tired, stressed and probably traumatised themselves.

I've started to notice little ways in which prison is seeping into my life outside of work. I'm uncomfortable in pubs. Or in any crowded space, especially if people are drinking, and there's more chance of a fight breaking out. But it doesn't feel as if it's interfering with the way I live my life. And not spending my days off in the pub isn't necessarily a bad thing. I've seen from other officers how that can become a problem in itself.

But I'm lying to myself. This world is interfering with my life. I still speak to my friends from home almost every day, but only by text. I ignore calls, I ignore FaceTimes. I hold my phone in my hand and watch as the calls come and go. But I can't bring myself to answer, because I can't talk. There are times when I come home, and I can't speak. I can't make my mouth move. It's as if I use all my energy during the day, everything I have, and then there's nothing left. I can't make conversation with my housemates. I don't want noise. I don't want to listen to anyone else's stories, their successes or problems or worries. None of it.

I just want silence. My own company. I don't want the hassle of any kind of relationship where I can't predict what's coming next. I want my own company, my own bed, my own plans – and nothing else. I want quiet. I want time. I want to run. I want books. Documentaries about anything, sports or nature or faraway cities, anything but prison. Because it's showing up too much now. It's there in my body language and the places I don't want to go and the conversations I don't want to have. I know how rude or standoffish I must seem when my housemates try to talk to me. But I feel as if I've expended all my energy in this place only a couple of minutes away that they have no idea about, that they walk past all the time, and here they are, talking about music and art and gossip, as if any of that matters when people are killing themselves down the road, and I don't care for any of it, and I'm not interested, and I can't pretend, and I just need quiet.

Silence.

Space.

***

I've been at Scrubs for two years when an advertisement is posted on the prison intranet for a temporary custodial manager position, to be based in the Visits department. Governor Olive encourages me to go for it. I think I'm ready for something different. C Wing has changed dramatically over the last couple of years. Officer Fitzgerald has left; he took VEDs. Officer Akash has resigned, saying the toll the job was taking on his emotional wellbeing was too much. He has young children, and the long hours and inconsistent finish times aren't conducive to family life. I don't blame him. I'm not sure they're conducive to any kind of life. I can't remember the last shift I finished on time.

I know none of this is healthy. So I plan a trip home, and talk to my friends there properly. I try to explain just how stressful work is. The kind of stress I didn't even know existed. We agree that I need a holiday. Maybe two.

As it happens, I end up taking four. A couple of months later, we fly to Spain, then a few weeks after that Vegas, and then, not long after that, Spain again. And before the year is up, I go on a raucous trip to Benidorm with fifteen other prison officers from Whitemoor. Brian and Bernard and Jade and everyone else. All of us together. In dodgy little nightclubs with strobe lighting and sticky floors and blistering heat. We sing karaoke at 3am; Jade turns out to be amazing at it. We swap shifts on the landings for shifts on the beach. We wince when Brian falls asleep and watch as the others solemnly carry him, still curled up and snoring on his sun lounger, and launch him into the pool.

And it helps. I feel better.

But the holidays end. And the real shifts start again. And it's all just the same as when I left.

So I go for the TCM post. To prepare for the interview, I read through the most recent inspection report on Wormwood Scrubs from Her Majesty's Inspectorate of Prisons. It makes for depressing reading.

The prison had a significant rat problem; we [the inspectors] saw them every day and night we visited the prison and a large rats' nest was very obvious in the grounds. Exercise yards… were bare and strewn with rubbish.

I think of C Wing and of broken drones.

Half the prisoners in our survey told us they had felt unsafe at some time in the prison and one in five told us they felt unsafe at the time of the inspection.

I think of Wesley. And all the others.

Drugs and alcohol were easily available (and the use of non-detectable new psychoactive substances was increasing rapidly) but there was no supply reduction strategy or action plan.

Everyone on the fours, Hashem, the change in atmosphere when a new batch of drugs made it on to the wing, the countless packages flying over the perimeter wall and the devastation they caused.

The number of assaults on prisoners and staff was double that at similar prisons.

Khan and Okowo, Tristan, Adam, Bekim. All the officers who have been punched and kicked and spat at.

We found prisoners who were too frightened to leave their cells and were not adequately supported by staff.

I think of everyone who is frightened of Flaherty and Gonzalez.

Only 13% of prisoners were attending activities off the wing.

I think of almost everyone on C Wing.
I wonder if I did enough.

***

After the report's publication, the Prison Reform Trust described Wormwood Scrubs as a place of 'Dickensian squalor'.

The only thing more depressing than reading about that squalor is living and working in it. Walking into it every day. Walking past those broken windows, and running past that rats' nest on the way to another alarm bell. Sitting in the office and listening as yet another prisoner asks for a cell move because they don't feel safe, or a wing move, or a transfer out of the prison altogether, and knowing that these requests take time and paperwork and negotiation, and that, even then, I can't guarantee a prisoner's safety. There's too much in the way. The phones and drugs and weapons and gangs and bullying. I can't guarantee anyone's safety.

I can't guarantee my own.

There are so many prisoners I've met whose lives are swallowed by statistics like the ones raised in that report. Prisoners whose lives revolve around drugs, whether taking them or selling them; prisoners living in filthy cells with holes in the windows and rats running around outside; prisoners who spend all day, every day in there and don't attend any activities; prisoners who self-harm or fight or both. I will remember some of these men well, but there are many more I will forget. They become nameless and faceless. They are lost in this place and in the prison system as a whole.

It isn't just the prisoners. For some reason, I don't allow myself to consider just how appalling the conditions I'm working in really are. I've told myself this is just what local jails are like, even though I know better, even though I've had the privilege of working in a place like Whitemoor. With my former colleagues, I don't talk too much about what Scrubs is like, because I know how it sounds. Eight or nine alarm bells a day? Only thirteen per cent attending activities? Less than two hours out of cells a day? If you come from somewhere like Whitemoor, that stuff is hard to believe. It sounds too far-fetched. But the Inspectorate's report puts it in black and white. Because this is real. This is how we are treating prisoners.

And then we wonder why the streets we release them on to are the same streets we hear about in the news, the same streets where people are shot and stabbed and beaten and robbed.

Although there is little mention of it in the report, the impact of these conditions is felt by the officers too. Of course it is. How could it not?

The constant exposure to violence, both interpersonal and self-harm, and the state of hypervigilance that is integral to surviving in these environments, is a heavy burden to shoulder. No one comes out unscathed. It's an old cliché to say that you need to be looked after in order to look after others, but it's one that is exemplified by the officers I work with at Scrubs. So many are fighting demons of their own, demons that the job has awakened, demons that their batons can't touch, that no cuffs can restrain, no planned removal can get rid of.

With all this in mind, I'm starting to wonder how productive it's really possible to be as senior officer of a wing like C Wing. It's a positive distraction throwing myself into the prep for the TCM interview, and it's a relief when I hear I've got the job.

14

Visits

A PRISONER FROM A Wing can't be booked on to the same visiting session as a prisoner from C Wing, because one is on remand for killing the other's mother. Gang-related.

A prisoner from D Wing can't be on the same session as someone from B Wing. They're co-defendants, in for exactly the same offence, but one got off with a drastically reduced sentence. So the other thinks he's a grass.

A C Wing prisoner can't be on the same session as a prisoner in Healthcare, because one has recently started dating the other's ex. And she's the visitor.

A prisoner from the IDTS landing is due to have a visit with a woman in her fifties, but intelligence suggests they've never actually met. Police intel shows she has a history of drug use herself, and has been visiting various men in prisons across the country. Under numerous aliases. Almost definitely a drugs carrier. She wants a visit on Wednesday, but that's our busiest day. It needs to be a quiet session, really, so the staff can watch her closely.

The logistics of the Visits department can be hard work. Theoretically, working in the Visits department should be like a holiday compared to C Wing. I certainly have more time. And my office is nicer, too. No mice. I even get myself a posh coffee machine. Most of the time, working in Visits is a good job to have.

Visits are championed within the Prison Service as being of vital importance to supporting a prisoner's rehabilitation. They provide an invaluable opportunity for the men to maintain family ties and stay connected with the outside world. And I see many instances where that seems to be the case. The majority of prisoners make the most of the time they have in the visits hall, the length of which is dependent on their behaviour. Prisoners on Basic, for example, are not entitled to as many visits as those on Enhanced, and those they do get are shorter. But even for those who don't get to spend much time in the visits hall – or perhaps especially for those men – it can be an emotional place. Those few hours a week are the lifeline they hold on to. There are bars on the windows, the tables and chairs they sit at are bolted to the floor, there are big red alarm bells on the walls and staff patrolling the hall, but there's also their elderly mum, dressed immaculately and clutching some weak coffee and snacks for the two of them to share. Or their wife, who has taken time off work and three trains to get here, and has dressed their twin toddler sons in matching suits so they'll look smart to see Daddy. Or friends, who clap them on the back and fill the room with energy and laughter. Or social workers, who aren't even meant to be here, who have come in on their day off to see how they're doing. Or nervous-looking men from local businesses who have received their CV and would like to discuss an apprenticeship with them. Even old schoolteachers, who saw their mugshots in the paper and just want to sit with them for a bit, to remind them of everything they are capable of. There are so many of these wonderful people, and there are moments when the two worlds collide, and the bars and bolts and neon bibs that prisoners have to wear all fade away, and they get a glimpse of the outside again.

The visits hall is an environment created by a collision of worlds: the world inside the prison walls, and the world outside as it is today. Despite the fact I spend my working days here, it's not a life I am part of. These are people and lives that I could never understand – and I don't even try to. I find it impossible to fathom. I see women passionately kissing their sons in order to transfer the drugs via their mouths. I see women who stroll into the visits hall carrying their newborn babies in designer outfits, their nappies stuffed with Class A drugs. It's through a combination of their carelessness, our good fortune and the expertise of the sniffer dogs that this particular method of getting contraband into the prison is exposed.

And it sickens me. All of it. The terror on children's faces as men around them brawl; the indifference on the faces of others who are used to it; the wearied resignation of women ordered to pick up juice cartons that their partners have just flicked on to the floor.

The overwhelming majority of prisoners are not like this. Many of them have done terrible things to end up in Scrubs, but there's context to that, and they're still bound by many of the same morals recognisable to most of us. They adore their children, they love their wives and girlfriends, and that's what keeps them going when their cell doors close at night. But it's the others, the ones who *are* like this, who take up so much of my time. I'm becoming resentful.

In a place where time is everything, I'm becoming bitter about how much of mine I seem to be wasting.

***

In my new role, I write policy documents, respond to prisoner complaints and oversee sick leave or HR queries for the staff under my supervision. I spend a lot of time in my office at the computer or on the phone. There are little wins, like the time when a visitor comes in with a block of cannabis resin the size of a brick strapped to his ankle. I don't know how he ever thought it would get missed in a search – and judging from the look on his face, I'm not sure he did either. The next time I see him, he's on A Wing, remanded for possession with intent to supply. In general, though, I find the work boring and repetitive.

I don't miss the chaos of C Wing, but I do miss the satisfaction I got from a decent conversation with someone who needed it. It's hard to find that kind of fulfilment from adjusting typos in yet another document about the 'Safe Systems of Work'. Though that stuff is undeniably important, I'm becoming disillusioned with the idea that the safety written about in endless policies ever translates to the wings at all.

Governor Olive and I are in my office together when an alarm bell sounds on A Wing. It's been a busy week there. A package was seen being reeled into a cell window a couple of days ago, and since then the incidents have been non-stop. Drugs and phones. So we run.

It's raining outside and I regret not putting my fleece on. I turn up my radio to make sure I don't miss a second alarm. About ten seconds later, I hear an officer scream over the radio: 'ALL AVAILABLE, ALL AVAILABLE.'

We run side by side through bloated puddles and rivulets of mud, past the empty laundry building and an unused workshop and a dead rat at the bottom of a drainpipe. The splash from the puddles soaks the bottoms of our trousers. We're both drenched when we get to A Wing.

As soon as we get inside, it's clear that things are out of control. A group of prisoners stand with their backs to the wall to let us through. The floor of the ones landing is peppered with cartons of juice and ripped paper that prisoners from the upper landings are raining down. A team of officers are restraining a prisoner in front of us, accompanied by a chant of 'Fuck the screws' coming from somewhere. The prisoner is covered in blood, and I can see a gaping cut exposing pink flesh on his cheek. He's been slashed. That's the initial reason for an officer pressing the alarm bell, but things have escalated quickly.

Prisoners on the upper landings are refusing to bang up. Governor Olive and I split; he takes the threes and I take the fours. Most of the prisoners return to their cells as soon as more staff arrive. Most walk in, but some stumble, the high from spice evident in the way they bang into the door frames on the way. When I reach the end of the fours landing, the A Wing dungeons, I come across two young prisoners, both probably in their early twenties, standing outside their cell. The shorter of the two nods and goes in when I ask. But the taller prisoner doesn't move. He stares at me. Immediately I can feel that something is wrong, and I know I've made a mistake coming to this part of the wing on my own.

I ask him to go back into his cell. He says nothing, but his eyes stay fixed on me. I slip my keys into my pocket so my hands are free. I could call for more staff, but I run the risk of not being heard among this din, and just inflaming the situation further. And I'm not even sure what the situation is.

'Is there a problem?' I say.

'Do you remember me, Miss South?' he asks.

I don't remember him. I wish I did, so I would have something, anything, to grab on to. Something to try to steer this moment, and me, back to safety. But I don't remember him, and I don't know what's going on.

His cellmate comes out. 'Leave it, Grover. Come back inside.'

Grover stares at me for a few more seconds. The air between us is charged with something. Rage. Hate. And then he walks into his cell. As I put my key in the lock, he grabs the TV and launches it at the door. The obs panel smashes. He screams at me. He calls me a cunt and a bitch and tells me to open the door so he can smash my fucking head in.

His cellmate sits quietly on the bottom bunk, muttering pointlessly, 'Leave it.'

**

A few days after this, I return to the wing to give Grover his nicking paperwork. I'd made a note of his cell location and found out who he was. Grover is twenty-four, his leg full of pins from a motorcycle accident. He's a short-term prisoner, but has experience of all the London local jails. He's a domestic violence perpetrator, on both his partner and young son. His current offence is for GBH on a male, suspected to be over a drugs dispute. It takes a while before I realise what my connection to him is. I'd rejected his application for a Family Day visit. He'd put a complaint in writing, and I'd rejected that, too.

Family Day visits are popular, and rightly so. They're a wonderful thing to be part of. Prisoners are allowed to have their partner and children visit for an entire morning or afternoon, and many of the strict rules that usually apply in the visits hall are relaxed. The prisoners are allowed to leave their seats, to explore the room with their children, and do arts and crafts activities set up by volunteers from local nurseries. These visits don't take place in the visits hall, either. Instead, they're held in a downstairs room with colourful paintings of Disney scenes on the walls, along with baskets of toys and books and crayons. There are still bars on the windows, but it's more soft play than prison.

But relaxing the rules also means providing a greater opportunity to smuggle drugs into the prison, and so the security criteria for allowing prisoners to take part in Family Day visits are stringent. A recent history of drug abuse will exclude a prisoner from Family Days, as will any serious violence in the last twenty-eight days. My reason for rejecting Grover is more specific than that, though. During his last visit with his girlfriend, he threatened to assault her in front of everyone and tipped a bottle of water over her head. To put him in a room with less security, and in such close proximity to so many young children, is too much of a risk. So, I said no. Twice.

Despite that, though, I'm surprised by his reaction. It's rare that I'm spoken to in that way by prisoners, even as a senior officer who often had to enforce less-than-popular rules. Being a custodial manager gives me more authority, but it also cuts me short in a lot of ways. It distances me from the very people that I have authority over. I'm stuck in that tiny office so much, and the prisoners I see in the visits hall change every day, so there's little chance to develop relationships. I was lucky that Grover's cellmate stepped in, but I didn't know him, either. He didn't do it because it was me.

I ask the staff on A Wing if Grover is locked up, and they tell me he is. I'm relieved. I walk up the steps to the fours landing, his notice of adjudication in my hand.

When I reach the fours landing, Grover is right in front of me. He wasn't locked up. A Wing has a lot of new officers, and maybe they weren't sure who I was referring to. But here I am again, isolated on the top landing with a man who hates me. And this time, I am very much alone. There's no all-available alarm bell ringing. There are no extra staff bursting through the gates.

'You've come to nick me, haven't you?' he says, motioning to the paper in my hand. His name is printed on the front in block lettering.

I can't really pretend otherwise. 'Yes. Were you expecting it?'

'I thought you would, yeah. It was a bad day, miss. You just rejected my application and didn't even come to see me to explain why.'

He's right. I should have come to talk about the complaint in person. But I'm so busy: busy with paperwork that feels endless and pointless and counterproductive; busy with filling in sick-leave records and calling yet another officer who's gone off sick because they're stressed and exhausted and depressed; busy with trying to arrange funding for a new tuck shop in the visits hall, because everyone is tired of sweaty ham sandwiches; busy responding to yet another alarm bell. And I'm tired: tired of trying to be in my office to get all this done, while somehow also being in the visits hall to support the staff; tired of trying to somehow find the time to fill in police witness statements for drugs found in nappies and SIM cards found in elaborate hair-styles and phones found in places no one wants to find them.

I'm so busy. I'm so stressed. I'm exhausted. I can't keep doing this. And I can't tell Grover any of it. I very much doubt he cares. He sees only his situation, his problems. The Grover in front of me today is different. He isn't happy with me, but it doesn't look like he wants to rip my throat out, either. I hand him the nicking and he accepts it. Before I go, I ask him, 'What do you think would have happened if that door had been open, Grover?'

He rests one arm on the railing and looks down. He shrugs. 'I don't know, Miss. I don't know.'

But I think he does know.

We both know.

**

That night, I dream that I'm standing in the chapel at Wormwood Scrubs. But as is the way in dreams, the chapel is in a completely different position. It's moved from its normal location just opposite the gatehouse and now stands in the centre of the green, one side facing C Wing. Inside, it's just as beautiful as it is in reality, with wide arches that sweep round the main hall and murals of saints and apostles and gospel scenes that were painted by prisoners over a hundred years ago. I'm standing in one of the arches. There's no light coming in through the stained-glass windows. The chapel is dark. It must be night.

I look out across the green to C Wing, at the rows and rows of cell windows. I notice that there is a man standing in each cell, looking back at me. I look closer, and see the noose tied round each one's neck. I watch as the first man steps off the table he is standing on – or perhaps it's a chair, I can't tell. His neck snaps. A clean, heavy click as his head falls into his chest.

I see the man in the next window jump. And the next. One by one, they look at me, and one by one, they jump.

Click, click, click.

Batons racking, ribs cracking, necks snapping.

Click, click, click.

**

On the intranet, I see that there's an opening for a senior officer position at HMP Belmarsh in south London. Belmarsh is a high-security prison, like Whitemoor. It's much smaller than Scrubs, and far more modern, too. It was built in 1990, rather than the 1800s. The wings are almost a third of the size of the wings at Scrubs. There's a larger staff, more funding for prisoner activities, more resources, more opportunities. Maybe less stress.

Prisons like Belmarsh and Whitemoor have more money spent on them for good reason. Patrol dogs, dedicated searching teams, ballistic vans, higher staff-to-prisoner ratios: these are all things Category A prisons have that others don't, and they all cost money. But what is the cost to the people inside all the other prisons? The places like Scrubs? The prisoners at Scrubs behave worse because there's little incentive to do otherwise. Staff shortages are so acute that they're not even guaranteed an hour out of their cells per day. The conditions in which they are kept are terrible and, unsurprisingly, their behaviour is much the same. It's inevitable. And yet, these are so often the men who end up serving life sentences in places like Whitemoor. A lifer very rarely has no prior convictions, no previous jail time.

If I were to get the job at Belmarsh, it would mean giving up my promotion. But I'm getting very little pleasure from writing reports that don't go anywhere or do anything, reports that tick a box, but I'm not convinced anyone actually reads. And all of that seems a bit pointless when I run to the fourth 'all available staff' of the week and the wings are complete chaos.

So I go for it, and I get it.

My last day at Scrubs is bittersweet. I'll miss so many of these people. I'm ready to go, but sad all the same. One of the prisoners draws me a picture of the entrance to C Wing, bordered by graffiti that reads, 'Good luck Miss South.' Another writes me a list of cockney phrases and their translations, saying

I'll need it at Belmarsh. I'll miss the camaraderie and friendships, and the sense of history that is everywhere at Scrubs. But there's plenty I won't miss.

I was idealistic when I became a prison officer. I'm not now. I know that Whitemoor is the exception, not the norm. I also know that, despite its many challenges, I've learned a lot at Scrubs. I believe that I'm a better officer because of it. But I've realised that that's not all I want to be. I don't want to take my work home. I don't want it to leak into my everyday life like it does now. My days off, my holidays, my nights.

And for what? So much of the work feels pointless. I could deal with all this if I felt like it was going somewhere, or that I was doing some good, as if there was some change happening. But the men released on Friday come back in on Monday. It's depressing. It's bleak. And all of this is so constantly in my thoughts. As much as I know that this is important, that I should be under no illusion about the reality of the system I work in, I know, too, that my life is becoming too enmeshed with those of the people I meet. Their stories, their traumas, even their deaths, are following me home. It's draining me of the energy and enthusiasm I had when I started this job. But that's the same thing that stops me from quitting altogether. I know prisons can be better. I'm hopeful that Belmarsh will be different.

As I walk out of Scrubs after that final shift, I look to my left and see the section of perimeter wall I leaned against during that strike in the summer. I was so sure of change then. John Howard and Elizabeth Fry watch me as I go. Their faces are carved into the stone pillars, looking out on to the car park and the bike rack and the traffic on Du Cane Road.

They were the most famous penal reformers of their day. I wonder what they would think if they could see inside Scrubs now.

All the ways it's changed, and all the ways it's stayed the same.

PART 3

15

Belmarsh

I MOVE OUT of my house share in East Acton, and find a new one in Brockley, south London, about a forty-minute drive from Belmarsh. My new housemates are three women, also in their twenties: two primary schoolteachers and an assistant at a legal firm, Jess. I click with her straight away. Maybe it's the nature of her work.

It's much quieter here. Everything feels much smaller. You can almost forget you're in London. There's a 1950s-style ballroom at the end of the road, a pub specialising in craft beer and a couple of cafés. I thought I'd miss the convenience of having a massive shopping centre within walking distance, but I don't.

HMP Belmarsh is probably the most famous prison in the country. There are cameras everywhere. The additional security is obvious here. Outside, inside, and even underneath.

A bombproof tunnel runs underground between HMP Belmarsh and Woolwich Crown Court. Prisoners are escorted through the tunnel early every weekday morning, for plea hearings, verdicts and sentencing. Some officers have told stories of seeing a ghostly figure walking ahead of them, a woman wearing a long coat belted at the waist.

The prison itself is situated on the site of the former Royal Arsenal, an old munitions factory. Women who worked there during the First World War were known as 'munitionettes'. They worked long hours in hazardous conditions, freeing up men to join the armed forces. But the hazardous conditions included TNT poisoning, exposure to harmful chemicals and the occasional explosion, and it wasn't uncommon for women to die as a result of their work.

There have been sightings of the same figure in different areas around the jail: in the Healthcare Outpatients Unit, where the corridors curl round past empty offices and unused toilets; occasionally in the chapel; and sometimes in the external passageway between the gym and education department. Dog handlers recount stories of their dogs refusing to walk down that short passageway, or standing stock-still and barking at something no one else can see.

The patrol dogs here are just as intimidating as they were at Whitemoor. But this time round, I find them more reassuring than anything else. I know what prison is like without them. Some mornings, I hear them before I'm even in the jail, as I walk up the tree-lined path beside the Visitors' Centre, that distant chaos of furious barking and tails thudding against metal kennels. The dogs are locked in the kennels while their handlers are searched by waiting OSGs, which happens every morning, every afternoon, every night shift, every single time they or anyone else sets foot in the prison. Everyone, from visitors to officers, to teachers to psychologists to drugs counsellors, is searched as soon as they come in through the gatehouse.

The gatehouse at Belmarsh is different to the one at Scrubs, but then most things are. At Belmarsh, those first few steps you take into the prison feel more welcoming, more organised, even colourful. Everything is painted bright blue. A flat-screen TV fitted to the wall alternates information about visiting times, the current 'culture of change' that the Prison Service are promoting and the new running club that the gym staff have organised. A triangle of square photographs shows the hierarchy of the prison's senior management team in suits and awkward smiles, topped with the governing governor. Bored-looking OSGs sit behind bulletproof glass and hand out temporary IDs to visiting staff: contractors and agency nurses and part-time chaplains. It's been a while since I've seen prison staff looking bored.

I pass through the airlock into the searching area, where queues of officers form beside piles of empty trays waiting to be filled with boots, jewellery, sealed drinks bottles and ID cards. There are no penal reformers carved into eighteenth-century brickwork here, but there are X-ray machines, portals, metal detectors, cages on the windows and cameras on the walls – and that early morning racket of barking that sounds like music to my ears. After the last two years at Scrubs, I know what I prefer.

There's a strange relief in being searched properly again. My ID is checked, my boots are tipped upside down, my bag is scanned and searched by hand. I step through the portal, and then my collar is turned up, my waistband turned in, the cuffs to my trousers lifted, my pockets patted down. Staff searches were rare at Scrubs. Perhaps once every six months. They were almost always an indicator that the security department was homing in on someone, their suspicions about a potentially corrupt member of staff about to be confirmed. And sadly, there were many of those. The lack of security infrastructure at Scrubs paved the way for so much corruption. But here, searching is as much a part of the daily routine as the sound of the dogs barking. Inevitably, contraband still gets in, but the risks are much higher. There are more eyes on you here. More eyes, hands and metal detectors. Scrubs didn't have all these additional security measures because, as a Category B prison, it isn't required to. That's the case for most prisons. Belmarsh is the exception, because, like Whitemoor, Belmarsh is a Category A high-security prison.

I collect my keys and step out into the sterile area. As is the case at any local jail, this time in the morning is busy. Court buses swing round a mini roundabout, their drivers leaning out of the window in stab-proof vests and waiting for the vehicle lock to be opened. The prisoners who aren't taking the tunnel to Woolwich

Crown Court will be travelling in these buses instead. Belmarsh serves a number of south London courts, the most famous being the Central Criminal Court, better known as the Old Bailey.

Only Category A prisoners going to the Old Bailey will be escorted by prison officers. All other prisoners going to court are supervised by staff working for Serco, the company outsourced to provide custody and escorting services for the Prison Service. Serco employees have minimal interaction with prisoners compared to prison staff, so it might seem a bit excessive for them to be wearing stab-proof vests. But escorts are a vulnerable time for prison security, and this includes court transport. While I was at Scrubs, a man was shot dead by police who suspected him of planning to ambush a court van on its way to north London. And shortly before I transfer to Belmarsh, a female Serco officer is killed by the prisoner to whom she was handcuffed.

Staff are darting in between the court buses, criss-crossing the asphalt to different gates and departments. Psychologists in chinos and blouses turn in the direction of Healthcare; a couple of physical education instructors in blue tracksuits head towards the gym; officers in black trousers and white shirts walk past them to the houseblocks. For some reason, the wings are called houseblocks here. I'm not sure why. Although it isn't just the name that's different.

On my way to Houseblock 3, I pass manicured bushes, palm trees, even a pond with a fountain in the middle and fish swimming serenely around it. These are perhaps not the bits you see in the documentaries referencing 'Britain's most notorious jail'. The cameras tend to skip the nice shrubbery and instead zoom in on the twenty-feet-high concrete walls, or the block lettering that reads 'HIGH SECURE UNIT'. But actually, as prisons go, the grounds of Belmarsh are, well, really nice. A lot of it is.

***

Firstly, it's clean. The cell windows have cages, so there's hardly any litter. And no litter means no rats, either. I don't see a single rat in all my time at Belmarsh. And there's greenery everywhere. Flowers and trees and neatly trimmed hedges that break up the concrete buildings and grey pathways that sweep round the sixty-four acres in which Belmarsh is set. The buildings themselves are modern and well maintained, red and brown brickwork with burgundy window frames. Not a smashed window in sight. Even the exercise yards look decent. They're spacious, with exercise equipment installed in the middle, and they're situated far enough back from the perimeter wall to prevent packages being thrown on to them.

The inside isn't bad, either. The wings are small, only 180 men, and divided into three spurs of sixty each. Unlike Scrubs, the exercise yards are separate from the spurs, as are the staff offices and treatment rooms. Little things like this are important; it splits the wings into self-contained areas that are more manageable and easier to secure. There are three landings rather than four, each with clear lines of sight from start to finish. The pool tables on the ones landing are covered with bedsheets each night to keep them clean. Just the fact that there's enough spare bedding to do this blows my mind.

Cameras watch you as you walk the external pathways from the houseblocks to the High Secure Unit to the astroturf; they follow you down the internal corridors to the chapel and education and visits hall. There are cameras pretty much everywhere. And perhaps most significantly, there are officers everywhere, too. Staff cuts haven't hit Belmarsh like they have Scrubs. At least, not yet.

I'm still finding my feet, just as I would be in any new workplace. But already I can feel some of my stress dissipating. When we unlock cells, I don't feel so much like I'm waiting for the first fight to break out. Coming to work doesn't have that feeling of inevitability to it, of pointlessness.

Belmarsh certainly isn't all fountains and fish. It's the only prison I ever go to that has triple cells: a bunk bed and one single, pressed to the walls. Cells feel tiny anyway, but in the summer, when the air is thick with heat and stale body odour and bad breath, and the windows only open a few inches, a three-man cell is not where anyone wants to be.

The prisoner population can be problematic, too. It isn't like other jails, where the prisoners fit into specific categories: lifers, sex offenders, young offenders. Belmarsh is one of very few prisons in the country that both holds high-security status and serves the local courts. This means it takes high-risk Category A prisoners, among whom, more often than not, are organised crime nominals or terrorists, but it also accepts men going in front of a magistrate rather than a jury. (Magistrate courts are for low-level offences, things like driving offences or theft.) Sometimes, the papers will focus on Belmarsh's High Secure Unit, describing the prisoners there as 'Category A', the 'worst of the worst'. But that isn't really true, either. There are Category A prisoners on all four houseblocks, living alongside the men who are in for robbery and minor assaults.

The High Secure Unit holds high-risk Category A prisoners, those men considered to have both the means and motivation to escape, and who have been deemed a high risk to the public should they manage to do so. The unit itself is like a self-contained mini prison. It has its own exercise yard and its own gym, not dissimilar to the Close Supervision Centre at Whitemoor. The men living in the HSU are unquestionably dangerous, but it's also arguably the safest place in the whole jail, with the fewest incidents.

So, Belmarsh isn't exactly how you might imagine the country's most notorious high-security prison to be.

The prison benefits from being staffed by experienced and knowledgeable officers. It offers a full regime, with a wide array of activities available to the prisoners. Admittedly, some of these are less than inspiring; the tea-pack workshop might just be the worst version of 'purposeful activity' I've ever come across. Worse than unpacking CDs at Whitemoor. But there are alternatives. One civilian worker comes in several times a week to run workshops aimed at supporting prisoners who want to safely leave the gangs in which they have become so embedded. He spends time with the men individually, too, and visits them on the houseblocks, talking through their options and mediating between those with conflicts. One prisoner will tell me that it's impossible to put a figure on how many violent incidents this man's efforts have prevented. The education department is open every day, the library is well-stocked, and there are numerous initiatives in which prisoners can engage. Things like business-enterprise courses or personal-development workshops. There are options here. By the time I left Scrubs, it didn't feel like there were any. My faith in the job had all but gone, but now it feels like it's coming back.

So, I'm excited to be here. I'm ready to get back to work, to feel as if there's some point to what I'm doing. I know how good this job can be. But I'm a little uneasy, too. I've spent the last few years in a difficult place. I know that burgundy window frames and posh gardens aren't enough. Neither is a full staff quota. It doesn't matter how many staff you have if they're there for the wrong reasons.

Ultimately, prisons rely on good people – the right people – and the funding and resources to allow them to do their jobs properly. The political rhetoric changes so quickly, and I have no idea which way it's going to go or how that will impact Belmarsh. The people running the Prison Service need to be making smart decisions, not taking away books. Prisoners need time out of their cells; they need support and opportunities, something to do each day. It's not much different for the officers. Prison staff need adequate training, proper mental health provision, to be listened to and heard, to feel like the hours they spend at work mean something. That it's all worthwhile.

I think we all need that. Without it, the palm trees are pointless.

16

Houseblock 3

A HIGH-SECURITY PRISON is probably not the first place you'd think of when wondering where to find love. But being in jail isn't enough to deter Cameron. He's already two years over his IPP tariff, and hasn't got time to waste. When he finally gets out, he wants a fiancée waiting for him. So where better to look than the prison newspaper? *Inside Time* is published once a week, and is available to all prisoners and detainees in the country. It's a good read. The content is mostly prison-related, covering updates on policy changes, inspection reports and case studies of prisoners describing their experiences inside – anything its readers may find interesting or useful. Lots of legal firms use it to advertise their services, and prisoners are also able to make contributions of their own, including letters, short stories and poems.

The centre of the ones landing on Houseblock 3 is where Cameron collects his paper and scans the pages for prospective partners. There's no Lonely Hearts section, so he has to be a bit more industrious than that. Instead, he starts with the poetry pages, where prisoners from establishments all around the country submit their work. He checks the Mailbag page, too, where prisoners write in about everything from how rubbish the food is at HMP Oakwood to the politics behind joint enterprise laws. The prisoner contributions are signed with the name of the writer and the prison they're from: 'Hannah S – HMP Styal', for example.

The papers are stacked in a busy part of the houseblock, the core from which all the four main areas stretch out, one on each side. Spur 1 to the left, Spur 2 in front, Spur 3 to the right, and the First Night Centre behind. The First Night Centre is small, barely even the size of a spur. It holds a few offices for staff to conduct day-one interviews and collate admission information, and a classroom where prisoners sit during the day-two induction talk. The interviews are held almost as soon as prisoners arrive in the FNC, and certainly before they're locked up for the night. Officers will ask about things like previous custodial history, any drug or alcohol abuse and thoughts of self-harm. This information is combined with what's on record to decide what sort of cell that prisoner goes into. The induction talk the following day is a PowerPoint presentation. It covers basic prison safety, things like where the alarm bells are located and what happens if you press one, and explains the regime.

Behind the classroom is a carpeted area with cushioned blue chairs and a TV. Prisoners wait here until it's their turn to be seen, and officers from elsewhere on the houseblock often find a reason to be here if there's a football game on. But most of the time, the FNC is quiet. The men filter in from the reception department a few at a time, and most of them are smart enough to know it's a good idea to observe what the houseblock is like, to see who's on it and where you might fit in, before raising your head too much. The FNC is where you see some of those early-day nerves.

The gates from the FNC open out on to the centre ones landing, where there's always people coming and going, and the general din of the houseblock seems to collect. Prisoners stand at the locked gates of Spur 1 and shout across to those on Spur 3 opposite; prisoners from Spur 2 stare across into the FNC to see if there's anyone they recognise; the cleaners wheel buckets of hot, soapy water across the linoleum; and at mealtimes, the clattering of metal trays and plastic plates signifies it's almost time to start queueing. It's here that prisoners collect their meals from the hotplate, here that they're searched on to the exercise yard, and here where leaflets are piled up on a table in the corner, including pamphlets about Samaritans or details of a new 'Foundations for Change' workshop starting soon – and, of course, the weekly newspaper that Cameron scrutinises in his search for love.

Cameron looks for a writer from a female establishment whose words he identifies with. He doesn't much like prison food either, so it could be that. And if she's also serving an IPP sentence, there's some common ground straight away. He's been inside since he was in his mid-twenties, so he's not perturbed by a violent background or a bad record. In fact, all that really seems to matter to him is something the paper can't tell him – what they look like.

I've been at Belmarsh for about six months when he bursts into my office in a ball of excitement. He's five foot nothing, slim – skinny, even – with a patchy goatee that splits when he smiles, and the loudest voice of everyone on the houseblock. I hear him before I see him. He rushes in waving a piece of paper.

'She replied,' he says.

'Which one?' I ask.

'Gina T from New Hall,' he says.

Prisoners who contribute to the paper often include their unique prison number, so Cameron had had all the details he needed to write to her. He pulls out the chair opposite me, then slides her response across the desk between us. Gina T has neat handwriting. She thanks him for saying nice things about her poem, and tells him a bit about life at New Hall. Cameron and I both agree it sounds better than most male establishments. She works in the hair salon. It's all looking promising, until I get to the bit where she makes a comment about him being six foot two, saying she likes tall men.

'Did you tell her you were six foot two?' I ask, looking at him with a raised eyebrow.

Cameron throws a hand in the air as if that's completely irrelevant. 'Keep reading,' he says, excitedly.

So I do. Gina T tells him about her sentence. She isn't IPP. In fact, she's due out in three months and twenty-two days. And this time, she's going to stay out. If their letter writing goes well, she says, she'll come and see him after she's been released.

'She's going to come all the way here?' I ask.

'Yeah, why wouldn't she?' Cameron grins.

'Do you know where New Hall is, Cameron?'

It's in Yorkshire.

'And what are you going to do about your height...?' I ask.

He waves his hand again like it doesn't matter – and I suppose it doesn't, really. I doubt they'll ever meet, or even that they'll continue writing for much longer, but five years inside is a long time, and Cameron is bored. Gina T probably is, too. It's a distraction.

***

I've been made to feel welcome on Houseblock 3 and at Belmarsh in general. Officer Nesse is one of many officers who have spent their whole prison career at Belmarsh, with no intention of transferring elsewhere. And why would they? The government cuts have not yet had much of an impact on Belmarsh. There's still more than enough staff here. It's still a safe place to work. Still a good job to have.

I'm particularly lucky to have been assigned Houseblock 3. Two experienced custodial managers oversee the running of the houseblock, and they're widely considered to be the best in the jail. Fair, but strict, with a keen focus on discipline. Discipline is important in any prison, in any unit, but perhaps particularly the First Night Centre. This is where a fluid and mixed population can become problematic. Lots of people coming in off the streets on the same night, each with their own issues or needs, and quite possibly conflicts.

An evening shift in the FNC might see a man detoxing from heroin come in alongside another with a serious alcohol addiction. Both will require close monitoring, especially in the first twenty-four hours. They'll need to be located in cells that have drop-down hatches in the doors rather than standard observation panels, so that nurses can easily pass them medication during the night. Staff will be regularly updating the system and checking Police National Database records to see who they're expecting, and what types of cells are available for them.

Next to be brought to the FNC could be men whose faces are plastered over the evening news, defendants in a high-profile case that's fast catching the attention of other prisoners.

Shortly after that, a group of prisoners from HMP Swaleside might come in, surly and pissed off at being forced to leave a jail where they've become comfortable. Next might be a prisoner on remand for serious domestic violence offences.

So, the FNC is busy. There's a lot going on. Working there involves careful organisation and liaison with other departments. It's certainly not the place you'd want lazy staff to be working. Fortunately, there aren't many of those on House-block 3.

Officer Nesse, Cameron and I walk downstairs to the ones. Cameron takes the steps two at a time, still buoyed by the letter and his budding relationship. I hear him telling another prisoner about Gina T as soon as he disappears on to Spur 2. Spur 2 is the IDTS spur and holds mainly drug users. That's why Cameron is located there. His index offence wasn't drug related, and he swears blind that he never touched the stuff before coming into jail, but there are lots of prisoners who form drug habits once they're inside. Now he takes methadone twice a day to try to break his heroin habit. Even for a prisoner who's never touched drugs before, the boredom and stress of this environment can make that first time much more tempting. Belmarsh isn't immune to this. Admittedly, it's much more difficult to get drugs into Belmarsh than other local jails, but there are still ways.

Officer Nesse and I stand outside the gates to Spur 1, putting on blue gloves in preparation for searching prisoners as they go out on to the yard.

'How many ACCT reviews have we got today?' he asks.

As with many of the officers on Houseblock 3, Officer Nesse has an area in which he specialises. He's an ACCT assessor, meaning he conducts initial interviews with prisoners who may be at risk of suicide or self-harm. These interviews can be difficult. They involve asking tough questions, things like, 'If you're thinking of killing yourself, have you made a plan? How would you do it?'

You'd be surprised at how honest many of the prisoners are. They'll share not just that they plan to hang themselves, but what they intend to use. Shoelaces, belts, even a turban. They won't just say that they want to set their cell on fire and die from smoke inhalation, they'll explain that they're stockpiling paper to burn and are planning to ignite it at night when there are fewer staff to respond. They won't just admit that they've been hoarding all their meds in preparation for an overdose, but that they're keeping note of when their cellmate is on a visit so they can take them at the best time.

It's up to officers like Officer Nesse to listen to this and assess the immediate risk that a prisoner poses to himself, and what can be put in place to protect him. These assessments are then followed by a review with the senior officer. All ACCT reviews should ideally be conducted with both an officer and a nurse present, as well as the senior officer chairing the review. This was rarely possible at Scrubs. Input from a nurse would be provided over the phone, if at all, and there were never enough officers to have one sit in on a review. But on Houseblock 3, these guidelines are taken very seriously. Officer Nesse sits in on almost all of my ACCT reviews. And I'm glad of it. We work well together. Not only that, but sometimes the things you hear during those reviews can be difficult to stomach. Having someone else in there with you eases that a bit.

Last week, we worked together on a review for a man in his early twenties who had been banned from travelling on public transport in London. Dean had been convicted of repeatedly exposing himself to women in isolated train carriages or on empty bus decks. There are many sex offenders unwilling to admit to their offence, but there are some, like him, prepared to discuss it. He admitted that his actions were about power and the gratification he got from seeing the fear on a woman's face when she realised she was alone and cornered. He admitted, too, that once the act was done, when he was home and alone, he felt overpowering shame and self-hatred. And now, in prison, he was struggling to cope with the reality of what he'd done and what kind of a person that made him.

The review was uncomfortable. Often these meetings can feel a bit like going through the motions. It's not uncommon for prisoners to make threats of self-harm if they're not given some tobacco, or moved to another houseblock, as an attempt to manipulate the system. But then there are reviews like these, where every question takes you into uncharted territory and the complexity of the person in front of you is laid bare. We'd gently invited Dean to talk about his fears, about what his crimes said about him as a person, and how that translated into such revulsion at himself. But as he carried on talking, openly discussing the issue, alarm bells started ringing in my head. His candidness might have appeared commendable, but the more he spoke, the more apparent it became that he lacked any real self-control, and the severity of his potential risk to women became clear. As I sat across from him, me in my uniform, him in his grey prison tracksuit, I imagined for a moment how it would feel if the situation was different. If I was sitting in an empty train carriage; if he was standing opposite me in the long coat he says he wears when he does what he does. If the power dynamic was reversed. For all his cries of remorse and self-loathing, I could see clearly just how dangerous this man was.

The trajectory of a sex offender often starts with lower-level sex crimes, such as indecent exposure, and over time can graduate to more serious offences, like rape. We'd asked Dean if his fears extended to this. That he might be capable of rape.

He'd replied, 'I've done some really terrible things.'

I've been in the Prison Service a while now, and challenging conversations aren't new to me. I've talked with Bolt about grief and what that can sometimes make you do; I've talked with Ben about the things that scare him, and what it's like to have a future as uncertain as his. I've talked with Attwood about religion and violence, how the two can become entangled. I've listened as Tristan told me about how the system makes him feel as if he can't change, as if he isn't allowed to be better, as if he will always be defined by the mistakes he's made. And though I've never worked on a sex offenders wing, I've come across many. And I've had many unpleasant conversations about how there are always two sides to every story, and inevitably theirs is always the truth. I rarely come across sex offenders who are honest about what they've done, or who don't try to minimise it in some way.

In this regard, Dean's ACCT review struck me as unusual. It made me a little cynical, too. It felt very sudden for him to be opening up in this way to an officer he'd just met.

A female officer.

The point of an ACCT review is to figure out how someone's feeling, what's going on in their head, and why that's causing them to want to take their own life. It can involve searching questions and painful answers, but, without that kind of candour and introspection, it's very hard for prison staff to provide appropriate support. We need to know what the problem is if we're going to try to solve it. It can feel strange asking someone such personal questions amidst the background noise of a busy houseblock.

Despite my professional exterior and the requirements of this uniform, despite my understanding of trauma and abuse and the shadows that hide in people's pasts, and the help they might need to overcome those, despite all of it, during this particular review, as a young woman who often takes public transport myself, the person sitting across from me was not someone I really felt like supporting.

Although Dean didn't make any requests for tobacco or a houseblock move, there was still a sense of manipulation about that review. Just a different version of manipulation. Maybe he gained some kind of gratification from saying those things to a female officer, and maybe the thoughts playing out in his head were very different from the words coming out of his mouth.

Truth be told, the words in my head were different to the words I spoke, too. I wrote the support plan and set up the referrals, but I wondered if I was just going through the motions. There has to be an element of self-protection in prison, and I don't just mean for the prisoners. Nor do I mean protection from the fights or hangings, those physical acts you see in front of you. I mean the kind of vicarious trauma you take on by hearing about it from others. There isn't much in the way of proper support systems for staff who may be experiencing this kind of thing, and what is available certainly isn't sufficient.

Now, standing by the gates with Officer Nesse, I have yet to really recognise this change in my attitude. I think I've just become hardened to certain things, especially when working with sex offenders. I see the prisoner in front of me and hear the things he's saying, but I don't really absorb any of it. I'll keep taking the train, and going on the top deck of the bus, and I won't worry.

'No reviews today,' I say, unlocking the gate.

***

On Houseblock 3, we're trialling a new piece of security equipment: the pole. I'm not sure what it's actually called, but both staff and prisoners only ever refer to it as 'the pole'. It's a freestanding metal cylinder, about two metres high, that flashes red if it detects metal or green if it doesn't. It's being trialled in place of the handheld metal detectors, which are starting to look pretty old now. For the pole to work, all someone has to do is walk past it.

It's just before 9am, and time for exercise. All the houseblocks alternate their regime from day to day. Work in the morning, exercise and association for all three spurs in the afternoon. Or vice versa. Today, on Houseblock 3, work is in the afternoon. The weather outside is crisp and sunny, not a cloud in the sky. I know, because I've been on the yard already to check. Any rain, even just a drizzle, and exercise would be cancelled. But it's clear, and the pole is being manoeuvred into position outside Spur 1.

An officer stands poised on each landing, waiting for the call to unlock for exercise. I'm joined by Officer Nesse and then Officer Barton, whose area of expertise is the FNC. He put together the PowerPoint presentation that the prisoners watch during induction. More often than not, he can be found in the main office opposite the classroom, rifling through prisoners' charge sheets and checking they're OK to share a cell. At other times, he'll be on the phone, negotiating with staff from another houseblock, explaining why they need to take a certain prisoner from us because we have no single cells left and the man in question has a history of same-sex attacks. There's not much about prison induction or cell-sharing protocol that he doesn't know. He could easily spend all day in that office; there's definitely enough work. But he always comes out to help search the prisoners on to the yard.

'Unlock Spur 1,' I call.

The prisoners emerge from their cells. Some are still wearing pyjamas or dressing gowns as they step into their doorways, holding plastic mugs of coffee and weighing up whether they should go out on the yard or back to bed. Others have been up for hours already, and dart on to the landings with their blue plastic bins, keen to empty the leftovers from last night's food into the industrial-sized black bins on the landings.

The top landing of Spur 1 is predominantly cleaners: Nashef cleans the showers and was once one of Britain's most wanted men; Frake cleans the staffroom and was a diamond dealer who staged a multi-million-pound robbery to claim the insurance; Lewis is the painter and helped his terminally ill grandmother kill herself because she didn't have the money to get to Dignitas. These men are already out, sweeping and cleaning and, in Lewis's case, counting how many tins of paint we have left. The CMs want the whole houseblock freshly painted by the end of this month.

It's just the top landing that houses the cleaners. The other two landings of Spur 1 are a mix of prisoners, different ages and offences and backgrounds. At the moment, we've got one of the prisoners involved in the Swaleside riot, a few young offenders on remand for a stabbing outside a youth court, another who recently transferred in from Broadmoor and loves bumblebees, and another whose name is Douglas but who, after losing part of his ear in a particularly nasty fight last month, has been renamed 'Lugless'. And Adrian, a particularly large prisoner with a fearsome reputation.

Adrian is located on the ones, single cell, because he's Category A. Category A prisoners can't share cells. His sentence is life, his tariff is twenty-eight years, his offence is money, mur-

der, two lives lost. I actually know a couple of his co-defendants from Whitemoor. Ordinarily, that's where Adrian would
be, at one of the dispersals. But one of the things that makes
him so feared is the same thing that's left him with a price on
his head and a target on his chest. He's staunch, uncompro-
mising, resolute. He won't do something just because everyone
else does. He won't follow the crowd; he won't change religion
just because you tell him to. That attitude is what's marked him
out. It isn't just prison officers who rely on compliance – the
self-imposed hierarchy among prisoners does, too. To break out
of that and refuse to be whatever someone considered more
senior than you demands can be a dangerous thing. It has been
in Adrian's case. He's no longer safe in dispersals. So he's here, on
the ground floor of Spur 1.

He joins the queue of prisoners lining up to circle the pole.
It flashes green for the first prisoner, green for the next, green
again. Then it's Adrian's turn to walk past, and the officers and I
hold our breath for a moment. Still green. The security department are certain that Adrian is in possession of a phone, but
they can't find it. They've turned his cell upside down multiple
times looking for it, bursting through the door during lunchbreaks, lock-up, the middle of the night. Each time, Adrian
seems to be expecting them. He never seems surprised; he
never seems nervous. He's never been found with anything. It's
highly unlikely he would be foolish enough to walk past the
pole with a mobile phone, but still we hope. Officer Barton
rubs him down and he heads out on to the exercise yard.

The officers on Spur 1 lock the cell doors of any prisoners
who chose not to come out for exercise, and then move on
to Spur 2. The pole is wheeled to the gates and we repeat the
same process.

One by one, prisoners come off the spur. Bakari, who has a
thing for white bread and asks for extra slices at every single meal.
Lennard, a repeat offender who can't seem to stop beating up his

girlfriend. Rahim, a heroin addict with a dodgy leg who used a crutch until we realised he was storing spice in the handle. Clancy, twenty years old, covered in self-harm scars and always one of the first out for exercise, just in case there's an old cigarette butt on the ground he can get his hands on. The pole flashes green, green, green for all of them.

Finally, Spur 3. The defendant in the Hatton Garden robbery starts making his way towards us, but changes his mind halfway and goes back to his cell, grumbling about the cold. A lifer who removed his victim's penis before killing him is the first one out. Then a young offender on trial for murder, whose cell is full of soft drinks, chocolate and crisps; his teeth are rotting and his cheeks are swollen with abscesses from poor hygiene. Next is the prisoner recently charged with the murder of an inmate at another jail. His trial at the Old Bailey starts any day now.

Green, green, green. The pole doesn't catch anything today.

***

Adrian walks slowly around the yard with another lifer. His head is bowed and his hands are clasped together behind his back. He's normally animated and talkative with staff, but today he doesn't even look up as he passes the corner of the yard where the officers stand. When the hour is up, I call the prisoners back in, spur by spur.

Most of them are keen to come in. It's cold out today, and they want to make sure they get a spot in the phone queue. Association starts as soon as they return to their spurs. The prisoners who decided not to come out for exercise are unlocked when those who did go on the yard come back in, and association begins straight away. Many of the prisoners are already lingering by the gates, keen to get back inside and make the most of their time out of cell. Adrian isn't, though. I call for the Spur 1 prisoners, and his friend leaves his side and heads to the gates. Adrian stays walking. Lonely laps around the yard.

'Come on, Adrian,' I shout, thinking he must not have heard.

The Spur 1 prisoners file past me. I call in Spur 2. Only six went out in the first place, so it doesn't take long. Adrian keeps walking.

'Adrian, inside please,' I shout again.

His head stays bowed.

Officer Nesse is beside me. He raises an eyebrow. 'What's going on there, then?' he says. 'This isn't like him.'

'No,' I agree. 'It isn't. Let's get the rest in first.' I say 'first' because I want the yard to be clear before deciding the right course of action. If a prisoner refuses to come in, the officers have two main options: negotiation or force. Ultimately, it's my call. The regime at Belmarsh is much better than it was at Scrubs, but it's still tight. It still runs to the minute. I need Adrian inside. If I do decide to restrain him, that would require a minimum of two officers to help me. Given Adrian's considerable size and strength, I'd want three. But three is also the number of officers it takes to open a spur for association. So if Adrian wants to fight, then sixty men miss out on association. And association isn't just about associating; it's phone calls and showers, too. I wait until the last prisoner has walked past me. Or almost the last. Adrian is still walking laps.

'Adrian,' I say, taking a few steps in his direction.

'I'm coming,' he snaps at me.

And he does. He's certainly not in a hurry, but step by step he walks back towards the gates, and moves past me into the corridor that leads to the centre ones, and back on to Spur 1. He walks in as if it was the first time I'd asked, as if he was always going to, as if it's nothing.

But I know that things like that, from people like him, are rarely nothing. To speak to staff in that way is out of character for Adrian. To ignore repeated requests to come in off the yard is as well. And none of the obvious explanations fit. He hasn't had an argument with an officer, he hasn't been refused something like permission to go to the gym or a place on a course, he hasn't had a visit cancelled, he hasn't been told to move cells, he isn't ill. But something's happened. To ignore it would be foolish. Paying attention to it is jailcraft. Moments like these are the ones that ring alarm bells in prison officers' heads; not the sort of alarms that make the lights flash, but often just as serious.

One of the great luxuries I have at Belmarsh is time. The alarm bell doesn't go every day, like it did on C Wing at Scrubs. So, when the prisoners have all returned to their spurs for association, I ask Adrian for a chat.

We walk up the stairs from the bottom landing to the middle, me in front and Adrian following. We pass the bubble, a small office with glass panels that looks out on to all three spurs. This is where the designated 'bubble officer' of the day ticks prisoners on and off the wing, collates numbers, and fields queries from prisoners shouting at the spur gates. Things like, 'Am I on education today, miss?' or 'Have I got a visit this afternoon? Who's coming?' It's just like the box office at Scrubs.

I poke my head through the doorway and let the officer inside know I've taken Adrian off his spur. Adrian follows, but says nothing.

***

Adrian and I sit opposite each other in my office. I keep the door slightly open.

We sit in silence for a moment. Something's wrong. He doesn't look himself. He looks pissed off and fed up and upset. So I ask him if he's OK.

And just like that, it all pours out of him. The weight of being who he is. The pressure of being the one everyone is scared of, when he's scared too. The constant fear of having to watch your back, the messages that filter in from prisoners in other high-security jails, warning him. The stress of knowing it's coming, but not knowing when. He tells me he knows why we watch the pole so closely when he's walking round it; he knows we think he's got a phone and that's the metal we're after, but he says we're focusing on the wrong kind. He's the biggest man on this houseblock, he's all muscles and brawn and sheer size, but none of that matters if the person coming after him has a shank. And he says they do, they will. At home, he was the man of the house. In prison, he's the main man on the houseblock. But inside, he's scared. And tired.

He has a young son. The implications of his crime are far-reaching. If his enemies can't get him, they'll get his family. So they're moving house, again. Moving school, again. He isn't the man of the house anymore. He isn't even in the house. He's let them down. It was all for nothing.

And it's then that I realise – because it's suddenly so obvious – that if security are right and he does have a phone, he isn't using it to intimidate witnesses or organise outside crime. He's using it to call his little boy.

***

Otis is fresh off the bus from the Old Bailey. He's wearing a grey suit and smart shoes. His blond hair is swept to the side.

I knew he was coming. The staff in the FNC phoned me in my office upstairs to let me know. He's just been found guilty of manslaughter. First time in. His whole life derailed in one night. Sometimes, these prisoners are referred to as 'poor copers'. They're the kind of men who inadvertently send out signals to others that they're vulnerable, that this environment is new to them and they don't yet know how to navigate it. More crudely, they're sometimes described as having 'victim written all over their face'. The point is the same. Belmarsh will swallow them up if they aren't supported.

Despite the many positive attributes I found at Belmarsh when I joined, it has always been a challenging place to be. Some of the prisoners here are unspeakably cruel, just as the papers say. Some of the things you hear about – the incidents that take place here and the people who perpetrate them, the mugshots that stare back at you and the helicopter footage of famous inmates being driven from the Old Bailey to the jail, the way the media describes life inside HMP Belmarsh – some of that is true.

I've talked favourably about the well-kept grounds and plentiful regime, and all that is true as well. Staff and prisoners are better able to manage the difficult incidents because the infrastructure in place enables them to do so. But no prisoner wants to be here. When the media says it's a holiday camp, that's the bit that isn't true. It's regimented and restrictive; this is prison. Everything is controlled. Your every move is monitored. You go to the shower when you're told. You wear the shoes you're told to wear. You use the phone when you're told you're allowed to. You stay locked in a room. All of that, against the ever-present backdrop of violence.

And over the last year, the cracks have started to show. The impact of staff cuts and benchmarking has finally found its way to the high-security estate.

Association no longer means all three spurs out at the same time. At first, it went to two spurs in the morning and one in the afternoon, or vice versa. But then staffing dropped further, and there were only enough officers for one spur out per day. The other SOs and I have drawn up a rota and, when prisoners walk past the bubble, that's what they ask about.

'Are we out today, guv?' rather than, 'Am I down workshops today?'

Because the workshops are closing as well. Classroom sizes are reducing, the library is only open on certain days. Even the gym is struggling. Less time out on the astro, and fewer prisoners when they do go.

No staff, no staff, no staff. It's all I hear. And as the staffing becomes less, the violence becomes more and the alarm bells do too. I didn't hear any of this at Whitemoor. There were always enough officers. We were clamouring for overtime. Now, the jail pretty much runs on overtime. Part of me wishes I could go back to then. More staff, more funding, more everything. I was happier. I was safer. We all were. But this is the Prison Service now. It's not a great time to be an officer.

And it's an even worse time to be a prisoner.

When I sit opposite Otis in my office, in his grey suit and nice shoes and red eyes, this is what he's facing. Everything about this place is uncertain, except for the fact that you can't leave.

Officer Barton has escorted Otis to my office. The printer is whirring as it spits out the latest incident report. A few prisoners are coming up, one at a time, to collect their evening medication, but other than that it's quiet. I say hello; Otis nods but doesn't speak. Officer Barton leaves.

Otis sits there. I find it hard to look at him. His knees are shaking and his bottom lip is wobbling, and I don't know what I can do. Maybe it's just the run of bad days we've been having recently, alarm after alarm after alarm, but I'm starting to feel like I'm not much use to the prisoners who actually need it.

What can I say? There's nothing I can do that will change his situation. He's twenty-two, a university graduate. He's never been in trouble with the police before, then, on one night out, something went horribly wrong, a punch was thrown and someone is dead. Now he's in a high-security prison, his hands are trembling, and I can tell he's just waiting for the click of the door so he knows it's closed. Then he can cry.

I look down at my desk, the surface dirtied with coffee stains, chewed biros and hastily scrawled notes on torn printer paper. The door finally clicks.

'How are you doing?' I ask.

He says he's struggling.

He says he didn't think this would happen. This wasn't supposed to happen. None of it. He says that when his cell door closed at 6pm yesterday, he asked when he would be unlocked, and the officer said, 'Not till the morning now.' And he can't get his head round that. What is he supposed to do? What is he supposed to do from 6pm until 7am the next day?

No one's ever asked me that before. In all the years I've been doing this, no one has ever asked me what to do behind closed doors. I don't know what the answer is.

He says he made himself a hot drink and then just sat and looked out the window. In that moment, he tells me, he knew he couldn't do it. He wouldn't survive this.

He says he doesn't know how people get through long sentences, like the one that has just enveloped him entirely. He asks me, 'How do they cope?'

I tell him honestly: there are lots of ways that people cope. Some use violence and anger to get through it; their fists are their language. Others become driven by the need to survive: extra courses, heavier weights, more miles on the treadmill. Others steady themselves in denial or escape into the ugly comfort of drugs. Some create entirely new worlds for themselves in their minds that inevitably lead to a stint in Healthcare, or maybe Broadmoor. And some don't cope. They kill themselves.

I don't say the last bit. Actually, I don't say the last few bits, because I can't see that helping. Especially as it's not just 'some' anymore, it's a lot.

So, what do I say? I say that he's going to have to get used to prison, because that's the truth. Last week, we had a slashing, a three-on-one assault that turned into an 'all available staff' with three officers injured and a nasty weapon recovered. It still had some of the victim's beard in between the razor blades. I wish I could tell him that this sort of thing is rare, an isolated incident that he doesn't need to worry about, but that's not the case. These incidents aren't infrequent like they used to be – but then, prisoners used to spend a considerable amount of time out of their cells each day. Everyone went on the yard; everyone had a shower and a phone call and a conversation. Everyone had a point to their day. Now the days blur into one another, the crude shudder of one shank barely distinguishable from yesterday's, the thunder of boots running to an incident becoming a frequent sound, wailing alarm bells accompanying staff from stabbing to brawl to hostage to hanging to fire to trauma to trauma to trauma.

I tell him to take one day a time. Don't borrow anything and don't lend anything. He should write letters home, and, as soon as his numbers are cleared, he must ring his family – that link to the outside world will be invaluable. And be smart, I tell him. Don't put yourself in vulnerable situations. Not all the prisoners in here are bad; many of them are decent guys who will look out for him and lift him when he feels himself buckling. Take one day at a time.

This is the first time I've worked on a wing with a First Night Centre. I find myself having these kinds of conversations a lot here. I've learned a lot over the last seven years, enough to know that for a lot of prisoners these first few weeks are the worst. The ones that feel insurmountable. But I realise he can't think even that far ahead right now. He needs to take it one day at a time.

And as I say it, as I try to prepare this young man for the strange and unpredictable and frightening world he now lives in, I think maybe I could use that advice myself. Because I'm getting tired. So tired.

Not just of what's happening at Belmarsh, but everything that's happened – at Whitemoor, at Scrubs, and now here, all of it blurring together. I'm tired of being shouted at, threatened, called a 'slut' or a 'slag' – or my personal favourite, a 'dirty sket who sucks dick for cheeseburger' – because I took your TV after you punched someone, or I won't let you on the yard with flip-flops on. I'm tired of feeling like those words barely even register now, so many times have I heard them hurled at female staff. I'm tired of being desensitised to it. Of feeling that this is just how the job is now. I'm tired of knowing that I'm surrounded by spice, of seeing it in the way the prisoners stumble and their empty expressions. I'm tired of putting people in the recovery position because they've taken too much, gently moving their heads away from the cupboard so they stop licking it. I'm tired of restraining people so mentally ill they wash their hair with butter and flood their cells because it reminds them of the 'monsoon in Bangladesh'. I'm tired of putting my hands on someone's wrists while the blood is spurting so high it drips from the ceiling. I'm tired of looking into that man's vacant eyes and asking, 'Why have you done this again, Euan?'

I am tired of then noticing the cuts on Euan's thighs and thinking I don't have enough hands to stem the bleeding.

I'm tired of asking for another shirt because mine has blood on. Again. I'm tired of shouting into my radio, 'I need more staff, batons drawn.' I'm tired of drawing my baton. I'm tired of using my baton. I'm tired of seeing a fist clench and knowing what's coming next. I'm tired of never knowing what's coming next. Of not knowing what I am running towards. I'm tired of going to see the nurse because I got hit with a plug in a sock while trying to break up a fight, or going to A&E because some lost angry eighteen-year-old whose parents failed him has spat in my eye (and then shouted, 'I've got Hep B, miss!'). I'm so tired.

But I can quit at any point. No one is forcing me to be here.

And then Otis comes up to me the next morning with tears in his eyes, and says he doesn't think he would have got through last night without talking to me first, and he promises to try to eat all his food today and get some proper sleep tonight.

It's then that I know I can't quit.

17

The Cells

OTIS DOES SURVIVE. He does cope.

He finds a way through those first few weeks, tumultuous as they are, and starts to settle into life at Belmarsh. He gets a haircut that's a bit more 'prison'. Grade two or three, with a bit of beard. He picks up some of the lingo the other prisoners use. He finds a good group of friends to spend time with.

One of those friends is Attwood. The same Attwood who worked in the kitchen at Whitemoor, who helped me out when a prisoner was giving me trouble on the hotplate, and who makes an excellent coffee cake. He's been transferred here from another dispersal jail, not because of any specific incident, but because lifers are moved about for myriad reasons. They could be transferred in order to complete courses only available at a certain prison, or because the security department are keen to disrupt any negative influence they may have, or even just to give them a change of scenery if they've been in the same place for a while. Often, this is welcomed by a prisoner in the dispersal system. Although those prisons are much better resourced and staffed, there are still some that don't even have toilets in the cells. During the night, the prisoners take it in turns to come out, one at a time, to use the communal toilets.

Some prisons have all single cells, like Whitemoor. Others have doubles and singles, like Scrubs. And at Belmarsh, there's a mixture of single-, double- and triple-occupancy cells, though the multi-occupancy cells are only marginally bigger than the singles.

The basic fabric of the cells doesn't really change from prison to prison. Four walls, a door with a glass observation panel, a barred window and at least one bed. It's how the cells are kept that differs, and that depends on the type of prison you're at, the sentence you're serving and who you're sharing with.

Most of the men I worked with at Whitemoor were lifers, so they treated their cells like a home. They organised their furniture the way they liked it, folded their clothes away neatly, burned incense on the windowsill and left out orange peel to keep the room smelling fresh. Almost all the prisoners had photos of family and friends pinned to their walls. Birthday cards, too, and sometimes drawings of their children that they'd commissioned other prisoners to do for them, copied from their favourite photographs. There were several talented artists on A Wing.

Of course, there were limits to just how homely a prisoner could make their cell. Furniture could be moved about, but never so that it obscured the obs panel or window. And redecorating wasn't an option, either. One man smuggled some black paint from the carpentry workshop back on to the wing and painted his entire cell black, including the ceiling. He spent the next day apologising to the SO and restoring it to its original cream. The generic design and interior of cells is deliberate. It's designed to make things harder to hide and the rooms themselves easy to search. So repainting them or adapting furniture is never going to be permitted. Of course, it's not lost on the officers that, for some prisoners, changes like this are less about hiding contraband and more just an attempt to take back a bit of control in this environment. To make them feel as if they have some ownership over the rooms in which they spend so much of their time. It's one of those things that people perhaps take for granted in their homes outside, a bit of DIY here or rearranging furniture there. A way of making your home a bit more pleasant, of asserting your individuality. But prison doesn't really allow for much individuality. The cells and everything in them are tightly regulated.

I didn't realise it at the time, but the fact that all the cells at Whitemoor were single occupancy made my job considerably easier. I had nothing to compare it to then, but it's obvious, really. If it's only you in a cell, you're far more likely to spend time making that space the way you want it. Particularly if you're serving a life sentence. There were no fights at night, because there were no cellmates to fight with. There were no arguments over the TV or when to switch the lights off.

Transferring to Scrubs was a real culture shock for me. C Wing had a handful of single cells, but not many. And C Wing had a handful of lifers, but not many. Prisoners would often be sharing with someone they didn't know, and cellmates would come and go regularly. A prisoner might be moved to another wing more suited to their needs, or transferred to another jail. They might be granted bail or released due to NFA, 'no further action', when the police decide not to proceed with the charge. The officers would try to allocate the most suitable cellmate they could, but the transient nature of the population made that difficult. It wasn't uncommon for a twenty-two-year-old to be sharing with a fifty-year-old, a short-termer to be in with a lifer, or for a man who'd lived in west London his entire life to be sharing with a non-English speaker. At Scrubs, the cells were not a home. They were dirty and poorly ventilated. Perhaps unsurprisingly, most prisoners did not invest the same time and energy into keeping their cells clean as those at Whitemoor did.

Many of the issues I came across at Scrubs are non-existent at Belmarsh. I never see a drone, for example. Nor do I find £20,000 worth of drugs hidden in one cell, as I did once during the emergency regime. But there are fights during the night – probably more, in fact, thanks to those triple cells.

And predictably, the less time prisoners have out of their cells, the more problems they have in them. The less time they have to make phone calls during association, the more mobile phones are found. And the less time prisoners have to do something, anything, that takes them out of those four walls, the more time they choose to spend smoking drugs inside them.

This isn't the case for everyone. Everyone is bored, but not everyone fights or gets high as a result. Two prisoners on Houseblock 3 construct a little basketball hoop out of the netting from laundry bags and attach it to their cell door, aiming scrunched-up balls of paper at it and cheering each time one of them gets it in. More than once, I find officers taking shots in there with them. Others make a game out of throwing raisins or Rice Krispies into the lid of a roll-on deodorant, increasing the distance with each throw. Some draw, some write poetry, some turn their mattresses into punch bags and train for hours on end. Or they commit to rigorous in-cell workouts, press-ups and burpees and the plank, anything to pass the time.

One of the problems with prisoners being locked up a lot is that they don't have the opportunity to talk through their disagreements with those in other cells. Instead, there's a lot of shouting from behind closed doors and acting up for the people listening. Arguments are obviously preferable to fights, but, with so little time to socialise, prisoners lose the skills and incentive to talk things through.

However, if the person you've got a problem with is the same man you're sharing a cell with, then those issues are either going to get sorted, or not. There is no middle ground. No agreeing to avoid each other or to be civil when you can't. The cells are too small, the air is too stale and the potential for irritating each other is too great. The propensity for violence is always there.

***

I've just finished the afternoon briefing when a new officer approaches me. She's been on the houseblock for about four months now, and is a hard worker, though her inexperience can be quick to reveal itself. She's perhaps a little too prepared to take what people tell her at face value. Perhaps not yet aware of how the truth can get warped here, of how disguise and manipulation can be a way of surviving. As the rest of the staff file on to their respective landings ready to unlock, she asks for a quick word.

She tells me that Simpson, a prisoner on Spur 3, had an accident before lunch. As she was locking him in his cell, she'd noticed some red marks on his face that looked like fresh burns. He'd told her that he was just being clumsy, not watching what he was doing, and had accidentally poured a cup of tea over himself.

There are two main issues with this. Firstly, any prisoner who sustains burn injuries needs to be seen immediately, not after an hour's lunchbreak. And secondly, no one pours tea over their own face. Not even the clumsiest of people. It's the equivalent of the infamous, 'I slipped in the shower, guv,' which has to be the most persistently used phrase prisoners use when found with facial injuries. In all my time working in prisons, I've never known anyone to actually slip in the showers. That's not how they got their black eye.

And Simpson hasn't got red marks on his face because he was careless with his tea.

***

By the time I reach Spur 3, cell 14, Simpson is in a bad way. I open the door and find him leaning over the sink, splashing water over his face and shoulders. The skin is peeling off. I can see patches of bright pink flesh on his shoulders, neck and cheeks.

It's obvious what's happened. Simpson has been 'hot watered', or 'kettled' as it's sometimes called. All cells have a prison-issue kettle inside. These incidents aren't common enough to warrant removing all the kettles, and being able to make their own cup of tea is one of the few home comforts prisoners have. But sometimes, that's not what they use their kettles for. Sometimes, they boil their kettles and then throw the contents over the victim. Sometimes, they stir sugar in with the water until it's caramelised, so that the mixture will stick to the victim's skin and intensify the burning. I've only seen this a handful of times in my career. It isn't a common assault. It's one thing to punch someone, but another thing entirely to potentially disfigure them for life. There's no coming back from this.

I take Simpson to the treatment room, where the nurse quickly assesses him and recommends he's taken to hospital. She gives him painkillers, which he accepts willingly, and treats his burns with an ointment that looks almost like plastic on his skin. He has a wet towel draped over his shoulder, which she removes, applying more ointment to the wounds on the back of his neck. Throughout all of this, Simpson does his best to stay calm. But he's trembling, too. He's clearly in pain, and the adrenaline of what's happened is yet to leave him.

He needs to go to hospital as soon as possible, but the preparations required for an unscheduled escort like this can be time-consuming. Additional officers need to be found to go with him, not easy in a prison struggling for staff. A governor needs to review his custodial record and decide the type of cuffs to be used. And a risk assessment needs to be provided by the security department. That's the bit that will take the longest. There's a lot of risk to assess with Simpson. He has as many enemies as he does friends, and is well-known in the local area. But he doesn't want to wait in the treatment room, where prisoners may see him as they come up for their medication. His face doesn't look the way it did this morning.

So we sit in my office. He holds cooling packets to his skin, but won't let me help him with the burns he can't reach. He's fine, he tells me. It's nothing. It was an accident. He sticks to his story as vigorously as the prisoners who claim they slipped in the shower. He dropped the tea while he was stretching, he felt dizzy for a second and lost his footing, he tried to swat a fly away from his face while holding the mug. The excuses come thick and fast. But I know him well. This isn't the first time we've sat in my office and discussed how someone has come to be injured, although Simpson isn't usually the victim. So, I wait it out. He can only lie for so long.

'There's an officer reviewing the CCTV footage as we speak,' I say.

Simpson shakes his head. 'You won't see it,' he says. 'It's not on camera.'

'So, it happened in your cell, then?' I ask. 'We'll still see the person who did it running out.'

He laughs wryly. 'No, you won't.'

'Why not?'

'Because he's still in there.'

***

Simpson was kettled by his own cellmate. As if this isn't bad enough, he was then locked up for lunch with that cellmate. He doesn't go into the details of why, though I piece together enough to ascertain that it is, of course, gang-related. But perhaps the most shocking bit of all of this is how it ended. Simpson didn't retaliate. He got scalding hot water thrown over him, and he didn't do anything back. When I ask him why, he says he doesn't know. He was a bit in shock, maybe, and all he could think about was getting as much cold water on his skin as quickly as he could. When I ask what the atmosphere was like in that cell during lunch, he says, 'Yeah, it was really awkward.'

After Simpson has been taken to hospital, I interview his cellmate. Knowles is a short, stocky young man with curly hair and a jumper that's too big for him. He walks into my office nervously, looking every bit like the first-timer he is rather than a man who's just potentially scarred someone for life. It's his first time in jail; he's not even been convicted yet. He's still got three weeks until his court case starts. Unlike Simpson, he doesn't beat around the bush. He admits what he's done immediately. When I explain that because of the seriousness of the incident, it will be referred to the police, and it's likely he will be charged with a further offence, he puts his head in his hands.

'I didn't know what else to do,' he says. 'He robbed my cousin outside. I didn't know what I was meant to do. I'd heard that's how you deal with people in prison. He didn't realise who I was, and when we got locked up together I knew it would get back to people if I'd done nothing. And I thought he would figure out who I was eventually. I didn't know what to do, miss. I was scared of him.'

It's rare that I empathise with the perpetrator of this kind of assault, but in this case I find myself feeling a bit sorry for Knowles. Not just because he was scared, but because I suspect he doesn't quite realise what's to come. No one has ever done anything like this to Simpson before. No one would have dared. It wasn't bravery that made his cellmate throw hot water over him, it was fear. And I can understand that Simpson was so taken aback by the suddenness of it all, he didn't retaliate. But he will.

**

Simpson, by some miracle, makes an almost full recovery. If you look closely, you can see the patches of discolouration on his face, but over the next few months the skin heals well.

Knowles is charged with GBH. He was barely even inside for a week, and he's picked up another charge before he's even been tried for the first one. If he's found guilty, that's at least another two years inside.

The day that Knowles kettled Simpson, Spur 3 hadn't been out for two days. Two days is a long time to be stuck in a confined space with someone you're afraid of. Maybe if Knowles had been out on the landings, getting to know other inmates and developing relationships with the officers on his spur, maybe he would have realised that people talk in prison a lot more than you might think. Maybe he would have realised that it was possible to discreetly mention that he might have a problem, and needed to move cells. We could have moved him to another houseblock within half an hour.

But that didn't happen. Instead, Knowles sat in that cell, letting his mind fester with fear and worst-case scenarios that might never have materialised. And now he has bigger problems to contend with. Simpson didn't know who he was before, but he definitely does now. And so do all his friends.

In trying to solve one problem, Knowles has created another one entirely.

***

Alarm bells can go off at all times in prison. Association is the most common time, not surprisingly. Freeflow is next. Mealtimes are also a flash point. Portion sizes and food that looks less than appetising can anger people quickly, and there are more opportunities to cause harm by the hotplate. There's hot food to throw and plastic cutlery to use.

The night shifts are less busy, but alarm bells still sound. Prisoners still fight when the doors close. Possibly the quietest time for violence is very early in the morning, when almost everyone is likely to be asleep. So it's a surprise to hear the warble coming through my radio at six on a bright Wednesday morning. I'm at my desk, reviewing the staffing for the day and checking which spur is due to come out.

'All outstations, we have a general alarm, Houseblock 3.'

That's even more of a surprise. I'm on Houseblock 3. I haven't heard any shouting. And then I do.

'Down here,' calls Officer Martin. He's fresh out of his probation and already one of the best officers we have. He has a way of talking to people that's very difficult to replicate. Prisoners trust him.

'Spur Two, bottom landing,' he calls again.

I start running.

***

When I reach the bottom of Spur Two, I see Officer Martin with his keys in the door of cell 10, ready to go. He waits until I'm almost at the cell and then shoves the door open. There are footsteps behind me as other staff run on to the houseblock from the ground floor entrance, through the First Night Centre and on to the spur. Hot on my heels are a couple of officers from the Dedicated Search Team, who were walking past the houseblock when the alarm went off.

We enter the cell behind Officer Martin. It's surprisingly calm.

There's a lot of blood, but no shouting. There's no noise at all, in fact. There are three prisoners in here, but no one to separate. One of them, Westmorland, stands at the back of the cell. He's looking at me, but his face is blank. His hands are by his sides, fists still clenched and red with blood. A prisoner in his sixties is curled up on the top bunk, shaking but unharmed. Conan, who normally sleeps in the bottom bunk, is kneeling on the floor. He's covered in blood and barely conscious.

A couple of officers help Conan out of the cell. I tell Westmorland to stay where he is and keep his hands where we can see them. We don't know exactly what's happened, but the state of Westmorland's fists is a pretty good indicator.

CM Grewal, the manager of the Dedicated Search Team, is now beside me, his eyes fixed on Westmorland. DST are a group of officers trained in specialist searching techniques, with expert knowledge in things like preserving crime scenes and detecting mobile phone signals. They're an ideal group of people to have with you during an incident like this, because the cell in front of us is most definitely a crime scene. There's blood on the floor and the sink, and some splattered over the pillow on the lower bunk as well. A toothbrush is snapped on the floor.

It's not entirely clear what's gone on, though it seems apparent that Westmorland has attacked Conan and left him badly beaten. There are a few competing priorities in this situation. Obviously, we needed to get Conan out of the cell, which we've done. We also need to get Grissini, the prisoner on the top bunk, out of the cell safely. Ideally, both these things would have been achieved without staff entering the cell, avoiding any contamination of evidence. But that wasn't possible with Conan. He couldn't have got out on his own.

CM Grewal steps forward and beckons Grissini out. He tells him to try to walk around the blood. And he tells Westmorland not to move a muscle. Westmorland looks blankly at him. His fists stay clenched. Once Grissini is out of the cell, CM Grewal locks the door so Westmorland is in there alone, but the complications continue. We need to remove Westmorland from that cell as soon as physically possible. He needs to be relocated to a cell with no access to running water, so he can't wash his hands or try to clean up the blood. Whichever cell he's relocated to needs to be empty, so he can't change his clothes.

He's beaten Conan so badly that he's almost unrecognisable, his face streaming with blood and snot. Westmorland's physical capabilities are evident, so any staff facing him need to be wearing full PPE kit for their own protection, but all of this takes time and it's still early. Most officers haven't even started work yet, and the ones that have need to stay with Conan, or escort him to hospital. He is the priority.

So CM Grewal makes a difficult call.

'We get him out now,' he says.

***

CM Grewal and five officers go in. No PPE. They stand in the entrance to the cell and tell Westmorland to walk towards them, one step at a time. He does as he's told, staying silent the whole time, dragging his feet through the blood as he goes. When he reaches the doorway, he turns round and puts his hands behind his back to be cuffed. Once cuffed, he walks slowly, but compliantly, to the segregation unit, where he's put in an empty holding cell and the cuffs are removed. As soon as the door locks behind him, he rips out the light fittings and smashes the window.

This time, when segregation officers enter the cell, they do so wearing full PPE. Shields, helmets, stab vests. And this time, Westmorland doesn't comply. He fights. It takes a while before he's restrained, and even then the level of violence he's demonstrating necessitates his relocation to the 'box', a bare room only found in segregation units, devoid of anything.

A team of officers re-enter the box several times over the new few hours in an attempt to safely relocate Westmorland to a standard segregation unit cell. Each time, he fights, and so each time, he stays. It's nearly the end of the day when he's eventually moved to a normal cell. And that cell is where he remains for the next few months. He's offered a shower and exercise each day, but only when there are six staff in kit to escort him. And when two police officers come to visit him, they give him the news through the obs panel rather than opening the door.

He's being charged with attempted murder.

**

Conan was blue-lighted to hospital. A bleed on the brain. What I thought was snot coming from his nose turns out to be brain fluid. One of the doctors who treats him likens his injuries to those of someone who had been involved in a high-speed road-traffic accident. He's in hospital for over a month.

Despite Westmorland being charged with attempted murder, the CPS choose not to proceed with the case. By this point, he has been found guilty of murder, the index offence for which he had originally been remanded, and so it is deemed not in the public interest to proceed with the attempted murder charge.

This isn't the first time something like this has happened in my career and, sadly, it won't be the last. Each time, it's incredibly frustrating. The decision is logical; trials are expensive and time-consuming and, even if Westmorland was to be found guilty of attempted murder, his sentence wouldn't exceed the one he's already been given for murder. Any sentence he did receive would most likely be concurrent, meaning it would run alongside his current sentence rather than resulting in additional time. So, in a way, it makes sense. But for the people there that day, who saw Conan and sat with him while waiting for the paramedics to arrive, or the officers who took photos of the crime scene and stepped gingerly around the blood, or the seg staff who fought and fought and fought, or Grissoli, who saw the whole thing, sitting on his bunk paralysed with fear and helplessness, there's nothing about that decision that makes sense.

We never really get to the bottom of what happened in there, though I'm later told that Westmorland was irritated when Conan got up to brush his teeth. The noise annoyed him. He told Conan to stop, but Conan carried on regardless. So Westmorland beat him to within half an inch of his life.

Westmorland is made a high-risk prisoner. He never shares a cell again.

***

There are incidents within cells, like the ones involving Simpson and Westmorland, that are unforeseen and shocking in their rarity. But others can feel entirely predictable. When the call comes over the radio that there's a Code Blue on Spur 1, cell 26, I almost roll my eyes. Ellison again.

Ellison is a habitual drug user. His index offence is drug related, and he continues to abuse drugs in jail, too. Staff refer to that as 'parallel offending', when a prisoner demonstrates the same kind of offending behaviour inside as they did outside. And when it comes to taking drugs inside, Ellison is probably the worst for it on the wing. He takes spice several times a week. He's almost always on Basic because of it, though that doesn't seem to bother him.

When he's not high, he's cheerful and outgoing, always joking with the staff. Many of the officers here have known him for years.

He's been in the same cell since I transferred here. Recently, he's had a few bad reactions to spice. Nothing too serious, but he's become incoherent, started to slur his words and vomited twice. That's what I'm expecting as I make my way downstairs to his cell.

It's hard to know what to do with someone like Ellison. He's in his mid-fifties. It's highly unlikely he's just going to stop taking drugs now. The Pathways team engage with him regularly, he's been offered a cell in Healthcare to support him with his addiction and other health issues, we've gone down the disciplinary route by removing his TV, but nothing changes. Even with his recent reactions to spice, he carries on taking it. He ignores all the warnings.

This time, though, it isn't a warning.

***

As soon as I look at him, I know he's dead.

The pallor of his skin, the way his body jerks with each compression, the blood that's started to pool at the bottoms of his legs.

His cell looks the same as it always does. Dirty socks balled up in the corner, old vape capsules discarded, a book half open on his bed, the diary he was given by chaplaincy on the table. This little room was his life. And now it's where staff desperately try to bring him back.

Two officers have already started CPR. That familiar beat of 'One, two, three...' rings in my head. I know this process well now, and the necessary management that surrounds it. So that's what I focus on. I ask the staff inside the cell if they're happy to continue, and they both are. CPR can be a traumatic and unpleasant task, but they're probably the best people for the job. Both are experienced, with recent first-aid training.

I ask another officer to open an events log, detailing what happens minute by minute. He stands in the corner of the cell, watching and writing, then checking his watch and writing again.

The houseblock custodial manager stands outside the cell with me. We delegate staff to different areas as they respond to the Code Blue. We need a couple on standby to relieve the officers doing CPR if they get tired. A few more to support the officers on the landings of Spurs 2 and 3. One to stand by the open gates to Spur 1 and wave paramedics on as they arrive. Spur 1, Ellison's spur, is locked up today. It was only by chance that Officer Nesse checked on him. Ellison hadn't pressed his cell bell. It wasn't time for a roll count. But a new officer is shadowing Officer Nesse today, and he'd asked to see what the inside of a cell looks like. The cell he chose was Ellison's.

It isn't long before the response team from Healthcare arrive, and shortly after that the paramedics arrive too. Prisoners from the other spurs cheer as they run on, the green of their uniform rich against our white and black. They ask Ellison's name as they enter his cell.

'Ellison, can you hear us?'

The officers inside kneel back against the cell walls, both sweating and out of breath, and let the paramedics take over the compressions. They unpack equipment from their bags, casings and packets strewn all over the floor. They're quick, thorough, efficient. This is a scene they've dealt with many times before.

Too many people crowding around can make these situations worse, so I check with the CM first and then walk away. There's nothing more I can do. Everyone has been given a job. Event logs, answering cell bells, extra boots patrolling landings. Standing outside this cell now, I'm just waiting. The whole spur feels frozen. Everyone's just listening for the same thing. A sudden breath or a cough. A splutter. Anything.

Less than an hour later, Ellison is pronounced dead.

***

That afternoon, I go with a chaplain to inform Ellison's partner. This is always done in person. The staff trained to make these visits are called family liaison officers, and our job is to tell a prisoner's next of kin what has happened and try to provide as much support as possible thereafter. But it's harrowing. Even for those families who have wondered if that knock on the door would one day come, it must be unbearable when it finally does. And that's only the beginning. As family liaison officer, you support the family through collecting the prisoner's personal effects, with making funeral arrangements (to which the Prison Service makes a contribution), and organising a memorial service to be held at the prison. It's a great privilege to be trusted with work of this sensitivity, but it's far from easy. Because while some deaths in custody might be somewhat expected, such as those of ageing prisoners in ill health, there are many deaths that aren't foreseen. Prisoners who hang themselves with no warning, leaving no note, no explanation, and a lifetime of unanswered questions for their loved ones. There are men who take drugs for the first time, never having dabbled before, and get a bad batch. And there are those killed at the hands of someone else. In a few months' time, a prisoner in Belmarsh will be beaten to death by his cellmate. It's hard to comprehend what it must be like to deliver that news, and harder still to imagine hearing it.

But after meeting with Ellison's partner, I decide then and there that I don't ever want to do this again.

We stand in the cold on her porch. We ring the doorbell three or four times. The curtains twitch. Eventually, she opens her door, but only enough to peer round it. I'm wearing my uniform and the chaplain has his distinctive white collar. She asks what's happened, why we're here. Has he been released?

We tell her. And she sobs. But they're not the tears I was expecting. She cries with relief.

I had no idea, because Ellison was always in for drug-related offences, but he used to beat her. He kicked down her door and smashed her windows with a baseball bat. Her home had become a cell of its own.

***

In the days that follow, the chaplain and I spend some time just the two of us, talking about what it feels like to break that kind of news to someone. We sit in a quiet office in the chapel, drinking tea made by Attwood. I can see him through the window. He vacuums the carpets, sweeps the floors and arranges leaflets on the tables, their glossy surfaces dotted with doves and swirling fonts about how to survive grief or living with loneliness. It's always good to see him. We've known each other for a long time now, since my earliest days as an officer. And we've spent a lot of time in this chapel, talking about everything and nothing. About Whitemoor, and how much we've both changed since then. But sometimes I wonder how far all this experience has really got me.

Because I should have got my head round this by now. I know the stats. I know about domestic violence. I know that the victims of so many of the men I work with are also their families. But it's always been at a distance. I read it in psychiatric reports or a judge's summing-up comments, or I hear it from the prisoner's perspective and on their territory. But all of that is so much more complicated when the victim is right in front of you. I rarely meet a prisoner's family – perhaps occasionally during a visit – and I almost never meet their victim. But so often they're one and the same.

I'm trying to reconcile the Ellison that frightened woman described with the one I knew. Because, in prison, he was no threat to anyone. If anything, the staff protected him. He was vulnerable in lots of ways. I'm trying to work out where this leaves me.

Being a family liaison officer is a skilled role, a trusted one. But I don't think it's a skill I want to have. I don't think I want to know as much as I do anymore. I don't think I should be trusted with this kind of thing, because I don't trust myself to leave it at the gate.

Leave it at the gate. Leave it at the gate.

All of it. Leave the fights there, leave the man who gouges out his own eyes, the man who sews his lips together, the man you thought you could trust but stabbed you in the back, the man who stamps on someone's head and then positions it carefully in between the cell door and the door frame, and slams the door against it again and again and again until the other prisoner I know so well gives me that look to say *Miss South go upstairs now*, and I go and I run and I see his head bounce and dent and I push the guy who's doing it off him and he screams at me that he deserves it because he killed his friend and who is the victim anymore, who is in the wrong, who is most damaged by this?

Leave it at the gate.

Leave it at the gate.

It's what the more experienced officers say. But now I'm one of those. And now the gate is moving. It isn't the cell or the wing or the yard or the prison or the car park, it's a frightened woman's porch, and it's Starbucks, where I sit with a cappuccino that goes cold before I even take a sip, because all I can think about is how scared she was.

But I don't tell anyone. I don't say a thing. Because the governors tell me to go for promotion, they offer me this course and that, and people think I can do this. I'm trusted to do it.

But I can't. I can't do this.

***

When I pull up outside my house that evening, I stay in the car.

I tell myself it's just for a few minutes, just to wind down a bit. But one hour passes, then two, then three. The sky changes from grey to blue to black. The streetlights come on. And I stay in the car. I remember the conversation I had with Anthony, the officer at Whitemoor, all those years before. How he told me that he'd sat in the car park for hours, frozen.

This is different, though, isn't it? I've made it into prison and back out again; it's home that I can't seem to walk into. But deep down, I know the reasons are the same. The women I live with are funny and kind and good company, but their days are so vastly different from mine that I can't figure out how to be a part of them. I don't know how to make the two worlds meet. I don't know how to inhabit both. I don't know how to go from screaming men to dead bodies to this quiet suburban street in Brockley with its butcher's at one end and off-licence at the other, and somehow exist in both spaces.

It's cold in the car and I don't have a coat.

I sit and think about things I don't want to think about, people I don't want to remember, moments I wish had never happened. I think about all of it. As far back as Whitemoor.

And I don't know why. I don't know why it is that certain things are so clear when others fade from my memory so quickly. I don't know why some things feel as if they only happened yesterday, when actually it's been years since Ben came into that office and shut the door, years since I saw his letter in front of me in an evidence bag, years since I felt so stupid and foolish. Why do I still care? Why can't I let it go? It's been years since Scrubs, since C Wing. Years since that fight. And in the time before and after, there's been so many fights, so many that I forget, that all start to look the same. But not that one. The way the blood spread so slowly from his head. It's been years since Tristan, since I tried and failed to help him. He was released and back in again within weeks. He never stood a chance. Years since Adam cried in my office. The same Adam who I now know is an inpatient at a secure hospital receiving psychiatric treatment. He was so violent, so angry, but so young and so vulnerable. But so many prisoners are, and so many things have happened, so many people have come in and out of my life – why is it these people I can't forget? It's been years since that awful week, years since Bekim's eyes bulged the way they did, his skin the colour it was, and yet that's the one I remember the most. Not the man who died, not the man who was left permanently disabled. Their faces fade. But not his. Why him? And, I wonder, why me? Is anyone else finding this hard? Is anyone else stuck in their car?

And now Ellison. But even now, just days after his death, I know I'm forgetting him. Despite two years of seeing him every single day, his face, his laugh, his mannerisms, are already fading.

But not her.

Her expression is imprinted on my memory. Her voice and her tangled emotions. Relief and fear. And I feel those, too. Relief that one shift is over. But fear because the next one is yet to start. I have to go back tomorrow.

I have to let all of this go. If I can't leave it at the gate, then I have to at least leave it in my car, on my uniform, my boots, my belt – anything but my head. I don't want this stuff in my head. I don't want to care anymore.

Anthony said this job will weigh you down if you're not careful. But I have been careful, haven't I? I take annual leave, I go on holidays, I don't do overtime, I have good friends outside of the job, I exercise every day. I run and run and run. But I can't get far enough away. The weight is too heavy. He said it weighs you down. And now my whole body feels too heavy to even move. My hand too heavy to open this door.

All of it. Too heavy.

Too much.

***

Eventually, I do go inside. And though it's too late for an early night, I fall asleep quickly. When I wake, I'm in the chapel at Wormwood Scrubs. One wall looks out on to C Wing. Rows and rows of cell windows. There's a man in each one. One by one, they jump, like dancers in a ballet.

I am struggling.

18

The Security Department

This job can weigh you down.
This job will change you.
My wife says I shout more.
I can't talk to my wife anymore.
Speak to your friends.
Only your colleagues will understand.
You'll end up being desensitised to it all.
If you ever stop feeling nervous when the alarm bell goes, you'll know
it's time to quit.
Don't drink too much.
Have a drink in the evening to wind down.
Don't do too much overtime.
Get as much money out of the job as possible.
Don't look up what everyone's in for.
Know who you're dealing with.

I'VE HEARD A lot of different things from different officers.
Everyone has their own way of dealing with the job. I
need to find mine. Maybe I need a change. At Whitemoor,
the general rule was that an officer shouldn't work on the
same area for more than four years. Aside from my brief
period as a Custodial Manager at Wormwood Scrubs, I've
been working on the wings for almost eight years. So I request a move.

***

A Wing at Whitemoor, C Wing at Scrubs, Houseblock 3 at Belmarsh. I've had great experiences on all three, but the hard times are getting harder. The governor of security accepts my expression of interest in a position in his department, and recommends I apply when the next space becomes available. I don't have long to wait. Within six weeks, I'm sitting behind a desk in the security office.

The office is like any other. Desks, computers, filing cabinets and lever-arch files stuffed full of paperwork. It's the little things that mark it out as the kind of office you'd only find in a prison, like the labels on the lever-arch files. There's a jar of treats on the windowsill in case the handlers pop in with their dogs. The smell is probably a bit different from an ordinary office, too. Typically, any contraband found is taken to the security office, so there are often some phones, maybe a weapon or two, and a few bags of weed in here. But even with all that, it's a world away from life on the houseblocks.

There are four senior officers working in here, including me, and the rest of the staff are former officers who've now taken a civilian role. Between them, they've worked at HMP Wandsworth, HMP Pentonville and HMYOI Isis. Some have been in the Prison Service since the nineties. When they were officers, they worked in the houseblocks, the Vulnerable Prisoners Unit, Healthcare and the seg. So there's a wealth of experience in this room. I'm lucky to be working with them, because there's a lot to learn in a prison security department.

Some days, I can be visiting the local hospitals to conduct risk assessments for prisoners with upcoming appointments; other days, I'm assisting DST with cell searches. Staff submit security reports throughout the day, and a big part of my role is to evaluate the information coming through and decide what to do with it. If I want to stay in the office all day, drinking coffee and going through reports, I can. If I want to get out and about, visiting different areas of the jail and being more visible,

I can do that, too. It feels like a breath of fresh air. I'm not bound to the regime anymore. My time is my own, and I'm trusted to spend it appropriately. The difference in how I feel is almost immediate. I start sleeping better, going to the gym more, looking forward to work again. I hadn't realised just how much I needed a break, but working in security gives me that.

The work can be unpleasant. Monitoring phone calls means listening in on some pretty horrendous stuff. Like the sex offender who repeatedly tries to pass explicit messages to the children he abused. His own children. Or the domestic violence perpetrator who threatens his wife over the phone. And it's not just the phone calls. I regularly meet with prisoners requesting to speak to someone from security, often because they want a move off the houseblock or a transfer to another jail, and approval from the security department tends to override everything else.

I sit in the segregation unit with one man who fiddles with the gold band on his finger and tearfully tells me that it belonged to his fiancée who's just passed away, that he's finding this sentence tough, that's why he punched the officer, and that's why he's in the seg, and can I please approve a transfer to a different jail. But I looked up his record before I came to see him. I am well aware of who this man is – and that the reason his fiancée is dead is because he killed her.

But even the more unpleasant aspects of the job are buffered by the fact I'm not in the thick of it. I might be having difficult conversations with challenging people, but I walk away afterwards. I respond to the alarm bells, but I'm rarely there when the incident first breaks out. And there's so much else to get involved with: intelligence gathering, planning operations, late-night searches and investigations into staff corruption. My new role is exactly what I needed. It energises me and exposes me to things going on behind the scenes that I had no idea about.

One shift sees me searching an eighteen-year-old female member of staff suspected of bringing drugs into the prison. She denies it up until the very last moment, right up to the point where I'm putting on gloves, and then produces several wraps of Class A drugs. There is a part of me that feels angry with her, for the violence and chaos that her actions have undoubtedly caused. But there is another part of me that wonders why we decided to give an eighteen-year-old keys to a high-security prison in the first place. I end up talking with the prisoner she was going to deliver the drugs to, a man in his thirties with a history of conditioning staff, and someone I've always got on with. To my surprise, he speaks to me honestly. He doesn't feel bad about what's happened, or the fact that she now has a criminal record that will stay with her for the rest of her life.

'It's a dog-eat-dog world in here, Miss South. If you see an opportunity, you take it.'

For her, he was the love of her life. For him, she was an opportunity.

There was a time when prison officers still on probation weren't permitted to work in certain areas, such as the seg or the High Secure Unit. But the shortage of experienced staff means that that isn't really an option anymore. And even in the areas where officers still in their first twelve months would have always worked, such as the houseblocks, there aren't as many experienced officers there to keep an eye on them these days. Not just to give advice, but to point out red flags that may not be so obvious to someone unfamiliar with this kind of environment.

My conversation with that prisoner gives me an insight into the methods some inmates will use to condition vulnerable staff, and also an extra layer of compassion for those who fall victim. Because they're targeted almost immediately, whether they realise it or not. A female officer who wears her hair down, who wears more jewellery than she's meant to, or who gets into a conversation about which man she finds attractive on *Love Island*, inadvertently identifies herself to prisoners as someone who might be worth approaching. Those are the kinds of conversations officers shouldn't be having, or aspects of their appearance they shouldn't be highlighting, but they're also the things that some managers let go, especially when faced with much more pressing and immediate issues. But my time in the security department educates me about the risks of letting things slide, and the collective responsibility we all have to look out for each other.

I see so much of this from the comfort of the security department, and the distance gives me a different perspective to it. One young female officer enters into an inappropriate relationship with a prisoner, and brings him both drugs and phones. She is later arrested and charged with misconduct in public office, and ends up serving time in prison. I don't think I would previously have had any sympathy. But I see from the letters she continues to write him that, for her, this is the real thing. She'll wait for him. She loves him. But I also intercept his mail, the letters he writes to his actual girlfriend and the mother of his children, and the way they mock the former officer. And I don't really know who to blame.

Male officers are also seduced by the money that comes from bringing in contraband, and the false illusion that doing so gives them a kind of status within the criminal community. Again, they are opportunities, easy targets. Corruption isn't limited to male prisons, either. Relationships between officers and female prisoners can be intense, often more so than in male establishments. Female prisoners are typically quicker to open up than men, more willing to talk about what it is that's brought them there. Some have suffered extraordinary trauma: rape, domestic violence, human trafficking, forced prostitution. There might be fewer incidents of interpersonal violence in female jails, but self-harm is commonplace. And the relationships female prisoners develop with the staff there to support them can be all-consuming and, occasionally, exploitative.

Prisons are full of damaged and manipulative people. If we're to have any hope of rehabilitating them, then the staff inside need to be upholding the highest possible standards. It's perhaps no surprise that during COVID-19, when OSGs are unable to physically search staff anymore, corruption increases. But I start to think that it isn't the lack of security that's really the problem; it's the lack of support and training that staff receive. We recruit people into an environment that is often dangerous and exploitative, but don't always provide them with the tools to navigate it. I'm almost a decade into this job now, but I still remember how I felt during those first few weeks at Whitemoor. I remember how intimidated I was, by everything from the prisoners to the barbed wire to the sound of the alarm bell, and I remember how isolating that feeling could be. I was fortunate to have been surrounded by such excellent officers. My confidence came from them. They made me stronger.

Having said all that, there are plenty of officers I don't feel sorry for.

***

A prison officer's job is multi-skilled. It's demanding. It requires you to be a lot of different things to a lot of different people. But if you get it right, it can be a huge privilege. People allow you into their lives and trust you with their vulnerabilities. The impact an officer can have is enormous.

Part of my role in the security department involves night shifts — a lot of them. I normally do a week of nights at least once every two months. When all the prisoners are locked up for the evening, and all the staff have gone home, a small group of disciplinary staff stay on.

I don't like doing nights. I never have. At Whitemoor, it was the boredom that made the hours drag. At Belmarsh, it's how vulnerable I am. We all are. Incidents at night have increased, but the number of staff on shift has reduced. There aren't even officers on the wing anymore. Instead, a small team of us roam around the jail, responding to incidents as they happen.

Which they do.

The prisoners still fight at night, they still fall ill and need to be taken to hospital at night, they still cut themselves and take drugs and start fires at night. The alarm bell still goes at night. There are just far fewer officers to respond now.

I stay in the gatehouse for the first few hours, working with the OSGs until their shift comes to an end and the last of the staff have left the prison. Then I make my way to the main jail, visit the houseblocks, do some paperwork, and that's pretty much it. When I've got everything done, I normally go down to the prison gym for a couple of hours. Not everyone does, so it's usually quiet. Sometimes, officers will go there to use the computers or watch TV on the screens in the weights room, but a lot of the time it's just me.

I run. I aim to do 25k over the course of my week of nights. I remember Abdul and the advice he gave me at Whitemoor about how to take time off my 5k: when to eat carbs, how to pace myself, when to sprint and when to go steady, and I run. It keeps me awake, gives me energy and quietens my mind. I feel safe in that gym. So it feels like a momentous betrayal when an officer using the computer turns out to have been watching me, making explicit remarks about my appearance and then feeding back to others. He makes comments about whether I'm worth having sex with, and what he would improve about my body.

Inevitably, his comments get back to me. And when they do, I feel embarrassed, exhausted and angry. Embarrassed, because how could I not be? I didn't realise someone was watching me while I exercised and passing judgement on my body. Exhausted, because I thought we were past this. I've been here before. His words bring back echoes of Officer Parry's, all those years ago: 'Women shouldn't work in prisons.' As if I should consider myself lucky to be permitted to work here, and accept that this is what some men do.

I know men like this. I've met many of them in prison, and they're not always the prisoners. I've stood awkwardly on the wing at Whitemoor, shielding my red face with my clipboard after overhearing an officer make a sexual comment about me. I was twenty-two. He was in his late fifties. I said nothing and just pretended not to hear. Which didn't really matter, because other people did hear it: the kind of people who aren't known for hiding behind clipboards when something happens that they don't like. I stood there, ticking off prisoners, and said nothing, as Bolt left his queue for the library and walked off the spur without permission, walked straight up to the officer, his broad chest almost touching the officer's paunch, and said, slowly and carefully, 'I don't like that. Don't do that.'

We all felt the hot irony of him telling one of us how to behave – and of us knowing that he was right.

But that was 2012. It's 2020 now. A lot has changed in that time. I thought we were past this – and yet here we are. It's happening again. I'm angry because I know the wider implications of my colleague's behaviour. To wear a prison officer's uniform is both a privilege and a responsibility. That officer's responsibility isn't just to me, it's to the public, who have the right to think that prison officers are professional. His responsibilities are also to the prisoners he works with, for whom he's meant to model pro-social behaviour. And they're to every officer who has to work with him and should be able to do so without feeling uncomfortable.

Divisions between staff are problematic, and this is the kind of thing that causes them. Part of me is tempted to let it go, because the whole thing is embarrassing, and I don't want to sit in the governor's office and be asked awkward questions. But at the same time, I'm the one in my office who always goes on about upholding high standards. So, I report him. It's the first time I've ever filed a grievance against a member of staff. He's interviewed, he admits it all and he's issued with a final written warning.

Not long after, I see him on one of the houseblocks and decide to talk to him about it. He's polite, but says he doesn't understand what the big deal is; he was only messing about, and his girlfriend at home doesn't have a problem with what he said. He misses the point entirely.

So I stay angry. And my mind betrays me yet again, and keeps replaying Officer Parry's words in my head, almost ten years later. The reasons he was wrong are still so obvious to me. But there's more to it now. The demographic in front of me has changed. I see a lot more men coming into prison for gender-based violence: rape, murder, honour-based killings, domestic violence.

I remember a prisoner's face when I spoke to him a couple of weeks ago about his poor behaviour towards a female officer. I've known this man for years, since my first days at Scrubs, and we have a strong relationship. I was disappointed to hear that he'd threatened a female officer, and it was important to me that I spoke about it with him. Because I know him well. Because I know he is better than his obnoxious and foolish words. So we sat opposite each other and had it out. Just me and him. We went back and forth. He said he would never have actually hurt her. I said that's not the point. But there was a moment when his face fell.

I said, 'You should be the man that women feel safe around.'

And for some reason, that was it; that was what made him get it. What goes on in his head is not the same as what goes on in hers. His words were so much bigger than he was giving them credit for.

I don't believe that prisoner really meant what he said. Maybe most men who use that kind of language towards women don't. But too many men do. And I've met a lot of them here. I know that their experiences in prison need to be characterised by change and challenge, and by being held accountable for what they've done. That can't happen without women being present, right in front of them, for every single day of their sentence.

They need to see women checking the yard. Pushing the lunch trolley. Changing the menu sheets. Collecting the mattresses. Tallying up their numbers. Responding to the radio. They need to see women working collaboratively with the male officers. They need to see women on the wings, running focus groups, delivering workshops, and as governors hearing evidence in adjudication rooms. They need to see all of it. They need to see the way women are treated by most men, by good men, by other prisoners and by their fellow officers. And they need to be called out when they fall short. That's what we're here to do.

But they can't see that if we aren't there. Removing women isn't the solution. Because women aren't the problem.

Right now, I'm sitting only a couple of metres from the room where I sat with that prisoner I knew from our time at Scrubs, but instead of him opposite me it's the officer who made degrading comments about me. Who just keeps saying it was a joke. I'm frustrated because I don't have the time, inclination or energy. I'm frustrated because he isn't even willing to hear me out, when so many others are. I'm frustrated because I have to accept that there are prisoners here who have more respect for women than some of the officers do.

Officers who are paid to be here, paid to have my back.

***

Prison officers always say that the worst time to be on nights is the week between Christmas and New Year. Two pretty tough bank holidays to get through if you're a prisoner. Typically, self-harm spikes at around this time, as does the brewing and consumption of hooch. Hooch is vile stuff, and more than a few prisoners who drink enough of it end up in an ambulance. All of this means that these are tough shifts for prison officers to work. There are inevitably going to be more incidents to respond to. And it's usually during the night, when prisoners drink the hooch they've spent the daytime brewing, or take the drugs they've spent the daytime sourcing. It's usually during the night when prisoners kill themselves.

The last time I worked that set of nights between Christmas and New Year was at Whitemoor. I've been fortunate to go so long without being detailed nights during that period. So when one of the security SOs asks if anyone is willing to swap so he can be at home with his kids, I say I'll do it. I owe him a week, anyway.

It turns out to be a terrible decision.

***

On the second night, a prisoner hangs himself and can't be saved. He's pronounced dead while I'm still in the gatehouse, several hours before I go to the main jail. There always has to be a senior officer on duty in the gatehouse, so I couldn't leave even if I wanted to.

The CM calls me to let me know what's happened, and to explain that the coroner is having a busy night and won't be able to collect the body for some hours yet. He tells me the name of the prisoner. Abel. I know him. He was on House-block 3 for a while. He'd asked me to come and see him the previous week. He didn't say what it was about. I said I would go back, but I didn't. I didn't have time. I was so busy.

And now he's dead.

***

I wave the coroners van in at 3am and go with them to collect Abel's body.

He's lying on the floor of his cell, beneath a white sheet. And then he's being zipped into a body bag and placed carefully into the back of a van. And then he's gone. Out of this place forever. He was only a few months from release.

On the way back to the security office, I take the same path I always do. I pass the houseblocks on either side, the palm trees with their shadows like fingers scraping the asphalt. Not for the first time, I think how liberating it feels to walk around on my own at night, and how strange it is that the only place I feel safe enough to do that is in the grounds of a high-security prison.

It's quiet. The air is still. There are no lights on in the cell windows. No planes flying overhead, even though London City Airport is just round the corner. But sometimes, when it's this quiet, that's when you need to listen the most. Or you miss something.

And now he's dead.

***

The next night, Balfour, a nineteen-year-old inmate, makes threats of violence from behind his door. He's in a single cell, so as long as he isn't harming himself there's no immediate need to open the door. But then he covers his obs panel with toilet paper so we can't see him. He starts off refusing to remove it, then refuses to say anything at all. He won't respond. Now we have to go in. He's as much a risk to himself as to anyone else. The CM checks his record for any previous violence or self-harm, and finds that he has a history of both.

The room the control and restraint kit is kept in reminds me of a school changing room. It has that stale smell of sweat and clothes worn by too many different people. There are rows of overalls and shelves of boots, helmets lined up in one corner and boxes overflowing with arm and leg guards in another. One side of the room is lined with wooden racks that hold big black hold-alls. I'm fortunate that one of those is mine. I joined the Tornado riot team at Whitemoor, and ever since then I've had my own kit. Inside, everything is freshly washed and nicely folded, ready to go after the last riot call-out to HMP Bedford a few weeks ago.

I've recently become a control and restraint instructor as well. I teach staff refreshers a couple of times a month, going over the basic locks and de-escalation techniques that underpin staff interventions. So it makes sense for me to be the officer with the shield for the planned intervention on Balfour. This means I'm going in first. It's nerve-racking, but I have a strong team behind me.

By the time we're all kitted up and have made our way to the houseblock, my adrenaline is pumping. It's 1am now, and the cold of the night is offset by my full kit and balaclava. My breath is steaming up my visor before I've even started giving instructions.

'Go to the back of the cell. Keep your hands where we can see them.'

Balfour doesn't answer. The CM shakes his head; he's been standing at Balfour's door the whole time and hasn't had a response. He checks that we're ready, and puts his key in the lock.

I call out to Balfour again. I let him know we're coming in. Nothing. The CM unlocks the door. I step inside the cell, the staff behind me peeling to my left and right. I raise the shield, ready for some kind of impact, but none comes. Something doesn't feel right. I can't see Balfour. He isn't in front of me. He isn't on the bed, or on the toilet, or on the chair. I can feel my panic rising.

Then I see him. I see his head first, suspended by a ligature that's attached to the bedframe. I throw the shield to the floor and shout, 'He's under the bed.' His eyes are closed. His body is limp. His mouth is open, with his tongue lolling to the side.

Someone hands me a fish knife, and an officer holds the ligature as I slice through it. We pull him out from under the bed.
The CM is suddenly in the cell with us. He yells for someone
to get the defib. The nurse is here too, thinking she was going to
be observing a planned removal but now required to administer
emergency first aid. The situation has changed in a second.

We find a pulse. And just as we do, Balfour starts coughing.
He coughs and cries and opens his eyes and tells us he's sorry. He
comes round so quickly, almost too quickly, and I wonder if
he was faking it. But in that moment, I don't even care. I'm
just so glad he's alive. I can't cope with another body. I can't see
another body.

***

The next night is New Year's Eve.

A high-profile prisoner is currently being held at Belmarsh,
and there's been a lot of press attention surrounding his impris-
onment. His supporters camp on the central reservation of
Western Way, just outside the prison. They stay out there for
weeks, living in cheap tents and holding up placards as cars
speed by. But on New Year's Eve, they come into the staff car
park and decide to hold a demonstration. It's close to 11pm
when they start to gather outside the gatehouse, lighting can-
dles and chanting about justice. All the day staff have left by
now, and it's just me in the gatehouse. I've switched off the
lights to make it harder for them to see me, but they press their
faces up to the windows, leering at me and banging on the
bulletproof glass. Pointless, but intimidating, nonetheless.

It's a relief when they leave the area outside the gatehouse
and start making their way around the perimeter wall. This
is a restricted area, and their presence sets off various alarms.
At one time, patrol dogs and their handlers would have been
stationed there, but the cuts stopped that. So the staff in the

control room watch the demonstrators on the cameras, and call the police. But it's New Year's Eve in a busy borough of south London, and the police have got enough going on. The demonstrators' behaviour is annoying and inconvenient, but Belmarsh is a high-security prison. The perimeter wall is pretty high. They're not about to get in. So the police don't come, and the shift carries on.

The demonstrators stop outside the area where they believe the political prisoner is being held. They set off flares that light up the sky, the bangs so loud they sound like gunshots. They chant louder and louder, yelling messages of support. But they've got it wrong. They're nowhere near the houseblock where the prisoner they're supporting is located. They're outside the Healthcare unit. He's not in Healthcare, but an eighteen-year-old with Asperger's is. And he's terrified.

A call comes over the radio for me to attend Healthcare as soon as possible. When I get there, two officers are already in his cell, trying to comfort him. He's trembling and crying. He isn't good with physical contact, but he lets us hold his hand.

The flares keep coming and the noise is too much; he can't cope with it. He scrunches his eyes shut and screams, then slams his head into the wall. The bang of the flares as they erupt is followed by the bang of his skull against the brick. Bang bang bang.

It's horrible to see. It's so upsetting. The whole thing is traumatic. It's one of the worst weeks of my life.

***

During my week off, I get a call from Rob, the segregation unit officer I worked with at Scrubs. We still speak most days, but this time he's calling with devastating news. An officer from Scrubs, one of my former colleagues, has passed away. He hanged himself. When I return to work, I read in the prison newspaper that a prison officer at HMP Parkhurst hanged himself while on duty.

Its 2021 and both staff and prisoners are hanging themselves in our jails.

***

I lose myself a little bit after that. I haven't spoken to him since the day I left, but my former colleague's death sends me reeling.

In the days that follow, I hear from several officers I haven't talked to since leaving Scrubs. Some are still there, some have transferred to different jails and some have left the job altogether. Despite the changing trajectory in everyone's lives, it feels like we have never been out of contact, and we settle into a rhythm of conducting welfare checks of our own. We rally round each other, sending daily messages and sharing our shock and despair. I'm so grateful for all of them.

But it all feels like too much. I can't sleep. And when I do, I dream of death and dying. I dream of threadbare ligatures, of plaited bedsheets and leather belts. I dream of Abel's body and his profile beneath a white sheet, the lump of his nose and the jerk of his feet. I dream of bodies hanging and ligature points that rotate in my mind like a gruesome carousel: bedframes, window cages, gates, all weighed down by bodies with dangling feet and a heavy head. My own head feels heavy. I dream that same dream I had when I was at Scrubs – I see the prisoners staring at me from their cell windows, then one by one jumping and writhing under the grips of their home-made nooses, their necks snapping, one by one.

My mind is submerged, drowning all day, every day in thoughts of hanging and what it is to hang. I see Balfour's head suspended from one end by ripped green fabric and dragged from the other by the weight of his still body. I see his eyelids resting shut, his mouth open and leaking drool. I hear the shield slam against the floor as I throw it. My voice sounds thick and slow as I shout, 'He's under the bed.' I feel the cold plastic of the little red fish knife as I hack at the ligature, the burning relief when it cuts, the hope when I feel a pulse on his clammy neck.

If I don't see Abel's dead body, I see him alive, standing at the back of the cell with his arms folded. He asks me to come and see him when I get a chance. I hear his voice, and I feel the way his eyes focus on mine. I hear my answer. My words sound pointless and empty. I never went back.

I never went back.

***

I'm in the security office when an email flashes up on my computer screen. It's Officer Nesse. 'Free for a coffee?'

He and Officer Barton have left Houseblock 3. They work in the Safer Custody Department now, helping staff manage their ACCTs and conducting assessments of prisoners in crisis.

I type back, 'I'll be there in five.'

By the time I get there, my coffee is ready and waiting. I don't end up drinking much of it, though. When they ask me how I am, the words just spill out of me. I can't stop talking.

I tell them everything.

I tell them I have nightmares, like a child struggling to wake up, these desperately intense nightmares, so vivid and frightening that I feel my body convulsing in fear and I hear the noise of rushed panicky breathing, so loud it wakes me up, only to realise the breathing is mine. I tell them I dream about child abuse and murder and sequences of men hanging themselves, one by one. I tell them I shake every time I hear a raised voice. I tell them I feel nervous if I see two men talking on the street, because I'm waiting for one to throw the first punch. I tell them I see violence when it isn't happening; I see violence when my eyes are closed; I see violence when I sleep. I tell them I see every prisoner as a vessel for more violence. I tell them I can't use public transport because I feel trapped. I tell them I eyeball the men in the queue in Costa in case they are looking me up and down, objectifying me. I tell them I can't stand in queues at all, in case someone gets too close and tries to touch me. I tell them I cross the road every time a man is behind me, in case he is following me. I tell them I won't go out on my own past 6pm. I tell them I bolt and double-bolt the door. I tell them I always wear my jacket at work, so I can put my hands in my pockets. So that no one sees them shaking. I tell them I don't even feel safe with the ninety-two-year-old in Healthcare who can't walk: the same ninety-two-year-old who raped his daughter for years, over and over again, and destroyed her life. I tell them I can't watch certain news bulletins, I can't watch the steady stream of prison documentaries on at the moment, I can't watch CCTV footage of a brawl in a pub, of a woman being stalked on her way home, of a fight in a shopping centre. I can't listen to a 999 call played on the news. I can't look at the images on the news of people injured, bruised, swollen, black eyes, blood spattered, I can't watch it. I tell them I have to change the channel. I have to leave the room.

I tell them I'm struggling.

I leave their office armed with advice and support, a slightly stale digestive and their own stories of surviving this environment. The more I talk and the more I listen, the more I realise that almost every officer I know has their own version of these feelings.

***

Amidst the harrowing and traumatic things that take place in such a short space of time, there are some more positive moments. Attwood is transferred to a Category C prison. I find out he's going on the morning that he's scheduled to leave, and by the time I get to reception his bus has left. I've just missed him. But I see Otis later that day, who tells me he had a message for me: 'Thank you for being my friend.'

Not long after, Otis himself is transferred to a Category C prison. By chance, he goes to the same one as Attwood. I check their locations and see that they're in cells next door to each other.

I also just miss Adrian on the day he's due to be transferred. We've been embroiled in a game of cat-and-mouse for the last few months. The intel developed by security was spot-on, and it became obvious to me as soon as I joined the department that he was indeed in possession of a mobile phone. But we still couldn't get it. I watched that man like a hawk. He knew exactly what I was doing. He never complained, not even when I burst in through his door at 2am with DST. He just yawned and said, 'Take a look around.' During lunchbreaks, we did the same thing. And at 5am, we tried again. The soles of his shoes, the U-bend of the toilet, the panels in the wall: we took it all apart. But nothing.

The day he leaves Belmarsh, I get a call from the senior officer at reception.

'Alex, we just shipped Adrian out,' he says. 'He asked me to tell you something.'

'What's that?' I ask.

'He said, "Check the light fitting."'

I've never moved so fast in my life. I'm in that cell within minutes of hanging up. The CM of Houseblock 3 helps me to take the light fitting apart. At first, it doesn't look like there's anything to see, until we feel around and realise that one end has a small piece of cardboard slotted into it. It's been covered in toothpaste so it's the same colour as the fixture. I stand on a chair to pull out the cardboard.

And there it is: a glossy white iPhone.

PART 4

19

The Outside World

D URING MY TIME at Belmarsh, I apply for a travelling fellowship with the Winston Churchill Memorial Trust, now
known as The Churchill Fellowship. The Churchill Fellowship
funds people to travel abroad and research something they're
passionate about, with the aim of learning from other countries
and bringing positive change back to the UK.

Anyone can apply, so I figure I have nothing to lose. The
issues of staff support and workplace stress in prisons have
weighed heavily on me for a long time. I know too many
people who were struggling, and I know all too well what
this meant for prisoners. Prisoners need to be supported by
consistency, structure and social connection, but that's hard to
achieve if the people meant to be supporting them are finding
things tough themselves.

After a long application process and a daunting interview
with a panel that includes the grandson of Winston Churchill
himself, I find out I have been successful.

My Fellowship project is entitled 'How Prison Officers Survive Prison'. Over the course of six weeks, I travel to Canada,
Australia and the USA. I visit prisons, universities, mental
health research centres and occupational stress clinics. I meet
with corrections staff, academics, police chiefs, neuroscien-
tists and forensic psychologists. In Calgary, I learn about how
a programme developed to support veterans with PTSD is
being adapted for correctional officers. In Melbourne, I spend
time at the Metropolitan Remand Centre, the site of one of

the worst riots in Australian penal history in 2015. I speak to the clinicians specialising in trauma, there to support staff through their immediate reactions to what happened, but also to address any gradual, residual effects of trauma.

Finally, I visit Huntsville in Texas. Huntsville is known colloquially as the 'prison town'. It's home to seven prisons and the busiest execution chamber in the United States. One of the prisons I visit is the Huntsville Unit, also known as 'The Walls'. The Walls is the oldest state prison in Texas, and it houses the state's executions chamber. The staff show me around the various residential blocks, the infirmary, and the workshops, where inmates create everything from saddles to cowboy boots to baton holsters for the correctional officers. They show me the execution chamber: the gurney with its thick white straps, the window on one side through which people watch other people die, the garish lime-green paint on the wall. When I ask why the room has been painted that colour, the CO shrugs and says, 'It's the only colour we had.' It is an unsettling feeling being in there, and I am glad to get out. The staff there speak to me at length about the work they do, and they are under no illusions about how emotionally difficult it is to spend so much time in this room. Or in the corridor that leads to it, walking men to their death.

Texas has seen a lot. Huntsville has seen a lot. Correctional officers guarding the watchtowers have turned their guns on themselves. Others have been shot with their own firearms by escaped inmates. There is a lot to learn from in Texas, and the emotional wellbeing of correctional staff is a massive priority, from their specialist crisis intervention team – a sort of elite version of our peer-support programme – to the focus on staff training opportunities.

Training for staff holds the same value as it does for prisoners. Purposeful activity, something to engage in, to learn about and develop from, and to be stimulated by. These are the things that build natural resilience, which acts as a buffer against the most challenging of days.

As impressed as I am by my time travelling, there are some things I feel less enthusiastic about. I feel uneasy looking at the array of weapons in the security departments of Canadian prisons, or in the boots of blacked-out cars in Melbourne as they patrol the perimeter walls. I feel unsettled by the guns slung over the shoulders of correctional officers in the watchtowers in Texas. When those same officers remark how unsafe I must feel at work without a weapon, I fervently disagree. There are plenty of things about the Prison Service that make me feel unsafe, but the lack of a firearm isn't one of them.

Though my research is predominantly concerned with the emotional wellbeing of staff, I spend time on the residential units in the three countries I visit, and gain some sense of what life is like for the inmates. Relationships between officers and prisoners seem strong in most places I visit, particularly in Australia. I see staff taking part in a monthly pizza night for the inmates, helping them cook and having interesting discussions. In Canada, there are various initiatives designed to support the Indigenous community within the prisons I visit. The staff here are clearly passionate about strengthening their bonds with the men they work with. It feels as if there is a greater distance between correctional officers and prisoners in Texas, but perhaps this is inevitable in a state where staff in the watchtowers are visibly carrying firearms. A state famed for its execution chamber.

I am in Huntsville on the night of an execution. I sit in a diner round the corner from the execution chamber, eating a burger called 'The Warden'. There are a few protesters on the road outside, but not many – certainly not as many as the documentaries make out. They march up and down outside the prison, waving signs and shouting. And when the deputy warden walks down the steps and confirms that the condemned prisoner is dead, and the protesters pack up their things and go, and the road is silent again, I realise that I don't believe in capital punishment. I don't think that anyone has the right to decide how someone else dies.

I realise that as much as we're getting things wrong in the Prison Service, there's a lot we get right, too.

***

Although my project is funded and endorsed by The Churchill Fellowship, I still see myself as a representative of the Prison Service while I am abroad. And I am proud to be one. I am proud to be part of a service that values interpersonal skills, communication and compassion. Proud to be part of a workforce that knows things could be better and wants to see that change happen, whether that starts with conversations in a briefing room or fiery debates in a Prison Officers Association meeting.

I conclude my Churchill Fellowship report with a list of recommendations for change: things like implementing annual mental health check-ups for officers and increasing staff training. Most of the proposals I make wouldn't need a huge amount of work or time or money to put in place. Others, like reviewing the psychological services that staff currently have access to, are bolder and more ambitious. But that doesn't make them unnecessary. And all of it deserves discussion, at the very least.

The person I want to discuss it with is the person who could make it happen.

***

After some persistent emails and more than one cancellation, I manage to secure a meeting with the Prisons Minister. I've waited a long time for this, for the chance to discuss my Fellowship with the person who can actually do something about my proposals. I've had my report professionally bound, I've rehearsed what I am going to say over and over, and I'm ready with stats and anecdotes and accounts of life as it is behind these doors.

The meeting is held in his offices in Westminster. I pass through security protocols not dissimilar to those I've become so used to from prison: metal detectors and turnstiles, ID checks and card-operated elevators. I move from one office to another, past rows of people tapping at keyboards opposite enormous screens, people in suits rushing about with files and harried expressions, and then into his office, where he greets me with a handshake and a polite smile.

We sit across from each other at a large, oval-shaped table in the centre of the room.

I speak for about fifteen minutes. I tell him about my career so far, the places I've worked and the people I've met, and what it has taught me. I explain what my Fellowship was for, why I'd felt it necessary in the first place, and the things I've learned from my time away. And of course, I share my recommendations.

When I finish talking, he smiles and says, 'Well, to be honest, Alex, that all sounds like fluffy things to make prison officers happy.'

I don't know what I say in response to that. I think I just fall silent for a moment.

He goes on to say that he visited Wormwood Scrubs recently, and saw a lot of officers standing around drinking coffee. He says that on one wing, he was chatting to the senior officer when a prisoner dashed in, grabbed a pen from the desk and then ran out again. He thinks that is the problem. That we aren't disciplining people for little things.

But his first comment is still ringing in my head.

Fluffy things to make prison officers happy?

I think of my colleague at Whitemoor when he saw two pale feet dangling from beneath a curtain, and the officer at Belmarsh who sobbed in the recess when he saw Ellison's body, cold, rigid and dead. The officer at Scrubs who only ever wore long-sleeved shirts so he could hide the scars on his arms. The alcoholic officer who passed out pissed on the pool table, numbed by the relief that drink brought him. The officer who flung himself into a river with weights tied to his own hands so he never had to surface. My colleague from Scrubs who took his own life. The officer from HMP Parkhurst who I read about in the prison paper.

I wonder now if the Prisons Minister would say any of this to the families of these officers. I wonder if he would say it to the families of all the prisoners who have taken their own lives in prison in the decade I've been doing this job.

Because every single one of them deserved better.

He's annoyed that they were drinking coffee? I think of all the times a trusted prisoner made me a tea that I never got to drink, because I was busy shouting or pressing the alarm bell or drawing my baton or doing CPR. The minister must surely realise that the only reason staff were able to have a coffee during his visit was because they'd locked the vast majority of prisoners in their cells? And that the reason they'd locked them away was because they couldn't run the risk of the Prisons Minister getting punched – or, even worse, slashed by one of the prisoners walking round with machetes made from bed slats hidden down their trousers? I've been present for several visits by politicians and dignitaries during my career, and not once have the prisoners been out on association during those times. Not once have we ever run the risk of a visitor getting assaulted.

Because it's not just home-made shanks that officers have to worry about, but real knives dropped off by drones, like Deliveroo for cons. That's what these people are carrying, and they are carrying them because they don't feel safe.

They. Don't. Feel. Safe.

Only a couple of weeks ago, I was discussing with one prisoner the latest government initiative to fight knife crime – printing warnings on chicken takeaway boxes. The prisoner said, 'If I saw one of those chicken boxes, and I hadn't got my knife on me, it would remind me to go home and get it.'

Prisoners know they can still get killed in prison, just as they can on the streets, and they protect themselves accordingly. With machetes, knives, knuckledusters and tuna cans in socks. And the Prisons Minister wants us to tell off a prisoner because he took a biro? A prisoner who I imagine came into ·the office and took the biro because he was probably a cleaner who gets on well with the staff. Staff who know him, who have probably worked closely with him to develop that relationship. I put myself in that situation and imagine Ullah coming in and quickly grabbing a pen – he would have run in and run out without saying anything in order to not interrupt us.

But I don't say any of that. I just sit there and listen to this man who has never worked in a prison as he tells me what the issues really are. I look at his expensive suit and his leather shoes. I remember the email sent round Belmarsh by the governor's secretary, asking old staff to search through their homes for any old uniform they don't need that could be given to new staff, as the Prison Service cannot afford to supply them with the basics.

We are sitting across from each other in his enormous, pristine office, framed by floor-length windows with stunning views of London. Compare that with Scrubs and the rat-infested wings or the carpet of cockroaches that scuttle away when you switch on a light, the broken windows that prisoners try to block with scouring pads, the constant shortage of toilet roll, the crumbling walls and holes in the roof. That's all I can think about.

I know now that I've had enough.

***

I left the Prison Service in 2021.

When the country went into lockdown in March 2020, I fell pregnant. I spent almost the entirety of the COVID-19 pandemic self-isolating for that reason. I was lucky not to be working in the prison during that time. A building made up of lots of confined spaces, with hundreds of people coming in and out, and hundreds more unable to leave, is obviously a very problematic environment to manage during a pandemic.

Staff were no longer physically searched, due to the social-distancing rules. While some prisons reported increased concerns about staff corruption because of this, in many ways it became almost pointless. Even if prisoners were able to get hold of contraband, it could only be for personal use. Otherwise, it wasn't worth their while. They weren't getting out of their cells often enough to distribute phones and drugs around the prison.

The nature of a prison officer's work changed, too. As only a few prisoners were allowed out of their cells at any one time, getting people out for showers and time on the yard had to be staggered and became more labour intensive – especially for a workforce affected by infection rates and high sickness levels in much the same way as the general population. PPE was not always readily available, and so issues around restraints and planned removals understandably became very contentious.

A lot was done to support prisoners at this unprecedented time, and rightly so, but there have been lasting effects that continue to impact an already stretched system. Due to court backlogs, there is now a dramatically increased number of remand prisoners in custody with a long time ahead of them before their trials begin.

Logistically, COVID-19 was extremely difficult for governors and senior management to manage. But as the various lockdowns lifted, some interesting truths were revealed. There had been real concerns that prisons would see a staggering increase in self-harm and suicide, and in violence between cellmates, or outside cells on the rare occasions when prisoners were able to socialise. But that didn't happen. Violence actually decreased during this time, because prisoners were leaving their cells less frequently. No one went to workshops, education or even visits. All of it came to a halt. Despite initial concerns, self-harm also reduced. This was due at least in part to the increased amount of support vulnerable prisoners were given. Specially trained officers, such as Officer Nesse, checked in on these men as often as possible, and provided them with resources to help pass the time. Things like activity packs, wordsearches, workbooks. Prisoners were also able to access more TV channels. Another reason for self-harm decreasing is probably that the prisoners weren't coming into contact with each other. They were bullied less, assaulted less, taxed less. All things that would usually contribute to low mood.

What many of us had known for a very long time was shown in stark clarity: prisoners want to feel safe. In recognition of this, senior management at HMP Belmarsh made bold changes to the running of the jail. Freeflow is now staggered, with the number of men in the corridors significantly reduced. Prisoners from rival gangs no longer have to worry about coming into contact with each other, or the social expectation that they will fight if they do. These changes have extended to the houseblocks as well. Fewer prisoners are now allowed out together during both association and exercise.

My friends and former colleagues at HMP Belmarsh tell me that these changes have been transformative, and have made a difficult job that bit easier. A strong recruitment drive has increased staffing levels to a far more manageable position, and retention levels continue to rise as well. There are still innumerable challenges within the Prison Service, but it seems as if things are improving. The impact of the disastrous decision to cut funding and resources in our prisons is still keenly felt, but perhaps not quite as badly as it once was.

I certainly hope so.

***

As I write, it has been over ten years since that day I first walked up the path to HMP Whitemoor. A lot has happened in that time. Certainly, no one needs to tell me how hard this job can be. But equally, I'm still its biggest champion. I've seen how much good is done behind those walls.

I've written a lot about how the cuts to public services have affected prisons. But it isn't just prisons. They've affected everything: housing, healthcare, employment, education. We all know this. After a while, the headlines all start to look the same. It's hard to remember the people behind these articles. The people behind these doors. I've said before that prison is a reflection of society, and I hope this book has demonstrated that. The things I've seen in prison are a magnified version of what those cuts do. For housing, look at the cells in which prisoners live. Broken windows and cockroaches. For healthcare, look at people like Hashem. Living in their own faeces, but there are no beds for them in hospital. For employment, look at all the empty workshops and non-existent courses. Look at the stratospheric rise in drugs and phones, because that's a guaranteed income. For education, look at Tristan and A.J., kids who are stabbed on the way to school, whose talents go unnoticed. The cycle just continues.

If we don't invest, then the damaged kids become the ones in Pupil Referral Units, the young offenders, the lifers. Ironically, it's at that point that we break the cycle. Go back ten years to when I first started at Whitemoor. Consider all the resources to which prisoners had access. For housing, look at their clean and modern single cells. For healthcare, look at the onsite forensic psychology team. For employment, look at the carpentry workshop, offending behaviour programmes, music-production software. For education, consider the countless men studying for their GCSEs, A Levels, Open University courses. So many of these men, most of whom had probably never been described as 'thriving' at any point in their lives, did just that.

They thrived. And that's absolutely the way it should be. But we could do more, for all the others. We should do more.

For a long time after that meeting with the Prisons Minister, I was frustrated with myself for not saying anything back when I should have. In some ways, I think this book is my response. The Prison Service is sometimes referred to as 'the forgotten service', and prisons themselves as 'hidden worlds'. But we can't let them stay hidden. There's too much we can't forget.

I don't want to lose these stories. They're too important. They provide a window into people's lives. That alone is invaluable. And they capture just a snapshot of ten years of our Prison Service, of life and work inside three vastly different jails, all affected by cuts and benchmarking and poor decisions, by outside politics and inside challenges. But also strength and bravery and hope.

I've learned a great deal during my time inside, from men like Ben, Bolt, Tristan, Attwood and Otis, who educated me on the complexity of our legal system, the flimsiness of loyalty and what it really feels like when the doors slam shut. Perhaps the most important thing they taught me was that the bars don't really exist if you can think outside them. Change is never impossible. You can be better. There's a lesson in that for all of us.

And to the men and women I've had the privilege of working with, many of whom have become lifelong friends, I'm so grateful. Working alongside you has taught me courage, resilience and compassion, and how to find all three in the darkest of places. Jailcraft, but life lessons too. You are so much more than a number.

For me, my time is served.

Acknowledgements

WRITING THIS BOOK has been one of the most fulfilling, insightful and challenging things I've ever done. It's got me through the pandemic, two pregnancies and some uncertain times. Throughout all of that, it's focused my mind in a way that not much else has. I'm only now beginning to realise just how invaluable that has been. There are many people who have helped and inspired me along the way.

Thank you to Daisy Larkin, without whom none of this would have happened. Her words of encouragement were the reason I wrote a memoir.

I am indebted to my agent, Sophie Lambert, who believed in this book from the beginning and shared my vision of what it could be. Thank you to Huw and the team at Hodder & Stoughton for everything you've done to make *Behind These Doors* a reality. I'm so grateful.

Hannah, for championing this book long before it was written and talking about it to everyone you've ever met. For always cheering me on in everything I do. Fran, for supplying some of the best memes in recent years and getting me through the deadlines and late nights. Vicky, for being a constant and unwavering support, despite being so many miles away. And thank you for pre-ordering the book within thirty seconds of it being made available online.

Charlie, for your constant encouragement. We've come a long way since writing our uni assignments by the oven.

Jade, for answering random existential questions about what it was like being in our twenties, and your friendship.

Buttrisso, for everything. Such a ten.

Jillius, for your endless support and enthusiasm. Thank you for being as excited about this book as I am.

Pete, for being my mentor and friend. Your advice and kind words are imprinted on my memory.

Nick, for all your support, particularly in those early years. Bring me sunshine.

Howard, for always being on hand to talk about things from a forensic psychological perspective.

Chris, for always having my back, sometimes quite literally at the expense of your own. Sorry your chapter got cut.

Mr Leggington, for being the best team mate and friend through some amazing and tough years. I hope I did some of our memories justice.

Henry, for your continued support and for pointing out the not inconsiderable difference between eight feet and eight metres.

Paul, for ending my time on the landings on such a high. We didn't know how good we had it.

The Open University; the confidence and curiosity my studies have given me is lifelong. Nothing seems out of reach. The Churchill Fellowship, for a once-in-a-lifetime opportunity and unforgettable memories. Thank you especially to Doug Dretke and Rick Hanson for giving me the best examples of what is possible.

To my mum and dad, for the endless calls and FaceTimes, lessons, laughter and wisdom. Thank you for supporting me in every way, always.

Jake, for the Moët. For the conversation, ideas, debates. The person I've wanted to emulate my whole life. And the Moët. Can I have some more Moët.

T, for looking only slightly nervous when I suggested quitting my job and focusing on writing a book. In the middle of a pandemic. With a toddler. While pregnant. There aren't enough words to tell you how grateful I am for everything you do.

And thank you to my children. My loud, bossy, extremely unreasonable and constantly awake children. You have given me the best reason to write this book and chase after my dreams. So that you do the same.

Ways you can help

There are some excellent organisations and charities dedicated to supporting people in prison, and in turn supporting prison officers.

Before becoming a prison officer, I volunteered with **Trailblazers**. Trailblazers train people to mentor young offenders with the primary objective of reducing their reoffending. They operate in various Young Offender Institutions around the country.
https://www.trailblazersmentoring.org.uk

I also volunteered with SOVA (Supporting Others Through Volunteer Action), and worked with ex-offenders in the early days of their release. SOVA have since changed their name to **CGL (Change Grow Live)**, and continue to do important work supporting people both inside and outside prison.
https://www.changegrowlive.org

The **Howard League for Penal Reform** is committed to creating safer communities with less crime, and ultimately putting fewer people in prison. Their work was instrumental in overturning the 2013 book ban that was implemented during my time at HMP Whitemoor.
https://howardleague.org

The National Association of Official Prison Visitors arranges for prisoners without family or friends to receive visits from Official Prison Visitors. OPVs are often the only contact

a prisoner has with the outside world. They are unpaid volunteers, and anyone aged twenty-one to seventy can apply.
https://www.naopv.com

Clinks supports, promotes and represents the voluntary sector working with people in the criminal justice system and their families.
https://www.clinks.org

I still believe in the power and potential of the **Prison Service** to change people's lives for the better. The role of prison officer can be an incredible job to have.

If you're up for the challenge, visit **https://prisonandprobationjobs.gov.uk/prison-officer**